Television, History, and American Culture

FEMINIST CRITICAL ESSAYS

Edited by

Mary Beth Haralovich and Lauren Rabinovitz

Duke University Press
Durham and London, 1999

Printed in the United States of America on acid-free paper ∞
Designed by Rebecca Filene
Typeset in Berkeley Medium by Tseng Information Systems, Inc.
Library of Congress Cataloging-in-Publication Data
appear on the last printed page of this book.

Television, History, and American Culture

Console-ing Passions

Television and Cultural Power

A Series *Edited by Lynn Spigel*

Contents

Introduction MARY BETH HARALOVICH AND LAUREN RABINOVITZ 1

Desired and Feared: Women's Voices in Radio History
MICHELE HILMES 17

Considering Monty Margetts's *Cook's Corner*: Oral History and Television History MARK WILLIAMS 36

Lucy and Desi: Sexuality, Ethnicity, and TV's First Family
MARY DESJARDINS 56

A Moral Crisis in Prime Time: *Peyton Place* and the Rise of the Single Girl MOYA LUCKETT 75

I Spy's "Living Postcards": The Geo-Politics of Civil Rights
MARY BETH HARALOVICH 98

Leading Up to *Roe v. Wade*: Television Documentaries in the Abortion Debate JULIE D'ACCI 120

Ms.-Representation: The Politics of Feminist Sitcoms
LAUREN RABINOVITZ 144

The Oprahification of America: Talk Shows and the Public Sphere
JANE M. SHATTUC 168

Averting the Male Gaze: Visual Pleasure and Images of Fat Women
JANE FEUER 181

Selected Bibliography 201

Contributors 211

Index 213

Introduction

Mary Beth Haralovich and Lauren Rabinovitz

Feminist TV History: The Politics of Critical Engagement

Feminism has never been unified. Feminism has always been feminisms—a variety of approaches that aim to improve women's lives and thus enhance the lives of the family, the workplace, the nation. An important deeper meaning of feminism is its effort to reconceptualize what counts as knowledge and power in general. This diversity has resulted in feminism defined and pursued not as a single political effort or as a series of political acts. Feminism aims to change culture through constructing and championing new ways of thinking about subjects from law to philosophy to literature to politics to economics to popular media. This volume on U.S. television attempts to demonstrate that a feminist politics of critical engagement in television history is crucial for understanding television's role in modern culture. Its purpose is to examine the social and industrial conditions affecting the struggle for representation on television—from the very presence of women on TV to the way television mediates civil rights, sexual liberation, and questions of individual identity.

There is a fundamental relationship between the feminist concerns that motivate the questions these writers ask and the feminist theories that frame their critical and historical methods. In any historical method, a theory of history frames how one looks at the past as it opens the past to investigation. Without feminist theory, how would the historical record allow the feminist historian to detect that record's ideological mystery? Theories of patriarchy enable feminist historians to make discoveries about everyday life, to bring to light the role women played in television production, to examine the practices that put forward particular representations of gender and race while gingerly avoiding others—to break historical silences about race and gender and sexuality.

Television, History, and American Culture: Feminist Critical Essays recalls the role of television in our cultural past as a nation. It illuminates how television participated in and mediated profound cultural concerns and discourses that engaged local, national, and global identities. The essays in this volume constitute a form of historical criticism. Each television scholar takes on a specific cultural representation that became available at a particular historical conjuncture for television and for the nation. Each writer examines the intertwined textual, social, and/or industrial conditions that constrained and limited television representation even as these conditions made representation available.

By attending to the essential interrelationship of television's textual practices and contextual conditions, the feminist historical criticism in this volume draws on and develops two decades of feminist television scholarship. From woman- and character-centered textual interpretations, through awareness of the complexity of audience and spectatorship, to redefining the role of consumerism in television's industrial practices, feminist television scholarship has enriched our understanding of the role of television as an agent of culture.

Feminist television criticism, which interprets and analyzes individual or group encounters with television programming, has relied heavily on models of textual interpretations and discourse analysis from film, literature, and media studies. The earliest books in television studies—such as John Fiske and John Hartley's *Reading Television* (1978), Charlotte Brunsdon and David Morley's *Everyday Television: Nationwide* (1978), John Hartley's *Understanding News* (1982), and E. Ann Kaplan's *Regarding Television—Critical Approaches: An Anthology* (1983)—applied semiotic and narratological approaches to show how television in Great Britain and the United States utilizes formal aesthetics within the parameters of TV's economic, industrial, governmental, and technological conditions and restrictions.[1]

These early interventions were important in a field that had been previously dominated, on the one hand, by pessimistic sociological critiques of television as an instrument of mass persuasion and, on the other hand, by quantitative analyses of television's messages and their effects on audiences. For example, Carol Lopate's "Daytime Television: You'll Never Want to Leave Home" (1977) and Mary Cassata and Thomas Skill's *Life on Daytime Television: Tuning in American Serial Drama* (1983), which were woman-centered and character-centered criticism, still relied on traditional methods in Marxist criticism and mass communication. Lopate criticizes television's content, saying that morning game shows (like *The Price Is Right* or *Let's Make a Deal*) present a bountiful world of consumer goods to excite housewives about the importance of their role as consumers and about material acquisitiveness as a family value. In addition, Lopate disapproves of afternoon serials for offering "bored housewives" the escape of fantasy and romance without discussing the solitude and isolation of their labor conditions.[2] Cassata and Skill's book is a meticulous statistical account of women's roles, occupations, and demographic status within soap opera fictions.[3] The beginning of a specifically feminist textual interpretation of television was a response to these older models of messages-effects and Marxist sociological criticism, to contemporary literary and film criticism that viewed popular entertainment as dense layers of complex meanings, and to feminism's political and cultural intervention in the 1970s.[4]

The first efforts of feminist television criticism were directed at deconstructing and countering the patriarchal implications of television shows featuring women or aimed at female audiences. Shifting the soap opera question away from traditional methods of TV inquiry, feminist scholars "reclassified" soap operas as a woman's genre and examined how the textual complexities of television melodrama contribute to meaning and interpretation. For example, Ellen Seiter's "The Role of the Reader: Eco's Narrative Theory and Soap Opera" (1982) and "Promise and Contradiction: The Daytime Television Serials" (1982) look at the patriarchal structures of a number of soap families as well as at a long-term story arc from *General Hospital*.[5] But Seiter argues that the strength of women's relationships and powerful women characters who control story lines allow for feminist pleasures in both the soap opera narrative and the cultural contradictions that it embodies. Two contemporary influential essays, Jane Feuer's "Melodrama, Serial Form, and Television Today" (1984) and Sandy Flitterman's "The Real Soap Opera: TV Commercials" (1983), also provide reasons why soap opera texts provide pleasure to so many women.[6] They expand the narrative and industrial contexts in which daytime dramas have meaning.[7]

The female spectator-auditor-subject, defined as one who can meaningfully engage with soap operas in ways that reinforce feminine and even protofeminist values, was introduced by Tania Modleski in "The

Search for Tomorrow in Today's Soap Operas: Notes on a Feminine Narrative Form" (1979).[8] In this influential critique of feminist film theory, Modleski argues that a model of contemplative spectatorship cannot take into account the realities of television viewing in the home: the gendered position of a busy housewife watching TV while working in a domestic setting. Although Modleski's female spectator is an imaginary one, constructed by the television text and defined monolithically by gender, inherent in her critique is the notion of television watching as an interactive relationship between text and spectator.

Feminist awareness of the processes of viewer identification continued to develop in studies on the progressive potential that television could have for women. Patricia Mellencamp's "Situation Comedy, Feminism, and Freud: Discourses of Gracie and Lucy" (1986) and Serafina Bathrick's "The Mary Tyler Moore Show: Women at Home and at Work" (1984) both examined how women comedic characters could become feminist role models.[9] Gracie Allen, Lucille Ball, and Mary Tyler Moore—three of the most beloved characters in television history—were recognized as talented performers whose visual and verbal comedy provided opportunities for critiques of patriarchy, appreciation of women's agency, and audience pleasure.

The female spectator's proficiency at interpreting characters to fit her needs became the center of much critical discussion. By further attending to how stars may elicit political resistance in female spectators, E. Ann Kaplan, John Fiske, Lisa Lewis, and Cathy Schwichtenberg all followed through on the original premise of Mellencamp's work: they argued that Madonna's music videos offered teenage girls feminist subversions of the constitutive categories of gender.[10] Lauren Rabinovitz's "Sitcoms and Single Moms: Representations of Feminism on American TV" (1989) held that a single television text always offers women a variety of political positions with which to identify.[11] Sandy Flitterman and Mary Beth Haralovich examined the text and production materials, respectively, of a popular male-buddy, action-oriented show (*Magnum, p.i.*) to illustrate that it, too, offered something to its female spectators—a heterosexually charged, powerfully erotic address.[12] Christine Gledhill, Lynne Joyrich, and Patrice Petro demonstrated how the role of the female TV spectator dovetails feminists' interests in both television and cinema; they claim that television (more than cinema) as a mode of address and a cultural institution caters to feminine viewing positions.[13] Debates on the nature and role of the female TV spectator were prominent throughout feminist TV criticism in such works as Helen Baehr and Gillian Dyer's *Boxed In: Women and Television* (1987), E. Deidre Pribram's *Female Spectators: Looking at Film and Television* (1988), "The Spectatrix" Issue of *Camera Obscura* (1989), Mary Ellen Brown's *Television and Women's Culture* (1990), and Andrea Press's *Women Watching Television: Gender, Class, and Generation in the American Television Experience* (1991).[14]

Opening the boundaries of reception to admit the female spectator encouraged feminist television critics to expand on textual models inherited from film studies in order to understand how context—social milieu, industrial processes, and history itself—envelops both the makers and the consumers of television texts. Drawing on British cultural studies and U.S. and British ethnographic audience research, a new generation of feminist TV criticism increasingly looked beyond the limits of film critical models that focused only on the textual process of meaning production and posited the female spectator as a purely ideal construct held out by the text itself. Trying to extrapolate a more dynamic and sociohistorically specific "audience," feminist TV criticism integrated text and discourse analysis with audience studies and/or industry research. Integrated methodologies, necessary to understand cultural limits and potential for active audience engagement with television, had been proposed in such studies as Stuart Hall's "Encoding/decoding" (1980), Tony Bennett's "Texts, Readers, Reading Formations" (1983), Tony Bennett and Janet Woollacott's *Bond and Beyond: The Political Career of a Popular Hero* (1987), David Morley's *The "Nationwide" Audience: Structure and Decoding* (1980), Angela McRobbie's "Settling Accounts with Subculture: A Feminist Critique" (1981), and Janice A. Radway's *Reading the Romance: Women, Patriarchy, and Popular Literature* (1984).[15]

Ethnographic audience studies attempted to show how actual audiences make meaning of television, particularly when television programming crosses the fluid boundaries of nation, race, and subculture. These studies are of special interest to feminist TV criticism because they locate cultural agency in subjects who are often "resistant readers" appropriating, remaking, or reinterpreting television. Instead of being mere effects of narrative and consumerist practices, audiences were conceived of as capable of interpretation, and "misinterpretation" was as valuable and legitimate as the "correct" meaning. Thus ideologies became fluid and heterogeneous rather than doctrinaire. For example, the transnational popularity of *Dallas* led researchers to query audiences in various cultures about their responses to what seemed to be a distinctly American show that especially represented both gleeful American material decadence and a cultural invasion of other countries' popular media. In *Watching Dallas: Soap Opera and the Melodramatic Imagination* (1985), Ien Ang discovered that while Dutch women maintained a disdainful attitude toward the Americanness of the program, they still expressed a strong sense of identification with the melodrama's tragic structure.[16] Tamar Liebes and Elihu Katz's focus-group discussions with different Israeli ethnic groups showed how they interpreted *Dallas* as a mirror of American life and a critique of Western morals and capitalism.[17] Television critics similarly applied such ethnographic methods to soap opera audiences around the world, to different racial groups watching the same show, and to fan audiences.[18] One of the most interesting self-reflections on the "ethnographic approach" occurs in Jane Feuer's "Reading *Dynasty:* Television and Reception Theory" (1989).[19] Feuer's participant-observer study of gay men collectively watching *Dynasty* in a gay bar demonstrates how the text may be rewritten according to subcultural demands and pleasures. She argues for how subcultural groups routinely denied access to the means of cultural production may produce their own expressions of identity by subverting and "overwriting" dominant cultural products with new meanings. In studies like this one, television critics learned to read audiences as well as television as the "object" for understanding television's produced meanings.[20]

Women's involvement with television was reconceptualized from being an effect of a patriarchal text to a social relationship within a dynamic framework of industrial and economic interests, cultural values, and mass entertainment. In "Women's Genres" (1984), Annette Kuhn calls for greater attention to this relationship between text and context and to the distinctive differences between the spectator, a position held out by the text, and the audience, real social groups of people.[21] In this regard, Kuhn cites as exemplary Charlotte Brunsdon's examination of how the lives of viewers of the British soap opera *Crossroads* activated a horizon of meanings that was critical for how they interpreted soap opera texts.[22]

Numerous feminist TV critics in the late 1980s and 1990s followed this path. For example, Julie D'Acci's *Defining Women: Television and the Case of Cagney and Lacey* (1994) used participant-observation to examine how television producers mediated the horizons of their viewers within the ideologies of network television production by appealing to the demographic capital of the program's upscale women viewers while turning down associations with lesbian representations.[23] Lynn Spigel's *Make Room for TV: Television and the Family Ideal in Postwar America* (1992) and Mary Beth Haralovich's "Sitcoms and Suburbs: Positioning the 1950s Homemaker" (1989) examine the broad range of 1950s cultural discourses about the utopian and dystopian effects of television in family life and the life of the nation.[24] Gloria Masciarotte's "C'mon Girl: Oprah Winfrey and the Discourse of Feminine Talk" (1991), Margaret Morse's "Talk, Talk, Talk—the Space of Discourse in Television" (1985), and Jane M. Shattuc's *The Talking Cure: TV Talk Shows and Women* (1997) analyze the feminist foundation and politics of the talk show through its feminine linguistic modes, star discourses, genre conventions, industrial production, and cultural borrowings.[25] Lauren Rabinovitz returned to the soap opera genre to demonstrate that the progressive and resistant pleasures feminist critics earlier aligned with soap opera viewing are constrained when one addresses soaps within a new cultural model; she reveals that the format is crisscrossed by the political economy of television consumerist address, fan and bridal magazine "intertexts" that purvey traditional feminine norms, and conservative reading practices.[26] By the early 1990s, in fact, feminist television criticism had so fully adapted to an integrative model that several books synthesized feminist TV and cultural criticism in order to interrogate television itself as society's most powerful and pervasive cultural institution and to challenge its expression of racial, sexual, and national barriers.[27]

Questions of text-context, of spectatorship as an ideal point of textual address, of audience as a demographic social assembly, of television's industrial practices—they have all animated feminist TV criticism and contributed to the rich terrain of feminist television history. The essays in this volume shed new feminist light on the ideological mysteries of the past by continuing to ask questions about power and authority and by merging feminist theory with methods from cultural studies, audience ethnographies, oral histories, industrial practices, and textual analysis. These critics look at television with a different eye. They focus on well-known, established aspects of television in order to identify the politics of institutional and cultural constraints. They bring forward the institutional and commercial conditions in which TV's creative artists work and thus bring to light individuals who negotiated space for women in front of the camera and behind it. They critically examine existing industrial, sociocultural, and textual theory through the "test" of past practices or microhistories. Thus, *Television, History, and American Culture: Feminist Critical Essays* counters prevailing assumptions that U.S. television is merely a commercially driven enterprise that harnesses creativity to the market. Instead, it argues for television's national power in defining, transforming, and giving distinctive contours to American culture.

Outline for a New Feminist TV History: A Drama of Action, Power, Social Bodies, and Sexual Significances

These essays all consider the role of human agency. Human agency is a fundamental feminist political goal, a position and contribution for social change as well as an essential aspect of the feminist historical lens. In these essays, women—whether producers, performers, or fictional characters—are not simply positioned as social victims on the basis of gender or as passive pawns of oppressive corporations, including the media industries. The historians in this volume argue for a feminist analysis that understands action and the potential for action as always foremost. The way that power works in practice is that it is always diffused, not located merely in the government, the ruling class, the corporate elite, or the institution of television. These historians assume Michel Foucault's definition of power: power and resistance to power are manifest in a number of ways.[28] Power and resistance are always in motion and never static, specific, and concrete. Mark Williams portrays how Monty Margetts negotiated the world of early broadcast TV in Los Angeles. Julie D'Acci shows how Marlene Sanders negotiated who could and could not speak on national television about abortion. Michele Hilmes investigates women broadcasters' struggle over the presence of women's voices in local and national radio. Mary Desjardins examines Desilu's effort to establish the voice of authority of the television producer and create an acceptable television image of Hispanic ethnicity. Mary Beth Haralovich finds that popular press coverage of *I Spy* focused on the role that Sheldon Leonard and Robert Culp played in civil rights activism when they introduced integrated lead characters for the first time on network TV. Jane Shattuc argues that the complex, powerful relationships that TV talk shows build with their audiences are the popular legacy of the political public sphere. Jane Feuer studies the controversy of providing delicately poised affirmative self-images of fat girls.

Feminist television history is not solely a woman-based view; its interest in relations of power also embraces the study of race and ethnicity. In their reach across five decades of U.S. television history, these essays collectively show that U.S. television has a long history of struggle over the representation and participation of people of color. The object of study of most television histories has been a nominally white TV even when significant public policy decisions, such as *Topeka v. Board of Education* (1954) and the Civil Rights Act ten years later, increased activism and pressured U.S. institutions to recognize constitutional rights to equality and cultural rights to increased media voices. These essays argue that committed individuals have been able to translate their popularity into institutional and therefore cultural power. From Lucille Ball in the 1950s to Sheldon Leonard and Robert Culp in the 1960s to Oprah Winfrey in the 1980s, stardom and good ratings have given individuals enough leverage with television networks to enable them to design their programs to include more liberal representations of race. Their status within the television industry granted them some power over representation that, in turn, allowed them to wield cultural power. The histories in this volume recognize that the entertainment industry operates as just such a site of negotiation while also functioning as a gatekeeper in the hegemonic process; they acknowledge the dominance of industrial racism while also discovering that pressures have been successfully applied to it.

The representations of race and ethnicity that result from these negotiations are necessarily complex and contradictory. People of color have been frequently perceived as sources of TV humor; racially and ethnically marked fictional characters test the terrain of assimilation and difference as part of the weekly pleasures offered by television series. The essays examine how the explicitly marked presence of their difference identifies the terms of both white cultural dominance and racial/ethnic separation and othering.

For some of television's creative producers, the centrality of these nonwhite characters in a TV series is a means of placing integration in a space of public viewing. As welcome as this may be, these essays also find that representation with less than full agency is not sufficient. By discussing the larger industrial and historically specific contexts in which a television series functions, this volume shows how U.S. television may contribute to change but also how its gatekeeper function serves powerful ideologies by limiting representations of race and ethnicity and protecting the economic dominance of the white consumer demographic.

Another important assumption of these essays and, for that matter, of television studies more generally is that U.S.-produced television, regardless of its international circulation (or perhaps because of it), is an institution that defines U.S. national culture and identity. In practice, however, people intersect with television and national culture in complicated ways, and these historians show that the national culture of television does not unequivocally lead to unified audiences and effects. Mary Beth Haralovich examines how network television's *I Spy* series identified with the liberal cause of civil rights as a means of national security in the Cold War and attempted to open television to African American lead characters, but its advances toward racially integrated television were limited and contradictory. Although *Peyton Place* produced new images of an independent female sexuality, Moya Luckett demonstrates how that effort depended on prevailing stereotypes of femininity to focus attention on conflicting interpretations of women and morality. These feminist histories show the complexities of television's participation in U.S. society and dispel the myth that television is a hypodermic injection that produces a unified national culture.

The essays also assume that a feminist methodology pays attention to the fundamental implication of gender and heterosexuality in U.S. popular culture. In the history of television, gender and heterosexuality have been essentialized as the same. These essays try to disentangle and understand the dynamics of the heterosexual imperative in television. Toward that end, the tradition of analyzing components of identity according to a structural paradigm of bipolarism is inadequate; binarisms of masculine/feminine, male/female, straight/gay, white/black are not sufficient for understanding subjectivity. The process of analyzing representations on TV becomes one of self-reflection and consciousness-raising about television's construction of these ideological dualities as universally essential. In *I Love Lucy*, a sitcom widely taken for granted as exemplary of the heterosexual couple, Mary Desjardins shows how an intertextual reading formation points to the limitations of understanding the 1950s as illustrative of narrowly prescribed gender roles. Lauren Rabinovitz's essay reveals that 1990s "progressive feminist" television sitcoms accept the heterosexual imperative and embrace it with all of its dangers. Jane Feuer's essay concludes the volume by assessing how the heterosexist bias of feminist film theory (particularly Laura Mulvey's essay "Visual Pleasure and Narrative Cinema") has blinded some feminist theorists to the televisual pleasures of a lesbian gaze. These essays cope with the heterosexual imperative by acknowledging and probing its ideological construction. They approach the individual television text within its wider field of popular discourse so that the text's ideological construction is always within and part of a historicized reading formation.

The Juncture of the Critical and the Empirical

Women's positions have always been significant in staking out television's ongoing, yet evolving, roles within American culture. As viewers and consumers, images and content, laborers and producers of television, various categories of women have assumed numerous vital functions in television's operations. But to speak to women, to speak as women, and to speak about women in the 1990s means to take up more than Woman as the subject of study. A feminist critical assessment of television's history requires that we examine TV's various segments, its industrial practices, and its interconnectedness to other forms of popular culture in order to analyze and question how this institution has constituted powerful knowledge—political, social, cultural—that affects who we are and how we might transform American society.

Television, History, and American Culture: Feminist Critical Essays therefore covers a sweep of time from before the diffusion of television sets in the 1950s until the present moment. This volume embraces many of the features of a changing television institution—its earliest struggles over whether television's role is local, national, and/or international; its maturation as a social institution as it takes on key issues of the 1960s (abortion, civil rights, and sexual revolution); and its dissemination of issue-oriented images in today's digital culture. Taken collectively, these essays draw out the threads of U.S. television's industrial, social, and creative textual practices, interweaving all three to answer questions of television and culture.

Notes

1 John Fiske and John Hartley, *Reading Television* (London: Methuen, 1978); Charlotte Brunsdon and David Morley, *Everyday Television: Nationwide* (London: British Film Institute, 1978); John Hartley, *Understanding News* (London: Methuen, 1982); E. Ann Kaplan, ed., *Regarding Television—Critical Approaches: An Anthology* (Frederick, Md.: University Publications of America, 1983).

2 Carol Lopate, "Daytime Television: You'll Never Want to Leave Home," *Radical America* 11, no. 1 (January–February 1977): 33–51.

3 Mary Cassata and Thomas Skill, *Life on Daytime Television: Tuning in American Serial Drama* (Norwood, N.J.: Ablex, 1983).

4 For an overview, see E. Ann Kaplan, "Feminist Criticism and Television," in *Channels of Discourse, Reassembled: Television and Contemporary Criticism, 2d ed.*, ed. Robert C. Allen (Chapel Hill: University of North Carolina Press, 1992), 247–83.

5 Ellen Seiter, "The Role of the Reader: Eco's Narrative Theory and Soap Opera," *Tabloid* 6 (1982): 35–43; Ellen Seiter, "Promise and Contradiction: The Daytime Television Serials," *Film Reader* 5 (1982): 150–63.

6 Jane Feuer, "Melodrama, Serial Form, and Television Today," *Screen* 23, no. 1 (1984): 4–16; Sandy Flitterman, "The Real Soap Opera: TV Commercials," in Kaplan, *Regarding Television,* 84–96.

7 Other important studies on soap opera and women's participation include Robert C. Allen, *Speaking of Soap Operas* (Chapel Hill: University of North Carolina Press, 1985); Dorothy Hobson, *Crossroads: The Drama of a Soap Opera* (London: Methuen, 1982).

This subject, so central to the growth and development of a feminist TV criticism, has continued to fuel significant feminist TV criticism regarding feminine discourse and feminist spectatorship, women's pleasures, genre, and women's culture. See, for example, Christine Geraghty, *Women and Soap Opera* (Cambridge: Polity Press, 1991); Martha Nochimson, *No End to Her: Soap Opera and the Female Subject* (Berkeley: University of California Press, 1992); Mary Ellen Brown, *Soap Opera and Women's Talk: The Pleasure of Resistance* (Thousand Oaks, Calif.: Sage, 1994); Laura Stempel Mumford,

Love and Ideology in the Afternoon: Soap Opera, Women, and Television Genre (Bloomington: Indiana University Press, 1995); Charlotte Brunsdon, *Screen Tastes: Soap Opera to Satellite Dishes* (London: Routledge, 1997).

In addition, contemporary studies took up other genres, seen as less central to women's experiences, as means for providing sexual pleasures and addressing the conventions of gender roles. See, for example, John Fiske, *Television Culture* (New York: Methuen, 1987); E. Ann Kaplan, *Rocking around the Clock: Music Television, Postmodernism, and Consumer Culture* (New York: Methuen, 1987).

8 Tania Modleski, "The Search for Tomorrow in Today's Soap Operas: Notes on a Feminine Narrative Form," *Film Quarterly* 33, no. 1 (fall 1979): 12–21.

9 Patricia Mellencamp, "Situation Comedy, Feminism, and Freud: Discourses of Gracie and Lucy," in *Studies in Entertainment: Critical Approaches to Mass Culture,* ed. Tania Modleski (Bloomington: Indiana University Press, 1986), 80–95; Serafina Bathrick, "*The Mary Tyler Moore Show:* Women at Home and at Work," in *MTM: "Quality Television,"* ed. Jane Feuer, Paul Kerr, and Tise Vahimagi (London: British Film Institute, 1984), 99–131.

10 E. Ann Kaplan, "Feminist Criticism and Television," in Allen, *Channels of Discourse, Reassembled,* 270–76; John Fiske, "British Cultural Studies," in Allen, *Channels of Discourse, Reassembled,* 304–18; Lisa A. Lewis, *Gender Politics and MTV: Voicing the Difference* (Philadelphia: Temple University Press, 1990); Cathy Schwichtenberg, *The Madonna Connection: Representational Politics, Subcultural Identities, and Cultural Theory* (Boulder, Colo.: Westview Press, 1993).

11 Lauren Rabinovitz, "Sitcoms and Single Moms: Representations of Feminism on American TV," *Cinema Journal* 29, no. 1 (fall 1989): 3–19.

12 Sandy Flitterman, "Thighs and Whiskers, the Fascination of *Magnum, p.i.*," *Screen* 26, no. 2 (1985): 42–58; Mary Beth Haralovich, "'Champagne Taste on a Beer Budget': Series Design and Popular Appeal in *Magnum, p.i.*," *Journal of Film and Video* 43, nos. 1–2 (spring–summer 1991): 123–34.

13 Christine Gledhill, "Pleasurable Negotiations," in *Female Spectators: Looking at Film and Television,* ed. E. Deidre Pribram (London: Verso, 1988), 64–89; Lynne Joyrich, "All That Television Allows: TV Melodrama, Postmodernism, and Consumer Culture," *Camera Obscura* 16 (winter 1988), reprinted in *Private Screenings: Television and the Female Consumer,* ed. Lynn Spigel and Denise Mann (Minneapolis: University of Minnesota Press, 1992); Patrice Petro, "Mass Culture and the Feminine: The 'Place' of Television in Film Studies," *Cinema Journal* 25, no. 3 (1986): 5–21.

14 Helen Baehr and Gillian Dyer, eds., *Boxed In: Women and Television* (London:

Pandora Press, 1987); Pribram, *Female Spectators;* Janet Bergstrom and Mary Ann Doane, eds., *Camera Obscura* 20–21 (1989), special issue, "The Spectatrix"; Mary Ellen Brown, ed., *Television and Women's Culture: The Politics of the Popular* (London: Sage, 1990); Andrea Press, *Women Watching Television: Gender, Class, and Generation in the American Television Experience* (Philadelphia: University of Pennsylvania Press, 1991).

15 Stuart Hall, "Encoding/decoding," in *Culture, Media, Language,* ed. Stuart Hall, Dorothy Hobson, Andrew Lowe, and Paul Willis (London: Hutchinson/Centre for Contemporary Cultural Studies, 1980), 128–38; Tony Bennett, "Texts, Readers, Reading Formations," *Bulletin of the Midwest Modern Language Association* 16 (spring 1983): 3–17; Tony Bennett and Janet Woollacott, *Bond and Beyond: The Political Career of a Popular Hero* (New York: Methuen, 1987); David Morley, *The "Nationwide" Audience: Structure and Decoding* (London: British Film Institute, 1980); Angela McRobbie, "Settling Accounts with Subculture: A Feminist Critique," in *Culture, Ideology, and Social Process: A Reader,* ed. Tony Bennett et al. (London: Open University Press, 1981), 113–23; Janice A. Radway, *Reading the Romance: Women, Patriarchy, and Popular Literature* (Chapel Hill: University of North Carolina Press, 1984).

16 Ien Ang, *Watching Dallas: Soap Opera and the Melodramatic Imagination,* trans. Della Couling (London: Methuen, 1985).

17 Tamar Liebes and Elihu Katz, *The Export of Meaning: Cross-Cultural Readings of Dallas* (New York: Oxford University Press, 1990). Another significant transnational study of *Dallas* is Alessandro Silj, *East of Dallas: The European Challenge to American Television* (London: British Film Institute, 1988).

18 On transnational soap opera viewing see Robert C. Allen, ed., *To be continued—: Soap Operas around the World* (New York: Routledge, 1995); Ellen Seiter, Hans Borchers, Gabriele Kreutzner, and Eva-Maria Warth, eds., *Remote Control: Television, Audiences, and Cultural Power* (New York: Routledge, 1989).

For an examplary study of how black and white audiences view differently the same television show, see Sut Jhally and Justin Lewis, *Enlightened Racism: The Cosby Show, Audiences, and the Myth of the American Dream* (Boulder, Colo.: Westview Press, 1992).

Studies of fan-subculture audiences include Henry Jenkins, *Textual Poachers: Television Fans and Participatory Culture* (New York: Routledge, 1992); Lisa A. Lewis, ed., *The Adoring Audience* (New York: Routledge, 1992). Earlier studies of fan subcultures, like John Tulloch and Manuel Alvarado's exemplary *Doctor Who: The Unfolding Text* (New York: St. Martin's Press, 1983), concentrated on the industrial, generic, and star contexts of the show's particular subcultural appeals.

19 Jane Feuer, "Reading *Dynasty:* Television and Reception Theory," *South Atlantic Quarterly* 88, no. 2 (spring 1989): 443–60.

20 For a comprehensive study of audience research and media criticism, see Virginia Nightingale, *Studying Audiences: The Shock of the Real* (London: Routledge, 1996).

21 Annette Kuhn, "Women's Genres," *Screen* 25, no. 1 (January–February 1984): 18–28.

22 Charlotte Brunsdon, "Crossroads: Notes on Soap Opera," *Screen* 22, no. 4 (1981): 32–37.

23 Julie D'Acci, *Defining Women: Television and the Case of Cagney and Lacey* (Chapel Hill: University of North Carolina Press, 1994).

24 Lynn Spigel, *Make Room for TV: Television and the Family Ideal in Postwar America* (Chicago: University of Chicago Press, 1992); Mary Beth Haralovich, "Sitcoms and Suburbs: Positioning the 1950s Homemaker," *Quarterly Review of Film and Video* 11 (1989): 61–83, reprinted in Spigel and Mann, *Private Screenings*, 111–42. Another study on this topic is Nina C. Leibman, *Living Room Lectures: The Fifties Family in Film and Television* (Austin: University of Texas Press, 1995).

25 Gloria-Jean Masciarotte, "C'mon Girl: Oprah Winfrey and the Discourse of Feminine Talk," *Genders* 11 (fall 1991): 81–110; Margaret Morse, "Talk, Talk, Talk—the Space of Discourse in Television," *Screen* 26, no. 2 (1985): 2–15; Jane M. Shattuc, *The Talking Cure: TV Talk Shows and Women* (New York: Routledge, 1997).

26 Lauren Rabinovitz, "Soap Opera Bridal Fantasies," *Screen* 33, no. 3 (autumn 1992): 274–83.

27 See, for example, Patricia Mellencamp, ed., *Logics of Television: Essays in Cultural Criticism* (Bloomington: Indiana University Press, 1990); Brown, *Television and Women's Culture;* Toni Morrison, ed., *Race-ing Justice, Engendering Power: Essays on Anita Hill, Clarence Thomas, and the Construction of Social Reality* (New York: Pantheon, 1992); Spigel and Mann, *Private Screenings;* Mimi White, *Tele-Advising: Therapeutic Discourse in American Television* (Chapel Hill: University of North Carolina Press, 1992); Alexander Doty, *Making Things Perfectly Queer: Interpreting Mass Culture* (Minneapolis: University of Minnesota Press, 1993); Beverley Skeggs, ed., *Feminist Cultural Theory: Process and Production* (Manchester: Manchester University Press, 1995); Barbara Caine and Rosemary Pringle, eds., *Transitions: New Australian Feminisms* (New York: St. Martin's Press, 1995); Lynne Joyrich, *Re-viewing Reception: Television, Gender, and Postmodern Culture* (Bloomington: Indiana University Press, 1996); Sasha Torres, ed., *Living Color: Race and Television in the United States* (Durham, N.C.: Duke University Press, 1998).

A collection of essays that chronologically samples feminist television criticism is Charlotte Brunsdon, Julie D'Acci, and Lynn Spigel, eds., *Feminist Television Criticism: A Reader* (London: Oxford University Press, 1997).

28 Although his discussions about power can be found throughout his work, Foucault most specifically defines power in *The Archaeology of Knowledge*, trans. A. M. Sheridan Smith (New York: Pantheon, 1972) and *Power/Knowledge: Selected Interviews and Other Writings, 1972–1977*, ed. and trans. Colin Gordon (New York: Pantheon, 1980).

Desired and Feared

Women's Voices in Radio History

Michele Hilmes

Television in the 1950s presents an already sedimented structure of decisions, definitions, and distinctions. It owes its facade to the outcomes of struggles that took place in radio during the previous three decades. Economic and regulatory structures, organizational practices, program forms, notions of scheduling, and ways of conceptualizing and addressing the audience carry over with little debate or disruption from 1930s and 1940s radio to television. Yet radio's legacy to television, though generally acknowledged, has not been sufficiently explored or theorized. Discussions of televisual structures and practices lack historical context and thus remain cut off from their historical roots, which naturalizes conditions that are in fact shaped by intense conflict and dispute.[1] Several recent studies revise received broadcast history and question such "givens" as the inevitability of the commercial system, the provenance of daytime soap operas, and the relationship of television to the female audience.[2] One topic that has received little attention is the role played by gender distinctions and definitions in shaping broadcasting's basic institutions and practices during its very earliest years.

Gender is rarely treated as a structural determinant in standard histories of radio.[3] Such important and basic characteristics of radio and television as the limited participation of women in broadcast production and management and the division of the day into gendered segments featuring gendered program forms are taken as merely reflective of the larger social condition, or are assumed to be based on purely economic decisions. Yet the fact remains that, although women have always been the primary audience of broadcasting's commercial address, their agency as active "speakers" and producers in the medium has been severely and deliberately circumscribed. Similarly, early broadcasters created a separate, restricted, and culturally disparaged genre of "women's programs" to fill up the daytime hours, thus defining and differentiating the interests of women as distinct from those of the "general public." Though recent research has begun to recognize the primacy of gender in televisual discourse,[4] the ways in which assumptions about gender were used to shape radio, and as a consequence television, remain unexplored.

Long before television arrived, with its already determined patterns of domesticated address and economic structures, there was a time in which broadcasting's address to women, and by women, remained up for grabs, and important battles were fought over possession of this emerging medium. Would women—only recently enfranchised—be allowed to participate in public discourse on the public airwaves? And in what capacity—as participants in carefully structured program forms controlled by men, or as writers, producers, and announcers in their own right? Would radio be recognized as primarily a "woman's medium" because of its place in the home and marketing function? Or would dominant institutions define and contain women's speech and concerns within designated "ghettos" of daytime and "women's" genres? The ways in which these questions were answered in radio's first decade helped shape television as a medium and continue to resonate today.

The period between 1922 and 1927 was a period of crisis and fluidity during which radio amateurs, the first stations, and interested parties from various fields experimented with structures and formats for utilizing the new medium. During this period, women entered into both radio institutions and discourses in relatively unrestricted capacities, frequently as announcers and station managers. Likewise, early station schedules show little sense of program differentiation by time of day or assumed audience. But by 1927, radio had begun to settle into the structures and practices later adopted by television. Male announcers, producers, and managers dominated the most publicly visible portions of the airwaves, with women pushed aside into those areas specifically designated as "female"—usually having to do with educational, children's, and "women's" concerns. Daytime, defined as the natural terrain of women, subsumed its early educational emphasis into the low-budget, culturally disparaged hard sell of the daytime serial projected into the private and "hidden" world of feminine domestic space.[5] Nighttime—though still with a predominantly female audience—became the territory of public, and male, authority, and its programs had a dual purpose: to sell not only the Sponsor's products but also radio as a public medium. Notions of gender played a pivotal role in these seemingly "natural" divisions and definitions.

The Feminine Mass

For radio and television, the discourse of gender has been used as a device to both institutionalize and conceal a tension lying at the heart of the broadcasting enterprise: the conflict between official public discourse laying claim to broadcasting's "high culture" terrain and radio's economic dependence on market forces dominated by the sale of products to women. Advertising studies since 1918 had confirmed that 85 percent of household purchases were made by women, making them the primary target for radio's increasingly commercial address.[6] Women became the audience at once most desired and feared in the structure of broadcasting: desired because their participation was central to the basic functioning of the institution, especially as it was colonized by the program production departments of major advertising agencies, yet feared because they occupied a discursive space linked to threatening concepts of the irrational, passive, emotional, and culturally suspect "masses."

By the mid-1920s, according to Roland Marchand, major advertising agencies had arrived at a definition of consumers as "an emotional, feminized mass, characterized by mental lethargy, bad taste, and ignorance":

> The growing consensus about audience emotionality helped fuse the other observed audience traits into a composite conception. Popular convention defined emotion as a particular characteristic of women —and the advertising audience was overwhelmingly female. In fact, nearly every characteristic commonly attributed to the masses was also conventionally a "feminine" trait—capriciousness, irrationality, passivity, and conformism.[7]

Marchand explains that these associations stem partially from the need of educated, upper-middle-class advertising men to distance themselves from the masses they somewhat cynically manipulated:

> As a last resort, in the protection of their self-esteem and as a psychological weapon against cultural engulfment by the tastes of the con-

> sumer masses, advertisers could always emphasize the stereotyped gender distinction between advertisers as men and consumers as women. This distinction shielded the advertising elite . . . from being debased by the vulgarity and backwardness of the consumer masses.[8]

Andreas Huyssen theorizes this feminization of mass culture more broadly, exploring "the notion which gained ground during the nineteenth century that mass culture is somehow associated with woman while real, authentic culture remains the prerogative of men."[9] This conceptualization had material consequences: "The universalizing ascription of femininity to mass culture always depended on the very real exclusion of women from high culture and its institutions."[10] Negotiations of high and mass culture played a large role in the development of radio. Broadcasting maintained a deeply conflicted social status as a public institution upholding official "high" culture yet given over to selling products for private profit to a mass audience. Its mass/private/feminine base constantly threatened to overwhelm its high/public/masculine function. Strong measures were required to defuse this threat—a threat perceived as feminine.

As active agents within broadcasting institutions and as audiences, women had to be carefully contained and set apart in an explicitly differentiated and subordinated category. This subordination occurred on three levels. Institutionally, women's actual efforts were segregated into certain corporate functions and away from others, reducing their options and restricting them to women's, children's, and educational areas. Definitionally, a separate genre of "women's programming" was created and enforced, a world of soap operas and homemakers' talks strictly relegated to daytime hours. And discursively, distinctive program practices were developed that literally contained and controlled the voices and experience of women. The institutional debate over female announcers in the mid-1920s and the creation in the mid-1930s of gendered concepts of audience and programming emerge as central to this history.

"Are Women Undesirable—Over the Air?"

In September 1925, the article "A Girl Reporter-Announcer Speaks Up: Radio in Days of Yore" appeared in the newly minted fan journal, *Radio*

Age. It describes the experience of Gwen Wagner at station WPO (Memphis, Tennessee) a full four years previously, in 1921:

> Our staff in those days consisted of two. My only assistant was a young chap by the name of Percy Root, who took care of the mechanical end of the station at night and, during the day, worked at something else. . . . For myself, I worked during the day as reporter on the newspaper which sponsored the station. In addition to my general assignments, I wrote all the material for the radio column, engaged the radio artists and arranged the programs. At night I went out to the studio and broadcast.[11]

Serving as combination station manager, talent bureau, program director, announcer, and publicist, Wagner's experience was not unusual for this period in radio's development. In the early 1920s many women went into broadcasting, both on the air as announcers and off the air as program directors and station managers.[12]

Bertha Brainard represents one of the earliest announcers in radio, debuting at WJZ (New York) in 1922 in a special show of her own devising, *Bertha Brainard Broadcasts Broadway*. She was appointed program director of the station in 1923 and station manager in 1926. Upon the formation of NBC, Brainard was made the network's Commercial Program Director and served in that role until her death in 1943. Judith Waller joined WMAQ (Chicago) in 1922 as its first station manager; she not only provided a certain amount of on-air announcing but is credited with instituting live baseball coverage from Wrigley Field, finding commercial sponsorship and network coverage for the innovative program *Amos 'n' Andy*, and initiating the famed University of Chicago Round Table, among many other achievements. She became Vice President and General Manager of WMAQ in 1929. Upon NBC's purchase of the station in 1931, her responsibilities shifted to Educational Director of NBC's Central Division.[13] Margaret Cuthbert announced and planned daytime talks on WEAF (New York) beginning in 1923 and was later promoted to Director of Women's Activities at NBC. Myrtle Stahl announced and answered audience mail at WDAP (later WGN) in Chicago, where she was hired as general program director in 1922 but later moved to the audience response division. Other early women announcer/programmers include Dorothy Gordon at WEAF (New York), later in charge of children's programs; Madge Tucker at WRC (Washington, D.C.); and V. A. L. Jones of KSD (St. Louis). There were many others, most of whom later specialized in either women's, children's, and educational or public service programming by the middle 1930s. This eventual direction and channeling of their efforts into areas deemed appropriate for women points to the central role that gender played in the definition of the social and discursive functions of broadcasting.

One of the earliest institutional responses to the destabilizing effects of women's presence in the industry was the 1924 controversy over women's suitability as announcers. From the beginnings of standardized radio operation in 1922 into the early 1930s, the station announcer occupied a key position in broadcast programming. Usually combining the functions of program producer, talent coordinator, and on-air host—and often expected to fill in with musical or comedic talent when guest artists failed to appear—the announcer became the most prominent figure in early radio, a celebrity in his or her own right. As program forms standardized and became more self-contained, the role of the announcer as the "glue" in the station schedule decreased. Early announcers went on to provide news and sports coverage, introduce programs, emcee musical variety shows, and serve as the voice of the sponsor during commercial breaks. Many women, such as those listed above, served as announcers on stations around the country. But by 1930, women's voices had virtually disappeared from nighttime schedules and could only be heard during daytime hours, when they were devoted specifically to what the broadcasters thought of as "women's" concerns.

The 1924 debate over women's suitability as announcers began with a letter sent to Jennie Irene Mix of *Radio Broadcast* magazine, one of the new breed of publications catering to the entertainment-oriented radio listener, as opposed to technical journals for set-builders and ham operators. Mix wrote "The Listener's Point of View," the first regular critical column on radio programs in the popular press. She reported that a phonograph record dealer had written in to say that the poor sales of recordings featuring women speakers caused him to speculate that the public would not accept female radio announcers:

> When the speaker is not seen in person, and if that speaker be a woman, her voice is very undesirable, and to many, both men and women, displeasing. . . . People will not pay good money to listen to

> the talking record of a woman's voice. Consequently, I believe that a vote of radio fans would show great disapproval of woman announcers and speakers.[14]

Does this mean, asked Mix, that "when a woman is speaking she may be fascinating as long as she remains in sight, and becomes displeasing the moment she cannot be seen although she may go right on talking just as delightfully as the moment before?"[15] To explore this issue, Mix invited the opinions of several station managers—all male—for the September 1924 edition of the magazine.

Two of the managers dismissed outright the idea of women's unsuitability, citing the many women on radio and improvements in the reproduction of higher-pitched sound. But most agreed that women announcers and lecturers suffered from a variety of handicaps. "Few women have voices with distinct personality. It is my opinion that women depend on everything else but the voice for their appeal," stated W. W. Rogers of Westinghouse and KDKA (Pittsburgh). Corley W. Kirbett, director of WWJ (Detroit), bluntly opined, "I do not believe that women are fitted for radio announcers. They need body to their voices. . . . When women announcers try to be congenial in their announcements, they become affected; and when they attempt to be business like they are stiff." J. M. Barnett, manager of WOR (New York), concluded, "For certain types of radio work I consider that a woman's voice is very essential; but for announcing, a well modulated male voice is the most pleasing to listen to," since women's voices tend to be "monotonous." Or again, according to M. A. Rigg of WGR (Buffalo): "There are many reasons why, to my mind, it seems advisable to use a man as announcer, especially during the heavier part of the work."[16]

In response, Mix defended women announcers by noting that most of these managers expressed their views as matters of personal opinion and not because they had been inundated with complaints from listeners regarding women announcers. She countered the criticism with an additional feature on the many women on-the-air announcers, including those at the stations of the managers cited above—such as Bertha Brainard of WJZ (New York) and Helen M. White at WGR (Buffalo). In 1925 Mix died unexpectedly. Her column was taken over by John Wallace, who revived the debate the next year when he commented on the results of a survey reportedly undertaken by John Popenoe, manager of WJZ (New

York), who was, perhaps not coincidentally, Bertha Brainard's supervisor. Stating that a poll of five thousand listeners showed that men's voices were preferred to women's by a margin of 100 to 1, Popenoe speculated:

> It is difficult to say why the public should be so unanimous about it. One reason may be that most receiving sets do not reproduce perfectly the higher notes. A man's voice "takes" better. It has more volume. Then, announcers cover sporting events, shows, concerts, operas, and big public meetings. Men are naturally better fitted for the average assignment of the broadcast announcer. . . . But perhaps the best reason suggested for the unpopularity of the woman's voice over the radio is that it usually has too much personality. A voice that is highly individual and full of character is aggravating to the audience that cannot see the face and expression which go with the voice. We resent a voice that is too intimate on short acquaintance, and the woman announcer has difficulty in repressing her enthusiasm and in maintaining the necessary reserve and objectivity.[17]

It is encouraging, I suppose, that in two short years women have gone from being perceived as having no personality on the air to having too much. But either condition seems to be a liability when the woman cannot be physically viewed.

This survey would be absorbed into general knowledge in radio circles, as demonstrated by a 1933 newspaper article by Martin Codell. Discussing the more numerous examples of female radio announcers in Europe and their relative absence on the U.S. airwaves, he concludes:

> First, there is an apparently unshakable prejudice among the broadcast impresarios against women announcers; they are convinced that women's voices do not have the proper appealing quality . . . [and] say is it impossible to send a woman out on an assignment like covering a baseball game or football game or political convention or such like news events. They simply are not physically or by experience and temperament suited to the job, we are told.[18]

This debate clearly expresses the view that there are dangerous qualities specifically linked to the feminine in this nonvisual medium. We can see in radio in the 1920s the already formed issue of what Amy Lawrence calls "the problem of the speaking woman." Lawrence, building on the work of feminist film theorists Mary Ann Doane and Kaja Silverman, identifies ways in which women's voices have been contained and subordinated within classical Hollywood cinema:

> Women's voices are positioned within narratives that require their submission to patriarchal rules. . . . Female characters are made to use language that silences them. . . . The cinematic conventions of visual and audio representation convert woman to spectacle, precluding her status as subject, and [place] women on the weak end of sound/image hierarchies. . . . The authorial voice is rarely heard as a woman's voice in classical cinema.[19]

Radio offered a sphere of purely aural representation in which women's voices would be similarly contained.[20] The insistence on women's bodies, appearance, and sexualized physical presence demonstrates that radio awoke the same culturally subversive possibilities as did classical Hollywood cinema. Yet radio's potential for freeing women's voices from their bodies threatened to evade the visual containment mechanisms of other media. Maintaining a visual referent controls the threatening possibility that gender might become obscured. If a woman who is heard cannot be seen, how can one tell if that disembodied voice is male or female? In a medium in which adult actors made a living playing babies and children, whites impersonated blacks, young performers played the elderly, and humans imitated animals, the potential for gender subversion was great indeed.

Popenoe's summary and the comments of radio station managers quoted by Mix also contend that radio technology is physically and naturally less suited to women's voices. A closer examination of studies done during the period reveals that this was true only in the reproduction of the highest notes of a soprano's singing voice and not in the case of a normal speaking voice.[21] Indeed, many early male announcers possessed voices in the tenor range, easily congruent with female tones. An invocation of technology, stereotypically a male preserve, reinforces radio's essential "maleness." Even qualities for which male radio announcers were commonly praised—intimacy, emotion, personality[22]—are characterized as not suitable when emanating from a woman.

Deviant Daytime

Along with the containment of women's voices, a definition of the primary business of radio programming begins to emerge in the statements of these station managers: to broadcast high/public/masculine concerns (i.e., news, sports, and politics) to a male audience. By this definition, the exclusion of women from announcing and central administrative jobs could be justified as a "natural" extension of women's separate social role and physical attributes. But over the next few years radio would develop quite a different economic base, one that depended on catering to female purchasers of products. During the late 1920s and early 1930s, programming practices began to respond to these new economic conditions. Advertising agencies moved into production of commercially sponsored programs with the important female audience in mind.

Station schedules of this period show far less program differentiation by day part than later became the rule. A mix of musical variety, talk, serial drama, and "serious" music programming filled both day and evening hours.[23] Only after 1933 does a firm distinction between day and nighttime programming take hold; for example, until the middle 1930s, several women's serial drama shows aired in the evenings. *The Goldbergs*, written and performed by Gertrude Berg, debuted on NBC in September 1929 as an early evening show, running nightly at various times from 7:00 to 7:45. Despite its high ratings and mixed audience it was moved to daytime in the 1935–36 season. *Clara, Lu and Em* originated in Chicago in 1931 and aired daily at 10:30 P.M. but moved to daytime in 1933. *Just Plain Bill*, a Frank and Anne Hummert production, began on CBS in 1932 at 6:45 P.M. five times a week but moved to 11:45 A.M. in the 1935–36 season. *Myrt and Marge*, another Chicago show, also aired at 7:00 P.M. from 1931 until 1937; it was one of the last of the nighttime women's serial dramas, and with its removal from evening schedules an era ended.[24] By 1937, no women's serials remained on the airwaves after dark. In contrast, daytime programming featured little else. *Variety* discussed the change in these terms:

> As regards daytime programs—a change has taken place here, too. . . . the daytime programs are now nearly all serials. This development is one of salesmanship, not showmanship. The serial for the housewife,

> like the serial for the child, is designated to sustain interest in a continued story, day by day, and with it bring sales. Crude, perhaps, as compared to the evening program, it nonetheless has not yet burned itself out.[25]

By 1936, according to *Variety*'s statistics, the network daytime schedule consisted of 55.3 percent serial drama, 16.1 percent "talks," and 11.4 percent juvenile programs. Evening schedules showed a preponderance of prestige comedy/variety and dramatic adaptation programs, types rarely found on daytime. *Variety*'s designation of daytime serials as "crude," equating women's levels of sophistication with those of children and drawing a distinction between them and the more "serious" programming of the nighttime hours, shows that the subordinate positioning of women's programming was central to emerging broadcast practices.

What was the basis for these distinctions that defined not only who the audience was but the type of program appropriate to them? Most radio and advertising reports agreed that the daytime audience was predominantly female, though most glossed over the fact that the nighttime audience also contained a majority of female listeners. Yet the mere gender of the audience did not necessarily mandate the kind of low-budget, culturally disparaged serial programming that most historians take for granted. Bertha Brainard, NBC's head of commercial programming, had proposed a very different view of daytime radio's female audience in 1932. In an internal NBC memo addressed to Roy C. Witmer, network sales director, she noted that rates for early morning hours had recently been raised to equal later morning and afternoon and suggested a further policy change:

> I am looking forward to the day when you and the sponsors realize that the daytime hours are our most important selling times and the rates for the daytime hours will be double those of the evening, in view of the fact that all our real selling will be done to the women in the daytime, and the institutional good will programs will be directed to the mixed audiences after 6:00 PM. I am such a confirmed feminist that I thoroughly believe this is going to take place, and in the not too distance [*sic*] future.[26]

Witmer scrawled a note on the bottom of the memo: "I'll go with you part way—day time rates equal to night time."

Here is a version of time-of-day distinction that envisions the daylight hours as the most valuable part of the radio schedule, more costly to the advertiser than the evening, and presumably receiving the main focus of commercial programming efforts. Yet daytime rates remained half of nighttime rates, and by the end of the decade daytime radio had indeed differentiated itself from its evening counterparts—by becoming synonymous with the vulgar "serialized drool" of the daytime serial and the trivial commercialism of the women's talk show.[27]

The growing distinction between daytime programming for women, as opposed to nighttime programming for a more "general" (male-characterized) audience, resulted from a complex network of definitions and decisions involving more than simple economics. Much of it has to do with radio's dual mission of public service and profit, and the conflicting ideas of appropriate audience and content that ensued.[28] This tension, between programming for profit and programming for public image, rests on both gender and class distinctions, but its central component is the image of the "feminine mass"—the lower- to middle-class buying audience considered as feminine—as distinct from that of the nighttime critical audience of public decision makers.

It is no coincidence that this discursive dilemma reached a crisis in the middle 1930s. Robert McChesney convincingly argues that the interregulatory years—between the Radio Act of 1927 and the final closure of debate after passage of the Communications Act of 1934—represent the only window during which serious debate over broadcasting's social and commercial function came close to effecting structural changes in the advertising and network-based system. Rebutting accounts of radio's origins that portray its commercial base as eagerly accepted by the U.S. populace or as a result of careful planning and debate, McChesney demonstrates that this was a period of intense lobbying and ideological controversy, with proponents of radio's educational and public service uses eventually outgunned by the commercial radio lobby, via Congress.[29]

Broadcasters during this period of contested credibility had two formidable projects. One was to exploit an economic base that clearly rested on the female purchaser of household products, a function that remains primary in television and radio today. The other, however, required the radio industry to convince regulators that their mission consisted as much of public service programming as of sheer commercialism, even in the hours sold to sponsors, in order to rebuff educational broadcasters' claims on the spectrum. According to McChesney,

> The commercial broadcasters had to convince the public and public officials that they were firmly committed to high-grade cultural and educational programming. . . . Establishing a commitment to cultural programming was seen as being of fundamental importance in keeping increased government regulation or even radical reform at bay.[30]

One way to achieve this end was to differentiate between daytime and nighttime programming, by which the daytime became the venue for a debased kind of commercialized, feminized mass culture—heavily dominated by advertising agencies—in contrast to the more sophisticated, respectable, and masculine-characterized arena of prime time. Networks distanced themselves from their daytime schedules, selling daytime hours in blocks to sponsors and taking very little part in their production. By removing those forms most closely associated with women—and usually produced and written by women—from the evening schedule, and by building up the nighttime hours with prestigious commercial productions and serious sustaining programs in which women's roles were nonexistent or marginal, the radio networks sought to improve their image of public responsibility through containment of the devalued feminine. Nighttime thus became the more highly "visible," public, and publicized part of the broadcast schedule associated with "normal" audiences assumed to be masculine. Daytime hours—increasingly ceded to the overly commercial, feminized address of the daytime serials—became the private, less "visible," even obscure site of practices marked out as deviant from the norm, despite their substantial audiences and important economic function.

However, while differentiation of the daytime audience and programming worked to justify the exclusion of women's voices and concerns from the more masculinized forms of the evening, it also provided a space in which feminine writers, producers, and listeners could function more freely, out of the public eye. Under cover of daytime, women's programs addressed a wider range of specifically feminine concerns and explored a greater range of female occupations and issues than standard prime-time fare, in forms developed specifically for this purpose and least likely to be penetrated, or understood, by male executives and critics whose discourse dominated mainstream radio. Under cover of cultural obscurity, women spoke to women about issues of concern to women—though rarely outside the ultimately confining and narrow role of home consumer imposed by commercial interests. Millions of female listeners tuned in to the struggles of the serials' women—heroines often torn between responsibilities of home and family and careers in the larger world—and responded in enormous numbers of fan letters. At the same time, the power of these texts was contained and denigrated in the mainstream press, in articles such as James Thurber's series "Soapland" in that bastion of elite culture, the *New Yorker,* and in Philip Hamburger's insidious and damaging satire of daytime radio talk show host Mary Margaret McBride that appeared in *Life* in 1944.[31]

It is within this tension between the publicly delegitimated space of daytime radio and the defeminized address of nighttime radio that the careers of female radio pioneers were built. For example, Irna Phillips, Elaine Carrington, and Jane Crusinberry were influential writers and producers of soap operas and other radio dramas, including *Today's Children* (NBC, 1933–49), *Guiding Light* (various networks, 1937 to the present), *Pepper Young's Family* (NBC, 1936–46), *The Story of Mary Marlin* (NBC, 1934–45), and many more.[32] Anne Ashenhurst Hummert and her husband Frank operated the largest production house specializing in serials in U.S. radio from the 1930s through the 1960s. Nellie Revell was a journalist who pioneered a daytime interview format program on NBC in 1935. Mary Margaret McBride, another journalist, developed the first successful ad-libbed magazine-format multiple sponsorship talk show in 1934 over WOR, moving to CBS, then NBC, with topics ranging from recipes to politics to arts and public affairs. According to the National Association of Broadcasters, by 1950 McBride's audience consisted of 20 percent of radio households—a fact conveniently forgotten when Pat Weaver "discovered" the magazine/multiple-sponsor format for television in the early 1950s.[33]

Conclusion

Gender as a structural determinant both in broadcasting history itself and in historiography has remained unexplored until only recently, when scholars began to focus on television's feminine audiences and their negotiation of televisual texts. Expanding these historical insights backward into the important but neglected decades of network radio—the prehistory of television—can reveal the struggles over conditions of production and reception and the terms on which these struggles took place. Early television, faced with the same regulatory dilemma as the radio industry of the 1930s, similarly sought to conceal the feminized commercialism at the heart of its enterprise and to emphasize its serious, high-culture address and public service functions. William Boddy's analysis of television's Golden Age reveals that the networks' positioning of themselves on the cultural high ground worked to displace advertising agencies from their former powerful roles and to keep Hollywood at bay.[34] A closer reading might also uncover the fact that gender functioned in this process in very much the same way as it did in the 1930s, when networks identified themselves with live character based dramas indebted to the legitimate stage and distanced themselves from commercial forms such as the daytime serial. According to Christopher Anderson's recent reexamination of the period, ABC went so far as to ban the serial form from nighttime:

> At the time . . . soap operas were a somewhat disreputable form of programming locked in the women's ghetto of daytime TV. In spite of ABC's concern with demographics, the network seemed convinced that the appeal of soap operas was too limited for prime time and expressly prohibited Warner Bros. from producing open-ended serials for *Warner Bros. Presents.*[35]

Not until the 1970s did the networks feel secure enough to experiment with the prime-time soap. Their success with such serials as *Dallas* and *Knot's Landing*—and Fox's current *Beverly Hills 90210* and *Melrose Place*—indicates that this form's exclusion from the evening hours has rested on something more than either demographics or economics. Recent controversies over "tabloid television" and talk shows also centrally involve gender distinctions. The discursive functions of gender must be considered along with more obvious factors if we are to understand the development of broadcasting practices.

Notes

1 Both William Boddy, *Fifties Television: The Industry and Its Critics* (Urbana: University of Illinois Press, 1990) and Mary Ann Watson, *The Expanding*

Vista: American Television in the Kennedy Years (New York: Oxford University Press, 1990) provide analyses of television industry practices and programs that could have benefited from increased attention to the decades of radio that preceded the period they discuss. For an extended critique of this historical omission, see Michele Hilmes, "Born Yesterday: Television and the Academic Mind," *American Literary History* 6, no. 4 (winter 1994): 791–802.

2 See Julie D'Acci, *Defining Women: Television and the Case of Cagney and Lacey* (Chapel Hill: University of North Carolina Press, 1994); Robert McChesney, *Telecommunications, Mass Media, and Democracy* (New York: Oxford University Press, 1993); Robert C. Allen, *Speaking of Soap Operas* (Chapel Hill: University of North Carolina Press, 1985); Lynn Spigel, *Make Room for TV: Television and the Family Ideal in Postwar America* (Chicago: University of Chicago Press, 1992); Lynn Spigel and Denise Mann, eds., *Private Screenings: Television and the Female Consumer* (Minneapolis: University of Minnesota Press, 1992); and Christopher Anderson, *Hollywood TV: The Studio System in the Fifties* (Austin: University of Texas Press, 1994).

3 This criticism would apply to such works as Christopher H. Sterling and John M. Kitross, *Stay Tuned: A Concise History of American Broadcasting,* 2d ed. (Belmont, Calif.: Wadsworth, 1990); Erik Barnouw, *History of Broadcasting,* 3 vols. (New York: Oxford University Press, 1966, 1968, 1970); and J. Fred MacDonald, *Don't Touch That Dial!* (Chicago: Nelson Hall, 1980). As Lynn Spigel notes, "Women . . . are systematically marginalized in television history. According to the assumptions of our current historical paradigms, the woman is simply the receiver of the television text—the one to whom the advertiser promotes products" (*Make Room for TV,* 5).

4 See, in particular, Spigel, *Make Room for TV;* Spigel and Mann, *Private Screenings;* and D'Acci, *Defining Women.*

5 See Allen, *Speaking of Soap Operas,* esp. chap. 1; Ellen C. Seiter, "To Teach and To Sell: Irna Phillips and Her Sponsors, 1930–1954," *Journal of Film and Video* 41, no. 1 (spring 1989): 21–34.

6 "Women in Advertising," J. Walter Thompson house advertisement, 1918, J. Walter Thompson Collection (JWT), Duke University, Durham, N.C.; for later iterations see "Importance of Women as Consumers and Employees," memo from Marianne Keating to Ruth Ritenour, 19 October 1964, RG 3, box 8, folder 19: Officers and Staff: Sidney Bernstein: JWT History: Women, JWT. See also NBC promotional brochures in the late 1930s and 1940s emphasizing these statistics in the E. P. H. James collection, box 1, folder 12, State Historical Society of Wisconsin, Madison.

7 Roland Marchand, *Advertising the American Dream* (Berkeley: University of California Press, 1985), 69.

8 Ibid., 162.

9 Andreas Huyssen, *After the Great Divide: Modernism, Mass Culture, Postmodernism* (Bloomington: Indiana University Press, 1986), 47.

10 Ibid., 62.

11 Gwen Wagner, "A Girl Reporter-Announcer Speaks Up: Radio in Days of Yore," *Radio Age*, September 1925, 30 ff.

12 Two studies of women in broadcasting, done in the 1940s, briefly delineate the careers of other female broadcasters, whose functions ranged from homemaker advice programs, children's shows, and public service, to writing for radio's ubiquitous daytime serial dramas, to sports reporting (in one unusual case). See Ruth Adams Knight, *Make Way for the Ladies: The Distaff Side of Broadcasting* (New York: Coward McCann, 1939); Francis Willard Kerr, "Women in Radio: A View of Important Jobs in Radio Held By Women" (Washington, D.C.: U.S. Department of Labor, Women's Bureau, 1947). Their existence points not to the lack of women in this field—indeed, both studies have trouble encompassing the magnitude of their task—but to the conflicted status of women and women's programming within broadcasting.

13 *Twenty Year Club of Radio Pioneers* (New York: Radio Pioneers, 1947), 17, 102.

14 "What Our Readers Write Us," *Radio Broadcast* 5, no. 2 (June 1924): 172.

15 Jennie Irene Mix, "The Listeners' Point of View," *Radio Broadcast* 5, no. 4 (August 1924): 332–36. I am indebted to Anne McKay for bringing this exchange to my attention some years ago; see her "Artificial Voice Amplification and Women's Struggle for a Public Presence," in *Technology and Women's Voices: Keeping in Touch*, ed. Cheris Kramarae (New York: Routledge and Kegan Paul, 1988), 187–206.

16 Jennie Irene Mix, "The Listeners' Point of View," *Radio Broadcast* 5, no. 5 (September 1924): 391–97. Exactly what is meant by the "heavier" part of announcing remains unclear.

17 John Wallace, "The Listeners' Point of View," *Radio Broadcast* 10, no. 1 (November 1926): 44–45.

18 "Women Announcers—Why Not? Weaker Sex Heard Often in European Air, but Only Few Make Grade Here," Martin Codell Collection, scrapbook no. 60, 1933, State Historical Society of Wisconsin, Madison.

19 Amy Lawrence, *Echo and Narcissus: Women's Voices in Classical Hollywood Cinema* (Berkeley: University of California Press, 1991), 169.

20 These concerns go back to nineteenth-century popular entertainment, as Robert C. Allen has shown. Tracing the process by which burlesque, originally populated by transgressive "talking women" who dressed in men's clothing and took male parts in satirical sketches, became transformed into a medium of female physical spectacle, Allen concludes, "The burlesque

performer's transgressive power was circumscribed by her construction as exotic other, removed from the world of ordinary woman. Her power to reordinate the world was similarly limited by largely depriving her of speech. . . . The appeals of burlesque became increasingly bifurcated: verbal humor provided usually by male comedians and sexual display provided by female performers" (Allen, *Horrible Prettiness: Burlesque and American Culture* [Chapel Hill: University of North Carolina Press, 1991], 237–38).

21 John F. Rider, "Why Is a Radio Soprano Unpopular?" *Scientific American*, October 1928, 334–37.

22 See Carl Dreher, "The High and Mighty Place of the Announcer," *Radio Broadcast*, December 1926, 180–81. During this period many books advising potential sponsors and others emphasize the desired qualities of emotion, intimacy, and personality in an announcer's voice and address; see, for instance, Edgar H. Felix, *Using Radio in Sales Promotion* (New York: McGraw Hill, 1927), 153–59.

23 See, for instance, "WJZ Logs," box 98, folder 11 (1924) and 25 (1927), NBC Collection, State Historical Society of Wisconsin, Madison.

24 See Harrison Summers, ed., *A Thirty Year History of Programs Carried on National Radio Networks in the United States, 1926–1956* (New York: Arno Press, 1971).

25 Edgar A. Grunwald, "Program-Production History, 1929–1937," *Variety Radio Directory 1937–1938* (New York: Variety, 1937), 28.

26 Bertha Brainard to Roy C. Witmer, 23 August 1932, NBC Collection, box 90, folder 13, State Historical Society of Wisconsin, Madison.

27 See Allen, *Speaking of Soap Operas*, for a further description of the soap opera's devalued critical reputation and suspect social status; also Jennifer Wang, "Are Soap Operas Only Suds? Discursive Struggles over Daytime Serials in World War II American Culture" (paper presented at Telecommunications Colloquium, Department of Communication Arts, University of Wisconsin—Madison, April 1995).

28 Here Nancy Fraser's critique of Habermas becomes particularly relevant. Fraser demonstrates how the liberal bourgeois conception of the public sphere—a definition in which broadcasting institutions were heavily invested—was constituted as essentially masculine, in inherent opposition to the feminine/domestic sphere: "New gender norms enjoining feminine domesticity and a sharp separation of public and private spheres functioned as key signifiers of bourgeois difference from both higher and lower social strata" (Fraser, "Rethinking the Public Sphere," in *The Phantom Public Sphere*, ed. Bruce Robbins [Minneapolis: University of Minnesota Press, 1991], 1–32).

29 McChesney, *Telecommunications, Mass Media, and Democracy*.

30 Ibid., 115–16.

31 James Thurber, "Soapland," reprinted in *The Beast in Me and Other Animals* (New York: Harcourt Brace, 1948); Philip Hamburger, "Mary Margaret McBride," *Life*, 4 December 1944, 47–52.

32 For an extended discussion of this history, see Michele Hilmes, *Radio Voices: American Broadcasting, 1922–1952* (Minneapolis: University of Minnesota Press, 1997).

33 For McBride's career, see Douglas J. Carr, "The Overlooked Radio Career of Mary Margaret McBride" (paper presented at the American Popular Culture Association, New Orleans, La., June 1988). For references that attribute invention of the magazine format talk show to Pat Weaver, see James L. Baughman, "Television in the Golden Age: An Entrepreneurial Experiment," *The Historian* 47 (February 1985): 185; Harry Castleman and Walter J. Podrazik, *Watching Television* (New York: McGraw Hill 1982), 48–49; Sterling and Kitross, *Stay Tuned*, 280; Thomas Whiteside, "Profiles: The Communicator, Part 1: Athens Starts Pouring In," *New Yorker*, 16 October 1954, 37 ff.; Thomas Whiteside, "Profiles: The Communicator, Part 2: What about the Gratitude Factor?" *New Yorker*, 23 October 1954, 43 ff.; Martin Mayer, "Television's Lords of Creation, Part 1. Strategic Thinking at NBC," *Harper's Magazine*, November 1956, 25–32.

34 Boddy, *Fifties Television*.

35 Anderson, *Hollywood TV*, 209.

Considering Monty Margetts's *Cook's Corner*

Oral History and Television History

Mark Williams

One of the most direct ways to discover and introduce questions of gender and sexuality within television history is to focus on the local level of production and consumption. A most important condition of such study, however, is that individual television stations have paid surprisingly little attention to the history of their programs and practices. The television industry in general generates vast quantities of records (correspondence, proposals, studies, reports, ratings, memoranda, etc.), yet has little space and seemingly less compunction to save or to preserve them. But there appear to be especially few extant records or files pertaining to the earliest years of local television. None of the Los Angeles stations, for example, has a prepared history, perhaps because most of them have undergone significant and sometimes regular changes of ownership. Even KTLA, perhaps the most historical-minded of local stations—it presents a documentary about itself roughly every five years—has disposed of a considerable mass of materials. Such self-produced commercial programs provide historiographic contexts and emphases commensurate with both the perceived "demands" of the television marketplace and the less obvious ideologies common to popular characterizations of "history."

As a supplement to newspaper coverage of the industry, trade press coverage, and scant academic work, personal interviews are the most immediate alternative method of research for early television. Many television pioneers are still alive, and most are willing to discuss their experiences. Although some degree of nostalgia, simple mistaken memory, or perhaps even self-interest is unavoidable, such interviews can provide otherwise unobtainable details and typically lead to new directions for further research.[1]

Interviewing veterans of the industry can also suggest a historiographic methodology that complements feminist considerations. The "history" revealed in one of my favorite interviews, with Monty Margetts, raises important questions about feminist historiography. Monty, a popular personality on early Los Angeles TV, hosted *Cook's Corner*, a notable show that was premised on her readily apparent inability to cook. In the oral history process, Monty and I encountered the circumstances of women working in early television and women working at home; the potentially subversive aspects of this cooking program; and our own questions about generations of women and their relationship to waves of feminism.

Oral History and Women's History

First advocated by Allan Nevins in 1938, oral history was adopted as an institutional mode of historical inquiry roughly a decade later by Nevins and others at Columbia University. Although initially compliant with the standard emphases in historical work on "great men" as subjects, research via oral history has, especially since the 1970s, been recognized as a potentially groundbreaking mode of feminist inquiry.[2] Katherine Jensen, for example, sees work in oral history as an instance of the symbiotic relationship between feminist scholars and community feminist activists.[3] As a mode of inquiry and research, oral history responds to various gaps in the understanding of women's lives, the historical disparagement of women's activities, unchallenged generalizations about gender roles and gendered behavior, and the call for history "from below" (which usually emphasizes issues of class, race, and region).[4] In addition, oral history allows women who might feel unconnected to "official" history (i.e., already understood momentous events) to be empowered to narrate their own lives. It is therefore a useful tool in examining historical discourses and activities assigned to the realm of the everyday, the quotidian, and the marginalized.[5]

The value of work in oral history nevertheless has raised various methodological concerns, including (1) how the unique experiences of individual women can be treated or understood in relationship to the analysis of groups of women; (2) the tendency (true in much grassroots history) to reiterate similar, uncritical, nostalgic renderings; and (3) complaints from traditional historians, who position oral history as a movement away from "writing" as an essential part of the deep structure of history and who are wary about the introduction of modes of evidence that are to some degree transient in nature and not readily replicable or verifiable.[6]

For those of us who are more willing to adopt oral history, one of the most important characteristics of this kind of research derives from an awareness that oral history does not so much "find" historical evidence as generate it. Susan Armitage notes that an oral historian actually creates new documents or texts, and the recognition of this has led to an insistence on self-consciousness and reflexivity regarding oral history's methods and processes.[7] For Dan Sipe, this suggests the importance of documenting "not only the interviewer's explicit information, but the . . . dialogic relationship between interviewer and narrator, the role of memory, and the function of narrativity."[8] Sipe calls for interrogating, in other words, how interviews themselves illustrate the construction of history as a process while also remaining "consonant with a conception of history based on multiple methodologies, varied forms of evidence, and diverse modes of discourse."[9]

Oral History and Television History

Attention to theoretical reflection about methodology is also essential to, and even endemic to, historical work on early television. The vast majority of the textual and material practices in early TV were so ephemeral as to be literally lost in the air, and the status of extant materials and information pertinent to its study is in no way stable or exhaustive. This historical work should also be wary of the ready closure or erasure of discontinuities in its construction through the assignment of easy causalities that seem to ensure a "certain" truth about the past and its representations. Oral history can reveal and investigate gaps, aporias, and margins in our historical understanding of television, particularly those related to issues of gender.

Although much of the best work in critical television studies concerns TV's address in positioning gendered spectators and the centrality of this address to understanding television as a sociopolitical and ideological force, these questions have not been central to much of the work in television history.[10] Typically emphasizing the growth and practices of the major networks, these histories also tend to focus on individuals such as network executives and prime-time stars and producers, who were almost always in this era white and male.

Women, of course, had a considerable presence in early television—at both the network and local levels—as performers in prime-time narratives and variety shows, and in much of the daytime programming. The women whose careers I have so far investigated in Los Angeles worked as producers and writers in addition to their role as hosts, primarily in daytime and (to a limited extent) evening "domestic" or "service-oriented" programming.[11] Women were generally outnumbered by men in the industry during this early period, and most were relegated to secretarial and clerical positions. In a 1951 study of the Los Angeles radio-television-advertising industries, Margaret Wade reported that over 50 percent of women employees had clerical jobs, and that while some women served as producers, there were no female directors in television and only one in radio.[12] But the early television industry's demand for programming, necessary to building a habitual and loyal audience, allowed for a relatively generous window of opportunity for potential on-air personalities.

Radio had already set precedents in the broadcast industry for hiring women as writers, producers, and hosts, especially in daytime programming, which was assumed to appeal to women in the home.[13] Both the domestic, service-oriented show and the daytime serial/soap opera had been created out of a tradition of women's fiction and journalism that spoke to women as a subculture separate from the masculine culture represented in business and politics. Robert Allen and others have argued that this philosophy of "separate spheres" spoke to concerns of women in the home as it simultaneously supported a capitalist, patriarchal society: women in the separate sphere of the home were supposed to discover their true role by transforming the home environment into a haven from the ruthless world of big business.[14] Allen, Tania Modleski, and Sandy Flitterman-Lewis have all argued that broadcast programming carried on the "domestic fiction" tradition by emphasizing a rhetorical strategy that invited participation and connectedness to others—an interpersonal emphasis—yet was formally fragmented so as to accommodate the conflicting, interruptible, distracted viewing habits of the presumed female daytime audience.[15] It should also be noted that, especially in the case of local programming, such an interpersonal address was crucial in creating and maintaining an audience that was characterized by its shared geographical space (and the problems common to that space), as a complement to the gendered positioning within the home. The suburbanization that was characteristic of so much of postwar America—and its potential exacerbation of male and female "separate spheres"—was epitomized by the Los Angeles sprawl, so that this regional television industry had both an audience (positioned to be mainly white and middle class) that was arguably predisposed to such interpersonal programming and also a financial stake in bringing this audience together as Angelenos.

Monty Margetts

Monty Margetts came to Los Angeles in 1945 to work in network and local radio.[16] Like many industry professionals who emigrated to Los Angeles, she had established herself over several years as a performer in a range of media. Born in Vancouver to English parents, she began her career as an actress in 1929 in Seattle, where she worked to lose her accent. She became an accomplished stage and radio performer, including regular appearances on the regional radio soap opera *Skyler's Square.* From 1937 to 1945, she worked mostly in dramatic radio in San Francisco, usually appearing on NBC. She also worked occasionally as a newscaster and in a Western/hillbilly music series called *Abby the Postmistress and Her Black Mountain Boys.* Her career took a more certain direction when her friend Helen Morgan, a newspaper and radio writer, wrote and produced an afternoon women's commentary show that featured Monty in the title role as hostess *Barbara Tate* (the character's name rhymed with the sponsor's). This 15-minute program was heard every weekday afternoon on NBC; it featured Monty in the guise of Tate but essentially portraying herself discussing topical women's issues "in a pleasant way."

When the producer of a new program to be produced in Los Angeles heard a tape of Monty's performance as Barbara Tate, Monty was hired for the radio show *This Woman's Secret,* to appear as Mrs. John Taylor, the hostess and announcer who introduced the different "personal" stories enacted each day by visiting actors. She also appeared regularly on such programs as Ralph Edwards's radio version of *Truth or Consequences* and dramas such as *The Whistler* and *Cavalcade,* establishing a reputation for her convincing, effective delivery of sponsor messages.[17]

Her first experience on television was in the 1948 KFI (Channel 9) Christmas show written by Peggy Webber, a friend from radio. (KFI was at the time affiliated with NBC, both in radio and on its early TV programs.) In early 1949, Ken Higgins, who was the director of the parent radio station, called Monty and asked her to appear in a new television show. In her account of the conversation, Monty's charm and sense of humor are quite evident, as are some of the nontraditional aspects of her persona and life experiences.

> He said, "I understand, Monty, you've done a lot of ad-lib shows on radio." I had come down here from San Francisco radio in '45 for General Mills, to do a regular daily show. So I just knew Ken very lightly—I'd done a couple of dramatic shows for him—so he called me about this. And I said, "Well, what is it?" He said, "Well, what I want to know is, can you cook?" And I said, "Is this sort of a new switch on the casting couch?" (laughs) There was a long silence. He said, "Now let's be business-like!" (laughs) He was a marvelous man. He said, "No, we are starting television here . . . and we want to get commercials on it," naturally, something that will pay money. So he said, "We've been trying out home economists in a cooking set, and they are rather dull. I thought, you're never at a loss for a word." I said, "Thank you, sir." (laughs) And I said, "But I don't know a damned thing about cooking." I was an only child, whose father was a newspaperman and we lived in apartments or hotels, and my mother didn't want me under her feet. That was fine with me, I just liked to read, and so I knew from nothing. I had lost one husband, and I think that was probably the reason. Because he said to me one day— I had learned in Seattle, because I liked it so much, how to do a very simple thing with filet of sole—and he said, "Monty, we've had this four times this week." Well, it was the only thing I knew how to fix! (laughs) I realize I should have known more. But fools walk in, so . . .

The new show, *Cook's Corner,* was an almost immediate success. It was highlighted by the fact that Monty had little or no familiarity with what was expected to occur in its traditionally feminine domestic locale. ("Some people eat lunch while they watch me," she was once quoted as saying. "I think that's real rugged of them.") [18] In other words, Monty became popular partly because she did not fit into popular stereotypes of femininity that other women on television were upholding. At the same

Monty Margetts, "When I started to 'cook'"; on the set at *Cook's Corner*, KFI-TV, Los Angeles, 1949.

time, her show is indicative of what feminist critics have argued concerning television's gendered spectators—that television's mode of address (interpersonal, with a connotation of "averageness") and programming (genres and schedules) make it possible for women to find or recognize points of resistance at the same time that it co-opts them as consumers.[19] This property of "doubleness," in which women "simultaneously adapt to male social structures and reject them," is a central property of how women's public and private concerns and experiences are intertwined,[20] and can be seen as embedded at the level of the program text itself.

Integral to the success of the show was Monty's respect for and uniquely frank address to her audience. From the very first program (initially only 10 minutes), Monty displayed an innate ability to connect with her audience, doubtless enhanced by her stage and radio experience, which was conjoined with a matter-of-fact recognition of generally unacknowledged aspects of the genre and production of her show: when she noticed on the monitor that she was being identified as "Mary something or other,"

Monty Margetts, *Cook's Corner*, now moved to KNBH (NBC-TV), Los Angeles, 1951.

she flatly denied the moniker and identified herself as Monty Margetts, scolding the crew for such a ruse. Being seen, rather than only heard, via this new visible medium meant she insisted on being referred to as herself, rather than as a fictional character. Such a candid and unguarded moment, indicative of her personality, helped induce the kind of interpersonal tenor on which women's programs depended. In the following excerpt, an awareness of this dynamic seems implicit in Monty's assessment of the commercial leverage that her overall address afforded. It is also important to note how quickly the interpersonal aspects of the show's address became interdiscursive as well.

> As my later husband said: "Stand you in front of a camera and you'll tell everything you know, and enjoy yourself thoroughly." And I'm afraid that's true. . . . But then people started writing in. When I got them [the letters], then I made a habit of taking maybe the worst one . . . the first one I read, I remember, was a woman who said what a mess I made of things—just awful! Just absolutely awful. So I read it, and I said, "You know the terrible trouble about this is it's all true. I do make a mess because as I've told you, I don't know about cooking. But

> sometime in your life you've got to learn. So I've decided to learn." I didn't say [it was] because I was getting paid for it—but I wasn't getting paid so much that it mattered a great deal anyway. Well then they started writing in, these nice people, telling me how to do things. So I started reading their letters, and taking their advice. Because I figured, if you're smart enough to take their advice, and tell the world that you're taking it, they will buy anything you sell them. And that was true. And that's what made the show turn very successful. I took the right to turn down sponsors that I couldn't [believe in]—because I did all the commercials ad-lib, I just worked it in, and worked the show around them, used them, you see. And as I said, if the things don't turn out, it's not the fault of any product, it's "yours truly" here, who doesn't know how to go about it.

Cook's Corner and Monty Margetts occupy a singularly interesting site for resistance within the strongly gendered address of early television. Monty regularly opened up the address of her show, to include the crew, who occasionally responded audibly to her efforts and suggestions; to read letters of criticism from viewers, sponsors, etc. on the air; and to read letters of encouragement and countercriticism from her viewers. In this way, Monty casually put on display many of the discursive regimes of television discourse and address, even including those of production.

The show's strongly interpersonal address began to include her regard for the audience not only on the air but also off the air. She often phoned viewers who had written in with especially good suggestions or recipes or had offered a solid defense from her critics. The "communal" aspects of local television were therefore an important, material aspect of her success and overall experience with the medium.

> Many personal things came out of it. It was such a (pause) it was very strange, because radio was not like that at all. You got letters . . . just nice housewives, and a lot of children. Oh my God, I must have had the intellectual appeal to a ten year old. Or smaller . . . I've always got along with women, all my life. I like men tremendously, but I mean, you hear women: "I like men, but I don't care for women." Well, I've always had loads of friends. And I'm a friendly sort of gal. So I think that was it: especially housewives who were tied down with children and that. The attitude seemed to be, they were so glad to have a friend

Monty Margetts's *Cook's Corner* set at KNBH (NBC-TV), Los Angeles, 1951.

to talk to them for half an hour. That's sounds kind of silly, but that's about what it amounted to.

These interdiscursive and interpersonal dimensions of the show were centered on and directed toward women, which Monty fully recognized and appreciated. *Cook's Corner* developed a reputation and a narrative expectation that something odd, if not crazy, was bound to happen in a prescriptively gendered domestic space (though Monty maintains that her mishaps were never on purpose). But the show was couched in empathetic terms of address rather than a purely comical or cynical tone—*Cook's Corner* was never intended to be a parody or satire of women's domestic labor.

While not precisely aware of the political implications of her format and address, the social effects of the show were obvious to Monty, as indicated in the previous quoted material. But when asked directly about her own gendered experiences within the television industry, she found the implicit feminism of my question offputting.

Q: Was it at all difficult or challenging in any way to be a woman in early television?

A: No! You see, (pause) how shall I put this? When all this women's lib came along . . . I've never truly (pause) I sort of wondered what the hell all the fuss was about. And I think, really, Mark, it's because I had a remarkable father. He was a darling man, an Oxford man, Christ Church. But he, along with Mr. Robert Cromie, a Scot—with Mr. Cromie's money, he founded *The Vancouver Sun,* which is still the leading paper there. But my father just took it for granted that I would get A's in school. He could not bear it when my mother's sisters, my aunts, used to talk baby talk to me, and he told them so, plainly. My mother was a marvelous mother. And I think I grew up in such a secure thing, that nothing has really bothered me that much. And I well remember, one of these days, coming home from the show when it was still at KFI. And for years, I didn't drive—I hated the thought of driving. And I was walking up the street on Cole Avenue, where we lived (this is before I married Harold), and the phone rang when I got in the house, and I answered it. Well, for years when I first came down here from San Francisco, I would wear a hat and gloves, like we did in San Francisco. And I was dressed that way, and I had my briefcase with all my papers for the show. And this masculine voice said to me, "I would like to paint your portrait." Well, I said, "How charming." I said, "Why?" "Because," he said, "I will name it Madame Importance. That's what you look like." And he banged up the phone—it must have been one of my neighbors. Well, I thought it was too funny for words. I loved it, and I told everybody I knew. But then when I began to think it over, I thought, well, I guess I must seem very, you know, self-important, or something. But it didn't bother me in the least. And finally, I got to the point where I became something I had never been before—not introspective, but sort of (pause) looking at myself a little more closely. And I realized that my reaction at times—talk about fools walk in—but I would defend anybody to the death if I thought they should be defended. It never occurred to me not to stick my neck out. So perhaps that has something to do with it.

Despite the "nontraditional" characteristics of Monty's television show, and their apparent basis in her social life, she responded just as the other women I interviewed when asked directly about gender in their televisual experiences. Like many women of her generation, especially working women, she holds little regard for the women's movement and the feminist basis of my question. This may be due in part to second-wave feminism's slight toward most women working before the 1960s. But it may be more generally due to a different level of tolerance for behavior considered appropriate for women.

Nevertheless, her response also indicates an ambivalence about patriarchal or masculinist positioning of women's "proper place." Significant here is a nostalgia for her father—who was supportive and even insistent about her not accepting traditional women's roles, and, therefore, important to her own self-understanding—but also, of course, the somewhat unmotivated subsequent shift of focus to the story about an anonymous male response to her mere appearance in public. This casual, unprovoked scolding reveals a distaste or even a threat in the caller's attempt to position Monty as an object. Such a recollection appears as a kind of return of the repressed, a material encounter that in its rather blatant enactment of masculinist entitlement policing a gendered social space seems to validate the feminist concerns and issues Monty was apparently disparaging.

But at this juncture of potential generational condescension, I am compelled methodologically, perhaps even ethically, to throw a flag. For it is in such instances of differentiated socialized knowledges and points of view that oral history's reflexivity and self-consciousness should be invoked. These instances represent moments that engage one of the central dialectics of feminist oral history methodology: the tension between the necessary contextualization and analysis of the discourses that comprise the interview versus a belief in the value and integrity of women's personal understandings of their own lives. Susan Armitage observes that women who are interviewed generally feel quite positive about their lives and activities, even in the face of social inequities; these histories tend to be strong and affirmative statements. Too rigid a set of expectations or historical framework can lead to an ill-considered hubris that violates the implicit mutual respect on which oral historians rely, and also to potential failures to recognize new points of view or unanticipated insights about the history in question.[21]

One can imagine, of course, interview situations in which all manner of mutual respect could quickly melt down. In this instance, upon reflection, and after listening to the tapes of Monty's oral history, I realized that in my enthusiasm to discover a potentially subversive woman's show in "post-Rosie-the-Riveter" Los Angeles, I had been less than attentive to aspects of Monty's interests, duties, and responsibilities within the culturally determined personal sphere, aspects of her life that she mentioned but did not particularly detail: her lifelong passion for reading literature and history, which led for a time to a position writing book reviews as head of the book department at a leading department store; her three marriages during an era in which the escalating divorce rate was considered a somewhat scandalous sign of threatening, burgeoning female sexuality; and most significantly perhaps, her hiatus from the television industry in the early 1950s—after having developed a considerable following—to care for her daughter and especially her widowed mother, who had contracted cancer.

Details such as these, which relate directly to gendered inscriptions of social behavior and cultural divisions of the public and the private, are central to the project of feminist oral history. The conditions of my own critical framework, engrained within lived male social experience, certainly played a delimiting role here and were compounded by the mobilization of divisions of public and private in an interview framed as pertaining to *broadcast history* rather than *women's history*.[22] These areas of Monty's life were cordoned off in some ways as personal and therefore not pertinent. Finally, I would suggest that it seems at least conceivable to me that, even though Monty was quite candid with me concerning various aspects of her career, these "personal" issues might have been more readily addressed and pursued had a woman conducted the interview, especially in light of the emphasis on gendered interpersonal address in Monty's life and career. This encounter can then also serve as a call for advocacy—a call for more women to engage in oral history research pertaining to broadcast studies.

Reflections and Conclusions

In an attempt to fully engage the advantages of oral history methods, especially the opportunity for reassessment and reflexive inquiry, I sent a draft of the above analysis to Monty and asked for her comments. In the course of a few notes of correspondence and a long phone call, some of the issues related to feminist methodology and generational difference took on new dimensions.

Overall, Monty was delighted with the essay and excited that her early work on television was receiving such attention. (At the same time, she reaffirmed that her career as an actress was not restricted to the cooking program and, in fact, continued for some thirty years after she returned to acting in the mid-1950s.) A true professional, she offered to send me personal materials related to her cooking show—including the photos that accompany this essay—and suggested, even before I could ask, that she sign a release for the use of my original and subsequent interviews with her. She was, years later, the same personable, intelligent, funny woman I had met conducting my original research.

As I had expected, Monty also had comments about the academic language employed in the analysis, and she detailed her combination of amusement and puzzlement about this matter:

> You'll forgive me if I have had many a snicker over the academic language. I've been through a good deal of this. There was a writer at Oxford, one of the professors, who used to write excellent best-selling mystery novels. Beautifully written. He was the big-shot in the literature department, so I decided to read some of the stuff he had written as the professor. Good God! I wrote him a nice letter, and I said, "Why don't you put it in journalistic phrasing, so that people can enjoy it?" But you'll forgive me . . .

Later, she added,

> I'm so delighted that you sent me this, because I'm so, I shouldn't say journalistic, but it's very good for me to have my nose rubbed in all this academic talk.
>
> Q: How so?
>
> A: You know, it's a good exercise. But I had made a note when I was just scribbling the other night, and I've written down "Why can't he just say 'Oral history is a way of recording broadcast history'?" (laughter) Of course, that's because I had a newspaperman for a father. . . . I get very hung up on words. I love them. They're fascinating, really fascinating.

Q: But there wasn't jargon that you found puzzling?
A: Oh no. No, it's just an exercise for me, because unless you go looking for it you don't run into it in the ordinary way of things.

A perhaps more significant reservation about the essay, which Monty related to the general topic of feminism, concerned the protocol by which I had referred to her in the draft.

A: Maybe this has to do with my whole feeling towards feminism, but I cannot stand being referred to by my last name. I am either "Miss Margetts" or "Monty." Not "Margetts." That makes me sound like oh, I don't know, the charwoman—no, even the charwomen gets called "Mrs. so-and-so." (laughter)
Q: Absolutely. I certainly wasn't trying to bother you.
A: Oh my dear, it irritates me when I read a newspaper and they refer to women by their last name. But that's strictly me, you know. I don't understand any of this ghastly stuff about feminism, or women's lib . . .
Q: Well, did that emphasis in the paper bother you?
A: It tickled me to death. Oh no, I liked the way you've handled it, as far as I'm concerned and my attitude. I like the whole way you've handled the thing. But this is just trivia, you know, on my part . . .

Such an attention to the preferred use of her proper name is indicative of the generational differences between us. The use of only her last name seemed ill-mannered or improper when referring to a woman, and seems to have had possible class connotations as well. But her equation of this practice with feminism is telling: it seems to indicate that she identifies the women's movement as allied with or even the cause of such gaps or differences in the "proper" attention to gendered address.

Perhaps not surprisingly, the one consistent point of dissonance or possible miscommunication in our conversation arose over the discussion of feminism in the essay. I later returned to the apparent contradiction in her remark above:

Q: I don't know quite how to address this, but I'm intrigued by the fact that you say that you enjoy the piece a lot, and yet it's a piece that's a little bit *about* feminism, which I think you suggested that you're not too crazy about.
A: How shall I put it? Let me put it this way. I read so much his-

tory, and have done so all my life. Men and women have been equally damned fools. But the world goes on. And I've never understood what the commotion is about women finally doing things, why men are so upset about it. I've never understood it since they started this woman's lib. And of course something that's come into the picture since you and I talked five years ago is this sexual harassment. Well for God's sake. Any woman with any common sense knows how to handle a man, if he's going to be forward or troublesome or overly attentive. She'd probably kill herself if he wasn't at all. I mean, there's so much fuss over what doesn't need fussing over. That's about the only way I can put it. Which is not very original, many people feel the same way. Because if men are smarter, well then they have nothing to worry about. They're so convinced that they are [smarter].

As was evident in the first interview, Monty's discussion of feminism, while at first seeming offputting or dismissive, ultimately complies with feminism, but a feminism that simultaneously adapts to and rejects patriarchal social structures. She is at once wondering aloud why men seem upset over women's achievements, and suspicious about men's presumptions of superiority. At the same time, she apparently feels that certain attention to women's issues, particularly those related to interpersonal relations (e.g., harassment cases), are excessive and overrepresented in the media. I discussed the issue of harassment with her at some length. Although Monty could appreciate the possibility of situations in which women might not have many options in dealing with unwarranted attention or abuse, her own experiences as an independent woman in the workforce seemed to override any outright sympathy for harassment victims.

Nevertheless, she apparently came to recognize upon reflection that her positions about feminism were not entirely consistent. In a subsequent note attached to some of the photos she mailed me, she added,

Re my attitude (so contradictory) re feminism:
I have always had a great admiration for Gloria Steinem.
I *loathe* Phyllis Schlaffly (spelling?)

What is most meaningful in this exchange about gender politics is the importance of discussing the terms of these politics in ways that allow for mutual appreciation of how they have played out in the lived social experiences of different generations. It was presumptuous of me to expect an easy agreement about feminist issues and to analyze our exchanges from a purely contemporary perspective. In the final analysis, this would have defeated the potential for genuine intervention that oral history can provide, and precluded the plurality of experience on which oral history within a feminist historiography insists.

Like television, and to some extent television studies itself, oral history has traditionally been considered as a kind of bad object within larger "official" and authoritative discourses of history and cultural analysis. But oral history can afford inroads toward issues that are central to contemporary historical inquiry: subjective history and its relation to historical issues of subjectivity, personal memory and popular memory, but also local and regional history in light of the principles of multiculturalism. In terms of television studies, oral history offers an alternative method of research concerning an apparatus of considerable power in the very shaping of subjectivity and popular memory, and a movement away from—though potentially supplemental to—the industrial and commercialized discourses currently prevalent in our historical understanding of this medium. Ultimately, oral history may be able to serve as a bridge for interdisciplinary approaches within television studies, introducing both empirical and methodological issues for analysis and affording the conditions for a rapprochement among feminism, textual analysis, and political economy. In keeping with the tenets of feminism, oral history can demonstrate to us and reacquaint us with the fact that the personal is not only political, but historical and dialogical as well.

Notes

1 Many contemporary broadcast scholars have recognized the value of interviews and oral history, as evidenced by conference papers and publications in the field that have appeared since this essay was accepted for publication. See especially Michael D. Murray and Donald G. Godfrey, eds., *Television in America: Local Station History from across the Nation* (Ames: Iowa State University Press, 1977), which presents a range of local TV histories, all of which rely on interviews as part of their research. A more commercial but neverthe-

less impressive effort is Jeff Kisseloff, *The Box: An Oral History of Television, 1929–1961* (New York: Viking, 1995), which culls brief excerpts from interviews with a wide array of TV veterans in order to approximate forgotten practices and experiences of television as it developed. (Monty Margetts is cited in Kisseloff on pp. 172–77.) Oral histories have also played an important role in several recent dissertations on broadcast and media history.

2 Signal contributions in this regard include two special issues of *Frontiers: A Journal of Women's Studies* (vol. 2, no. 2 [summer 1977]; vol. 7, no. 1 [1983]), each of which includes extensive bibliographic and archival information. See also Sherna Berger Gluck and Daphne Patai, eds., *Women's Words: The Feminist Practice of Oral History* (New York: Routledge, 1991); Michael Frisch, *A Shared Authority: Essays on the Craft and Meaning of Oral and Public History* (Albany: State University of New York Press, 1990). Two major journals devoted to oral history are *Oral History Review* and *International Journal of Oral History*, each of which has published essays related to women's oral history. See, especially, Kathryn Anderson, Susan Armitage, Dana Jack, and Judith Wittner, "Beginning Where We Are: Feminist Methodology in Oral History," *Oral History Review* 15 (spring 1987): 103–27.

3 Katherine Jensen, "Woman as Subject, Oral History as Method," *Frontiers* 7, no. 1 (1983): 85.

4 See, for example, Susan Armitage, "The Next Step," *Frontiers* 7, no. 1 (1983): 3–8; and Staughton Lynd, "Oral History from Below," *Oral History Review* 21, no. 1 (spring 1993): 1–8.

5 Within the broader field of television studies, it should be noted that interviews with women viewers have been central to developments in cultural studies approaches to the medium. See, for example, Mary Ellen Brown, ed., *Television and Women's Culture: The Politics of the Popular* (London: Sage, 1990); David Morley, *Family Television: Cultural Power and Domestic Leisure* (London: Comedia, 1986); Andrea Press, *Women Watching Television: Gender, Class, and Generation in the American Television Experience* (Philadelphia: University of Pennsylvania Press, 1991); Ellen Seiter, Hans Borchers, Gabriele Kreutzner, Eva-Maria Warth, eds., *Remote Control: Television, Audiences, and Cultural Power* (New York: Routledge, 1989).

6 See Paul Thompson, *The Voice of the Past: Oral History* (London: Oxford University Press, 1978).

7 Armitage, "The Next Step," 6.

8 Dan Sipe, "The Future of Oral History and Moving Images," *Oral History Review* 19, nos. 1–2 (spring–fall 1991): 80.

9 Ibid., 87.

10 See, for example, E. Ann Kaplan, ed., *Regarding Television—Critical Approaches: An Anthology* (Frederick, Md.: University Publications of America, 1983); and Patricia Mellencamp, ed., *Logics of Television: Essays in Cultural Criticism* (Bloomington: Indiana University Press, 1990).

11 In addition to Monty Margetts, I have been fortunate to interview the late Lenore Kingston Jensen, a veteran of radio and early TV on several stations and the godsend who was crucial to contacting the majority of my oral histories; Dorothy Gardiner, a central member of the regular troupe of early personalities at KTLA; Ada Leonard, hostess and bandleader of an all-woman orchestra on KTTV; and Betty White, whose renowned television career began with various local shows in Los Angeles.

12 Margaret Helen Wade, "A Descriptive Study of the Jobs Held by Women in the Radio-Television Industry in Los Angeles" (M.A. thesis, University of Southern California, 1951), 50–53.

13 See the essay by Michele Hilmes in this anthology for a more detailed analysis of these practices and their evolution.

14 Robert C. Allen, *Speaking of Soap Operas* (Chapel Hill: University of North Carolina Press, 1985), 133–51.

15 These concepts are discussed thoroughly in Tania Modleski, "The Rhythms of Reception: Daytime Television and Women's Work," in Kaplan, *Regarding Television,* 67–75; and Sandy Flitterman-Lewis, "The Real Soap Operas: TV Commercials," in Kaplan, *Regarding Television,* 84–96. Modleski, in particular, points out the ideological consequences of such fragmentation.

16 This information is taken primarily from an interview with Monty Margetts by the author in Los Angeles on 20 February 1990. Since none of her shows exist on kinescope, the analysis presented here is based on descriptions within oral histories, primarily that of Margetts herself, and trade press coverage of her programs.

17 "Monty Moves In," *Radio Life,* 24 August 1947, 38–39.

18 "What's Cooking?" *Radio-Television Life,* 17 February 1950, 3.

19 See, for example, Beverle Houston, "Viewing Television: The Metapsychology of Endless Consumption," *Quarterly Review of Film Studies* 9 (summer 1984): 183–95; and Modleski, "The Rhythms of Reception," 67–75.

20 This concept is borrowed from Marcia Westcott, "Feminist Criticism of the Social Sciences," *Harvard Educational Review* 49 (November 1979): 422–30. See also Anderson, Armitage, Jack, and Wittner, "Beginning Where We Are," 126.

21 Armitage, "The Next Step," 3–8.

22 Kathryn Anderson has reflected on a similar experience in which her train-

ing as a historian skewed her initial attempts at women's oral history, impeding her attention to the significance of relationships in the women's lives she was documenting. Significantly, the practice of oral history is what led her to this methodological insight about gendered experience and historical inquiry (Anderson, "Beginning Where We Are," 109).

Lucy and Desi

Sexuality, Ethnicity, and TV's First Family

Mary Desjardins

I Love Lucy is widely recognized as perhaps the single most successful and best-known program in television history. In its 30-minute format, it ran on CBS from 1951 to 1957; additional 60-minute shows entitled *The Lucille Ball–Desi Arnaz Show* ran from 1957 to 1960; in one form or another, the program has reportedly never been out of syndication in the United States, and it has also seen wide international distribution. Not surprisingly, it has attracted a variety of critical attentions, especially regarding the history of the show's production, its place in the sitcom genre, and its status as a significant series of texts that represent conflicts of gender and ethnicity in 1950s patriarchal culture.[1]

I Love Lucy is full of swapping, switches, and transformations usually motivated by Lucy's desire to get rich, get even, or get into show business. In the 1952 episode, "Lucy Fakes Illness," Lucy convinces Ricky she has suffered a nervous breakdown because he will not hire her for his new act. She assumes a range of new identities in her "mental illness," from a tricycle-riding child to a Tallulah Bankhead look-a-like. In the 1953 "The Indian Show," Lucy swaps places with Ricky's dancing partner to prove that recent motherhood has not ended her aspirations for performing. In a famous 1954 episode, "Lucy Is Envious," Lucy wants former schoolmate Cynthia Harcourt to think she is wealthy. To earn money for Cynthia's charity drive, she and Ethel dress as Martians for a film publicity stunt that requires them to frighten tourists on top of the Empire State Building.

Lucy's desire to be in Ricky's place, her imaginative masquerades, and her defeat by Ricky's punishments are constants of the program. In groundbreaking essays about the program, Patricia Mellencamp and Alexander Doty suggest that these narrative patterns in *I Love Lucy* elicit viewer pleasure and recognition from Lucy's "symbolic castration" *and* her resistance to such infantilization. For Mellencamp, spectatorial pleasure from Lucy's antics replaces spectatorial anger at her gendered "containment."[2] Doty argues that "the expert physical comedy Ball brought from her film and vaudeville performances" into the construction of Lucy Ricardo "renders both performer and star image ideologically problematic" because Lucy Ricardo is ultimately figured as a rebellious child.[3] This current critical positioning of *I Love Lucy* as relevant to feminist concerns is not surprising, since reading the 1950s in terms of women's negotiation of patriarchal norms of femininity is now a typical strategy of feminist social historians.[4] And as representative of a growing body of work on how 1950s views of race and ethnicity interacted with 1950s positionings of gender, Caren Kaplan has focused on the role of Desi Arnaz/Ricky Ricardo to complicate the notions of ethnicity and disempowerment in *I Love Lucy*.[5]

The aforementioned works yield significant insights about the relation between the textual dynamics of the show and the complex gender and geopolitical relations of the 1950s documented by social historians. However, because these arguments rely mainly on textual analyses of episodes of the *I Love Lucy* program, they have limited explanatory power in considering how Ball and Arnaz were circulated at the time *as a star couple* and how discourses about *I Love Lucy* at that historical moment might have encouraged multiple readings of the program and the stars.[6] For instance, the contradictions and negotiations of gender, marriage, work, and ethnicity norms rehearsed by *I Love Lucy* were rendered more explicit and more complex at that time in the appearances Lucille Ball and Desi Arnaz made on other television programs in the 1950s, such as Ed Sullivan's *Toast of the Town* (CBS, 1948–71, renamed *The Ed Sullivan Show* in 1955) and *The Bob Hope Show* (NBC special, airing periodically since 1948). An examination of these programs suggests that the more "adult," more loosely narrativized genre of the comedy-variety show, with its sexually risqué jokes, its open promotional function, and its generally parodic stance, revealed the tensions between the "reel" and the "real" of this show business couple.

This essay concludes with a consideration of *Lucy and Desi: A Home Movie* (NBC, 1993) to suggest how the program and its star couple has fascinated—even obsessed—the viewing public for almost fifty years. This documentary special featured home movies as well as interviews with the Arnaz family, friends, and coworkers. It was produced by Lucie Arnaz Luckenbill as an attempt to understand the relation between her parents' troubled marriage and their work as performers and producers. Through disclosures of family and friends, the television special provides a confessional rewriting of Lucy and Desi of the 1950s that is simultaneously nostalgic for and self-consciously critical of the family of that era.

Although *I Love Lucy,* like other situation comedies of its time, ultimately does the cultural work of promoting the patriarchal nuclear family with husband/father working outside the home and wife/mother taking care of house and children, the television appearances of Ball and Arnaz in the 1950s expose some of the disparities between the myths and the realities of gender and work in that period. In order to promote Desilu productions, these appearances work by making comparisons between the reel-life marriage and careers of Lucy and Ricky Ricardo and the real-life marriage and careers of Lucille Ball and Desi Arnaz—working, cross-cultural couple, parents, business partners in a media empire made possible by the success of the Ricardo family.

In 1954, the cast of *I Love Lucy* appeared on Ed Sullivan's *Toast of the Town* in a skit built around Sullivan's attempt to get them on his show. By the time of this appearance, Ball and Arnaz were enjoying great success from *I Love Lucy:* the show was the top-rated program on television. Arnaz had assumed the title of executive producer of *I Love Lucy* in 1952, the birth of Desi Jr. in January 1953 had stolen the headlines away from Dwight D. Eisenhower's presidential inauguration, Desilu was expanding into television production, and Ball and Arnaz had starred in the box-office hit *The Long, Long Trailer* (MGM, 1954). *I Love Lucy* ancillary products—from dolls and comic books to cookbooks and sheet music—were enjoying great popularity, and stories about the Arnazes' off-screen family and work life appeared in magazines like *TV Guide* and *Life.*[7] The Sullivan skit does little to suggest rifts in this successful image, but the fiction it creates of the "real-life" family underscores the constructed nature of the "reel" Ricardo family.

The skit opens with Lucy and Desi in a simply furnished living room presumed to be part of their Beverly Hills home. The couple is dressed casually—Desi in his stockinged-feet, Lucy in robe and curlers. Desi is

Lucille Ball, Desi Arnaz, and Ed Sullivan on *Toast of the Town* (1954).

reading the Sunday paper, Lucy is knitting baby clothes, which she holds up for Desi's admiration:

Desi: "Lucy . . . again? We've already done that bit!"

Lucy: "Don't be silly! This is for Eve Arden's baby."

Desi's characterization of a potential pregnancy as a "bit" not only reminds us of the historic *I Love Lucy* episode featuring Little Ricky's birth but of how the Arnazes' own lives have provided material for the television program.[8] Through Arnaz's remark, we see the Ricardos as fictional characters and the Arnazes as performers who have to negotiate the demands of "real life" with work, as they did when Ball became pregnant during the show's second season. But the difficulties of those negotiations are smoothed over by the skit's focus on the "ordinariness" of this star couple.

For instance, after they receive a phone call from Sullivan requesting their appearance and announcing an imminent visit to their home, they madly dash around the room cleaning. Lucy is afraid of being seen as a slob:

Lucy: "What's the matter with you? We don't want him to see the house looking like this!"

Desi: "What the matter with it? It looks fine to me."

Lucy: "For Heaven's sake!"

Desi: "Honey, why don't you let him see you the way we really are? You know . . . natural, with no pretensions?"

Lucy: "The show's called *Toast of the Town,* not *Crumbs of the Town!*"

They change into evening clothes and rehearse responses to Sullivan's request that emphasize their modesty and surprise. In contrast to the usual configuration of Ricky and Lucy, Lucy and Desi are *equally* foolish as they both preen narcissistically while claiming no interest in their fame.

Vivian Vance and William Frawley (Ethel and Fred Mertz on *I Love Lucy*) appear one at a time after Sullivan's arrival, each offering the explanation that he or she was just strolling through the neighborhood. Vance and Frawley (who, apparently hated one another in "real" life[9]) are depicted as having a friendly relationship with the Arnazes outside the confines of the show, which works to naturalize their relationship *in* the show and represent them all as "just plain folks." Their performances also make the skit resemble *I Love Lucy,* in which the Mertzes' past as vaudeville entertainers is often central to the show's plots. Here, they bring out music and vaudeville costumes that they just "happen" to have with them in order to "audition" for Sullivan.

Much of the work in drawing parallels between the off-screen lives of the *I Love Lucy* cast and the sitcom itself is displaced onto the performances of Vance and Frawley. They behave as they do in *I Love Lucy,* whereas Ball and Arnaz do not. Although Ball and Arnaz do perform comedically, the *Toast of the Town* skit suggests parity between the couple. Such a relationship conforms to the image they liked to project to the public: press releases and captions for photos of the couple emphasize their roles as president and vice president of Desilu productions (Ball was second in command, although legally she had creative control on *I Love Lucy* over Arnaz), Ball as comedic genius and Arnaz as business genius. At this time, infantile Lucy Ricardo and volatile Ricky Ricardo were not to be confused with Ball and Arnaz.

However, a later appearance by the couple on *The Ed Sullivan Show* (as *The Toast of the Town* was called after 1955) suggests cracks or tensions in the construction of the personas of Lucy and Desi as star couple. Lucy and Desi made this 1956 appearance to promote their newly released film, *Forever Darling* (MGM, 1956), which the couple produced through their Zanra (Arnaz spelled backward) Production Company. In their third and

Lucille Ball tries to find a scene of "married bliss" from *Forever Darling* on *The Ed Sullivan Show* (1955).

last film together, Ball and Arnaz play Susan and Lorenzo Vega. Susan, a spoiled woman from a rich family, feels neglected by her workaholic chemist husband, Lorenzo. Susan's guardian angel (James Mason) intervenes by advising her to pay more attention to Lorenzo's work. After she takes his advice, the squabbling couple rekindles the romance in their marriage.

Lucy introduces a film clip from *Forever Darling* by comparing the marriage of characters Susan and Lorenzo Vega with her blissful marriage to Desi: "I'll just say *Forever Darling* was a joy to make because it depicts complete married bliss . . . the happy, serene everyday home life of two people just like Desi and me. They have such complete understanding of each other." But the film clip is a scene in which the characters are fighting. Susan, who has accompanied Lorenzo on a research trip to a swamp, has upset the couple's raft and ruined Lorenzo's samples. He shouts, she wails, and they both flail in the murky water. When the clip is over and Sullivan points out that the scene hardly depicts a blissful couple, Lucy and Desi desperately search among their cans of film for a happy moment from the movie but are unable to find such a scene before the commercial break. In this way, the Arnazes appear more like the Ricardos than the equal partners promoted earlier by Desilu.

Although these comic moments of marital discord in film and television skit are reminiscent of *I Love Lucy* and, therefore, suggest a promotable slippage among the Arnazes, the Ricardos, and the characters in

Forever Darling, it might have also resonated (as it most certainly does now) with the increasingly prevalent rumors of discord between Ball and Arnaz. In 1955, *Confidential* alleged that the Arnazes' marriage was stormy. It recycled gossip from the early period of their marriage when Ball filed for divorce in 1944. It claimed that Desi now had a drinking problem and frequent liaisons with call girls. Readers were asked to imagine a hot-tempered Ball with a "flat-iron in her hand" ready to strike Desi when he returned home after a night of carousing.[10] The *Confidential* article exhibits a relish in revealing the problems in the Arnaz marriage, never losing an opportunity to use exclamation points, alliteration (e.g., calling Desi a "duck-out daddy"), or offhand racist remarks (Desi as "Latin Lothario"). Robert Harrison, the magazine's publisher, claimed that his four million readers liked reading about the "truth" behind Hollywood stars' public images.[11]

The Arnazes' next variety show appearance, on *The Bob Hope Show* in 1956, is pertinent to this scandalous context, as they parody *I Love Lucy* through sexually risque jokes and situations. Bob Hope introduces the skit in a playfully indulgent monologue: "You know I've known Lucy long before Desi, and I've often wondered what would have happened if she married me instead of Desi—if I were the husband in *I Love Lucy.*" Hope here mixes Lucille Ball with Lucy Ricardo and Desi with Ricky. In addition, Hope introduces a rivalry with Arnaz/Ricky: "I know one thing, she wouldn't be doing those crazy things if I were her husband." The curtain then opens on a re-creation of the Ricardos' home—not the Arnazes' home.

In the skit that follows, Ball and Vance play Lucy and Ethel respectively, but Hope plays Ricky, Arnaz plays Fred, and Frawley plays Captain Blighstone, the owner of the trained seal that Lucy is using in an audition. This skit repeats a plot device of *I Love Lucy,* since, once again, she is trying to crack the world of showbiz.

Hope projects himself and his aggressive comic persona into a scenario with the Ricardos, assuming a place in the scene of marital discord and desire presented weekly in the sitcom but dislocating the matches between characters and actors. This comic mismatch between stars and characters calls attention not only to the romantic movie partnering of Hope and Ball in previous films but also to the fictional constructions and to the functions of coupling itself in *I Love Lucy.*[12]

Lucy, Bob Hope as "Ricky Ricardo," Desi as "Fred Mertz," and Vivian Vance as "Ethel Mertz" on *The Bob Hope Show* (1956).

Hope continues to dominate Desi, who in the skit is playing Fred Mertz, through racist jokes and through making fun of his accent:

> Arnaz (as Fred) expresses look of surprise when the trained seal throws a hoop over his neck.
> Hope (looking at Arnaz): "What happened? Did you just come back from a 'wetback' luau?"

Hope plays Ricky without any signs of Cuban ethnicity, and this portrayal gives him power over both the "reel" and "real" personas of Arnaz. His racism raises the specter of the racism in *I Love Lucy*, which Mellencamp argues is evident in the way Ricky is never given complete symbolic mastery because of his accent, but Hope's racism also trumps that show's racism in its explicit aggressivity.[13] At one point, Arnaz-as-Fred says that Hope-as-Ricky lent him his golf clubs but did not give him any "balls," surely a sexually charged joke in terms of its extratextual reference. Ball apparently appealed to Hope to give Arnaz and his band a job on Hope's radio program in 1946 so that she and Arnaz could be together (i.e., so he would stop philandering on the road), and it has been suggested that Arnaz wondered if Ball and Hope had ever had an affair.[14]

The risqué antics here may recall the rumors of adultery in the *Confidential* article, but Arnaz is potentially the cuckold this time. The sexual joke also connects Hope's racism to masculinist, heterosexual competition, potentially exposing links between patriarchal control of gender and racial definitions at this time. This linkage remains hidden within the textual dynamics of the *I Love Lucy* program, which stages its understandings of gender and race in struggles between a husband and wife.

Hope's film star persona was based on the feminized man. He frequently acted the coward who had trouble getting the girl in such films as *The Princess and the Pirate* (Goldwyn, 1944), *Monsieur Beaucaire* (Paramount, 1946), and the Road movies with Bing Crosby—*Road to Singapore* (Paramount, 1940), *Road to Zanzibar* (Paramount, 1941), *Road to Morocco* (Paramount, 1942), *Road to Utopia* (Paramount, 1945), *Road to Rio* (Paramount, 1947), *Road to Bali* (Paramount, 1952), and *Road to Hong Kong* (United Artists, 1962). As a variety show host (not unlike his USO host persona), Hope is transformed into a sophisticated wielder of sexual and racist jokes.

This specific skit, which exemplifies the variety show's parodic stance, suggests what is repressed from the family sitcom—sexual desire. The narrative line, which has Hope-as-Ricky trying to discover Lucy's scheme, is interrupted repeatedly by bedroom farce. Lucy puts Captain Blighstone (played by Frawley, the oldest and least sexualized of the foursome), in the Mertzes' apartment. Consequently, she suggests that the Mertzes sleep in her apartment. But Lucy Ricardo keeps slipping into Lucille Ball every time Ethel/Vance seems to be enjoying Desi-as-Fred too much. Not only does this remind us that Lucy Ricardo is a fictional construct and that Lucille Ball has a real-life relationship with Desi, but it also initiates the possibility of Ethel/Vance's sexual desire, an issue rarely broached in *I Love Lucy*, in which the Mertzes have a decidedly nonsexual marriage.[15]

In its emphasis on a mobile sexual desire, this fantasy of seduction subverts the fifties domestic sitcom, which insists on monogamous heterosexual coupling. Homoerotic possibilities between Hope-as-Ricky and Arnaz-as-Fred even surface in this fantasy as they end up sharing a bed and jokes together (just like Hope and Crosby in their series of films together). Yet, despite this skit's foregrounding of sexuality and the way it permits the characters to try out alternative conceptions of their sitcom identities, it does not effect a complete reversal of engendered power. Hope-as-Ricky evidences desire for Lucy, Ethel and Lucy are rivals for Desi-as-Fred, while he and Hope-as-Ricky enact a rivalry over mascu-

Desi-as-Fred eyes Havana U. alum Bob Hope-as-Ricky, *The Bob Hope Show* (1956).

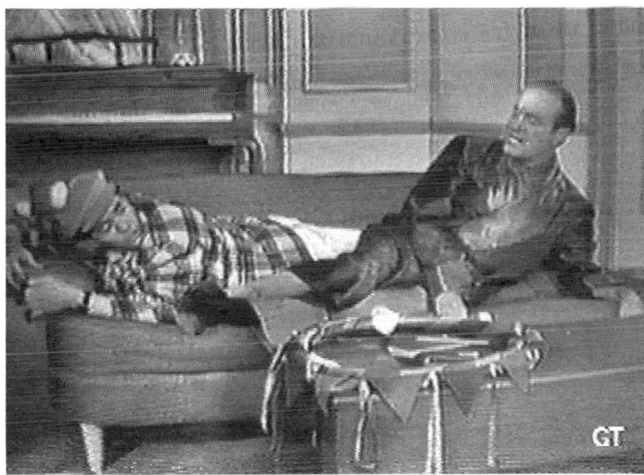

Bob Hope-as-Ricky and Desi-as-Fred bed down for the night, *The Bob Hope Show* (1956).

linity. In other words, heterosexual patriarchal prerogatives are stabilized through the centering of the women's desiring of the men and the men's competition through "exchange" of the women. When the men do bond, it is not necessarily homosexual but homosocial—they joke about what they perceive to be their sorry lot as husbands tied to manipulative and silly women. Desi-as-Fred listens to Lucy's scheming, turns to Hope-as-Ricky and says, "I feel sorry for you." He turns and looks at Ethel nodding at Lucy's series of lies and adds, "I feel sorry for me, too." This homosocial bonding between Hope-as-Ricky and Desi-as-Fred not only stabilizes patriarchal heterosexual prerogatives; arguably, it also mitigates the racist power Hope has over Desi in its display of men united against women.

The television appearances of the *I Love Lucy* cast in the 1950s were made to promote the show and the expanding Desilu empire of media productions. The tensions between the Arnazes' on- and off-screen personas and between 1950s gender norms and the demands of work surface in the need to promote Lucy and Desi as married stars, business people, *and* as fictional characters, the Ricardos, who *do* ultimately support contemporary familial ideology. By the 1990s, however, stardom and "fifties families" had become objects of scrutiny. Behind the public facade of success and happiness lies the "truth" of stardom as well as of the "fifties family." Both recent star studies and social histories have revised our notions of the 1950s through their exposure of the myths about gender and success that had previously sustained the familial ideology and public institutions of that period. Social historians have pointed to the oppressive roles that men and, especially, women had to perform—often at the cost of their own psychological well-being—in order to create the domestic version of the 1950s state's "containment" policy toward "alien," other ways of life.[16] Similarly, both academic star studies and best-selling star biographies since the 1950s have emphasized the repressive nature of the Hollywood studio system and its promotional operations. In these revisions, "Hollywood stardom helps produce an abnormal personal life."[17] In light of these rewritings, growing up in a "regular" or a star family of the 1950s was a matter of "preventing the outside world from learning the harsh realities of family life."[18]

This recent revisionism is the context for *Lucy and Desi: A Home Movie*. This NBC special was produced as a counternarrative to CBS's *Before the Laughter*, a 1991 made-for-television movie based on the Arnazes' life before *I Love Lucy*. Lucie Arnaz Luckenbill argued that *Before the Laughter* oversimplified her parents' problems and made Desi into a villain. She claimed CBS and her parents were like family to one another and that she "felt raped" when they did not give her final script approval.[19] Arnaz Luckenbill's feelings of "rape" and betrayal are better understood if we remember that *I Love Lucy* was responsible for CBS's great success as a network *and* for the couple's children. Lucy wanted to do a show with Desi so they could be together and have a family.

Using home movie footage, *Lucy and Desi: A Home Movie* makes claims

Lucy and Desi: A Home Movie (1991)

In a scene from their home movies, Lucy and Desi Arnaz embrace, *Lucy and Desi: A Home Movie* (1991).

to provide access to the authentic Lucy and Desi because it is not merely a representation of the "behind-the-scenes" life of Lucy and Desi with actors impersonating the star couple as in *Before the Laughter*. Instead, it consists of home movies that bear an indexical relationship to the actual Lucille Ball and Desi Arnaz. It supplements this veneer of realism with interviews of friends and family. These people, Lucie Arnaz suggests, are never interviewed about the couple and are now glad to express what they, in Lucie's words, had kept "bottled-up" all those years.[20] This strategy might support the 1950s discourses (such as their appearance on

The Toast of the Town, which defined Lucy and Desi as "ordinary" folks rather than stars), but it also complicates this picture, at least insofar as it tries to particularize Lucy and Desi in terms of class and ethnicity.

For example, Desi's Cuban heritage is described here by friends and musicians who either share or understand that heritage. Their emphasis on the importance and popularity of Desi's Latin music contributes to the documentary's strategy of portraying Desi sympathetically and reevaluates his place as an entertainer alongside Lucy. An extended discussion of the mothers of both stars attempts to understand them in terms of differing class and cultural/ethnic backgrounds. Lucy's desire to have her mother and other family members participate in Desilu business and the Arnaz family life in California is understood by interviewees as Lucy's reaction to the devastating effects that working-class and Depression hardships had on her family's survival in hometown Jamestown, New York. Desi's life-long economic protection of his own mother is explained in terms of his upper-class background, Cuban exile, and the Latin tradition of extended families.

Yet *Lucy and Desi: A Home Movie* suggests the illusory nature of the equation between domestic togetherness and happiness. The interviewees emphasize that there was always trouble between Lucy and Desi and the threat of dissolution in this coupling and family. Their testimonies are affectionate, yet they provide "honest" assessments of the problems and contradictions faced by the couple. Their words are sometimes used in support of visuals that illustrate the couple's love and happiness; at other times, they work in counterpoint to these images, indicating tensions not visible from promotional photos and home or promotional movie footage.

In this way, the documentary uses home movies to critique rather than celebrate 1950s familialism. Lucie Arnaz Luckenbill suggests that the image we have of the 1950s family from such TV programs as *Father Knows Best* (CBS, 1954–63) and *The Donna Reed Show* (ABC, 1958–66)—she singles these shows out by name—gives a false impression of family perfection and security. As Patricia Zimmermann has argued in her study of home movies of the 1950s, these amateur productions, usually photographed by the family patriarch, elevated and worshiped the family in its most "secluded interactions."[21] In contrast to what is depicted in these home movies—Lucy and Desi cavorting at parties at their ranch home, cuddling with the children, acting as the patriarch and matriarch of Desilu's company picnics—interviewees comment on Lucy's and Desi's work pressures and even on family togetherness (including having children). They identify these factors as contributing to a difficult marriage, because the family was supposed to compensate for the harsh realities of modern life in which both parents desired recognition and self-fulfillment.

The failure of Desi and Lucy as patriarch and matriarch of the Arnaz family suggests the loss of the nuclear family as a master discourse of contemporary life.[22] *Lucy and Desi: A Home Movie* reveals this loss in sometimes very obvious ways. Looped images, which repeat images of Lucy and Desi gesturing affection, punctuate commercial breaks. A sentimental song (in both English and Spanish) describes melancholy, irrational love affairs likened to the off-kilter movement of the stars in the universe. Lucy and Desi are figured in this stylistic "rearrangement" of the home movies as a besotted couple unable to ever truly separate or be together.

Similarly, in his interview, Desi Jr. states that this program is about "recovery, a spiritual recovery" from various "addictive behaviors." Young Desi describes his attempts to get his father into alcohol and drug abuse programs. The elder Desi's addictions are offered up as one reason the children are now mourning the loss of the family, the loss of their parents to each other, and even the loss of this family to us, the "viewing family." Desi's Latin heritage again resurfaces in a positive, albeit more stereotypical, manner, as Desi Jr. recalls how much his father had appreciated the joy and sensuousness of everyday living. But the home movies function to shore up this loss, because they combine with confessional strategies that elicit the "truth" about this couple and, in doing so, act as therapy for the interviewees and, presumably, for us. As with anyone's home movies, they preserve an image of the family of the past for the family of the present, making that "prior" family and its private interactions available to explain the origins of present problems and dysfunctions.

The Lucy and Desi documentary in the 1990s and the television appearances of Lucy and Desi in the 1950s expose the work that goes into being a star couple negotiating the personal and social pressures associated with family and career. As these television portrayals suggest, the Arnazes' desires for family happiness and business success as well as their problems in attaining those were key components in their stardom. The 1950s skits promote these aspects of their stardom as a way to promote

Lucie Arnaz and Desi Arnaz Jr. discuss their family on *Lucy and Desi: A Home Movie* (1991).

I Love Lucy and its Ricardo family. This promotion not only centers and validates family as a key site for audience identification, it also constructs and holds it up as a market for the developing television industry of that time. Although the 1990s documentary centralizes family in its subject matter and audience address, it makes an intervention in the familial ideology that sustained the earlier portrayals of the Ricardos and the Arnazes. This ideology is seen to work only at great cost to its subjects and is materialized in certain media fictions, such as the sitcom and the home movie. Yet, the looping of certain home movie images of Lucy and Desi and the sometimes emotional testimony from loved ones of the Arnazes also suggest the difficulties in rewriting mythologies of the family. In that way, *Lucy and Desi* is compatible with both the recent social histories and star studies that have interrogated the oppressiveness of familialism in patriarchal culture and the tenacity of our desire for family and its place in our fantasy life.

Notes

Thanks to Mark Williams for help with illustrations and just about everything else.

1 For discussions of the show's production history, see Bart Andrews, *Lucy and Ricky and Fred and Ethel: The Story of "I Love Lucy"* (New York: Dutton, 1976),

revised as *The "I Love Lucy" Book* (New York: Doubleday, 1985); Desi Arnaz, *A Book* (New York: William Morrow, 1976); Patricia Mellancamp, "Situation and Simulation: An Introduction to *I Love Lucy,*" *Screen* 26, no. 2 (March–April 1985); Thomas Schatz, "Desilu, *I Love Lucy,* and the Rise of Network TV," in *Making Television: Authorship and the Production Process*, ed. Robert J. Thompson and Gary Burns (New York: Praeger, 1990); Coyne Steven Sanders and Tom Gilbert, *Desilu: The Story of Lucille Ball and Desi Arnaz* (New York: William Morrow, 1993); and Jess Oppenheimer (with Gregg Oppenheimer), *Laughs, Luck . . . . and Lucy: How I Came to Create the Most Popular Sitcom of All Time* (Syracuse, N.Y.: Syracuse University Press, 1996).

For an examination of *I Love Lucy* and the sitcom form, see David Marc, *Demographic Vistas: Television in American Culture* (Philadelphia: University of Pennsylvania Press, 1984); David Marc, *Comic Visions: Television Comedy and American Culture* (Boston: Unwin Hyman, 1989); and Patricia Mellencamp, "Situation Comedy, Feminism, and Freud: Discourses of Gracie and Lucy," in *Studies in Entertainment: Critical Approaches to Mass Culture*, ed. Tania Modleski (Bloomington: Indiana University Press, 1986), 80–95.

For analyses of *I Love Lucy* and gender, sexuality, and/or race, see Mellencamp, "Situation Comedy, Feminism, and Freud"; Alexander Doty, "The Cabinet of Lucy Ricardo: Lucille Ball's Star Image," *Cinema Journal* 29, no. 4 (summer 1990): 3–34; Alexander Doty, *Making Things Perfectly Queer: Interpreting Mass Culture* (Minneapolis: University of Minnesota Press, 1993); Tinky Weisblat, "Will the Real George and Gracie and Ozzie and Harriet and Desi and Lucy Please Stand Up? The Functions of Popular Biography in 1950s Television" (Ph.D. diss., University of Texas at Austin, 1991); Andrea Press, *Women Watching Television: Gender, Class, and Generation in the American Television Experience* (Philadelphia: University of Pennsylvania Press, 1991); and Gustavo Perez Firmat, *Life on the Hyphen: The Cuban-American Way* (Austin: University of Texas Press, 1994).

Although she does not perform an in-depth analysis of *I Love Lucy,* in "From the Dark Ages to the Golden Age: Women's Memories and Television Reruns," *Screen* 36, no. 1 (spring 1995), 16–33, Lynn Spigel uses the popular memory of the program as one example of how the televisual past and women's history are recontextualized in the present.

2 Mellencamp, "Situation Comedy, Feminism, and Freud," 94.

3 Doty, "The Cabinet of Lucy Ricardo," 12.

4 For historical accounts of the fifties in terms of negotiations of gender roles, see Wini Breines, *Young, White, and Miserable: Growing Up Female in the Fifties* (Boston: Beacon Press, 1992); Stephanie Coontz, *The Way We Never Were:*

American Families and the Nostalgia Trap (New York: Basic Books, 1992); Brett Harvey, *The Fifties: A Women's Oral History* (New York: HarperCollins, 1993); Maxine Margolis, *Mothers and Such: Views of American Women and Why They've Changed* (Berkeley: University of California Press, 1984); Elaine Tyler May, *Homeward Bound: American Families in the Cold War Era* (New York: Basic Books, 1988); Lynn Spigel, *Make Room for TV: Television and the Family Ideal in Postwar America* (Chicago: University of Chicago Press, 1992).

5 Caren Kaplan, "The 'Good Neighbor' Policy Meets the 'Feminine Mystique': The Geopolitics of the Domestic Sitcom," unpublished paper delivered at Console-ing Passions: Feminism, Television, and Video, Los Angeles, April 1993.

6 Doty, "The Cabinet of Lucy Ricardo," does look at extratextual discourses on Lucille Ball but focuses on those about her film stardom before *I Love Lucy* rather than those produced about the couple or at the time of the television program. Weisblat, in her dissertation on star couples, does not discuss their other television appearances, but she does discuss print discourses about Ball and Arnaz at the time of *I Love Lucy*. Although her dissertation is informative and well researched, I find her readings of these discourses monologic (see Weisblat, "Will the Real George and Gracie . . .").

7 *Time* recounted Ball's career and the courtship and early marriage of Lucy and Desi in "Sassafrassa, the Queen," *Time*, 26 May 1952. On January 19, 1953, the very date of the double "birthday" of Desi Jr. and "Little Ricky" Ricardo, *Newsweek* published its article on how the Arnaz family negotiated Lucille Ball's/Lucy Ricardo's pregnancy on the air ("Desilu Formula for Top TV: Brains, Beauty, Now a Baby," *Newsweek*, 19 January 1953). *Life* covered the January 19th birth of Desi Arnaz Jr. on February 2, 1953. The Arnaz family appeared on the cover of *Life* for April 6, 1953, with the photo caption, "TV's First Family." The inside article, "Lucy's Boys," detailed Lucy's recovery from childbirth in January 1953 and the use of twin babies to play "Little Ricky" on *I Love Lucy*. Between April 1953 and December 1955, the Arnaz family and the *I Love Lucy* television program were subject to several articles in *TV Guide*, including the very first issue of the magazine: "Lucy's $50,000,000 Baby," 3 April 1953; "TV Guide Goes Backstage," 1 May 1953; "That Funny Looking Lucy," 9 October 1953; and "Still in the Driver's Seat," 10 December 1955. See also "At Home with Desi and Lucy," *Los Angeles Examiner Southland Living Magazine*, 26 April 1953, which gives postwar Los Angeles readers a glimpse of the Arnazes' idyllic life in their San Fernando Valley ranch home. In 1954, Eleanor Harris wrote *The Real Story of Lucille Ball*

(New York: Ballantine Books, 1954), the first book-length biography of Ball, based on material originally published in *Reader's Digest* earlier that year.

8 Lucille Ball was not, contrary to television mythology, the first actress to act on television while her pregnancy was visible and publicly known. In 1948, Mary Kay Stearns was pregnant in the *The Mary Kay and Johnny Show*, also starring her real-life husband. But Ball's pregnancy took place at the right moment: when her show was the top-rated program and when television was now reaching millions of homes rather than a few thousand.

9 This information, which has become part of the *I Love Lucy* mythology, appears in Andrews, *Lucy and Ricky and Fred and Ethel;* and Arnaz, *A Book.*

10 Brad Shortell, "Does Desi Really Love Lucy?" *Confidential* 2, no. 6 (January 1955).

11 Robert Harrison, "*Confidential* vs. Hollywood," *Confidential* 5, no. 4 September 1957.

12 Hope and Ball had made two movies together before this television appearance. *Sorrowful Jones* (Paramount, 1949) and *Fancy Pants* (Paramount, 1950). They later made *The Facts of Life* (United Artists, 1960) and *Critic's Choice* (Warner Bros., 1963).

13 Mellencamp, "Situation Comedy, Feminism, and Freud," 90. As is well known, the networks originally did not want Desi for Lucy's costar because of his Cuban ethnicity. In *Life on the Hyphen,* Perez Firmat has suggested that Desi/Ricky used Spanish for his own masquerades—for example, to disguise his swearing.

14 Perez Firmat, *Life on the Hyphen,* 187. In the rough draft of his autobiography, Desi apparently claims he suspected a Ball-Hope affair.

15 Vance was required to wear dumpy clothes, and she was contractually held to maintain a weight heavier than Ball's in order to reinforce Ethel's lack of sexual appeal (see Andrews, *Lucy and Ricky and Fred and Ethel*).

16 See Coontz, *The Way We Never Were,* 33.

17 Mary Beth Haralovich, "Too Much Guilt Is Never Enough for Working Mothers: Joan Crawford, *Mildred Pierce,* and *Mommie Dearest,*" *Velvet Light Trap,* no. 29 (spring 1992): 51.

18 Coontz, *The Way We Never Were,* 34.

19 Timothy Carlson, "Lucy Movie Was Planned as a Tribute—but Her Family Says It's Been a 'Nightmare,'" *TV Guide,* 9–15 February 1991.

20 In her introduction to the home movie footage, Lucie Arnaz Luckenbill says, "I was often surprised by people's candor, and how much they were willing to tell me . . . almost as if they had bottled it up for so long and they were so glad somebody finally asked."

21 Patricia Zimmermann, "Hollywood, Home Movies, and Common Sense: Amateur Film as Aesthetic Dissemination and Social Control, 1950–1962," *Cinema Journal* 27, no. 4 (summer 1988): 30.

22 Mimi White discusses the apparent paradox of the contemporary therapeutic discourse signifying both loss and recovery in *Tele-Advising: Therapeutic Discourse in American Television* (Chapel Hill: University of North Carolina Press, 1992), 21.

A Moral Crisis in Prime Time

Peyton Place and the Rise of the Single Girl

Moya Luckett

With its love affairs, illegitimate births, and narratives of unrepressed desire, *Peyton Place* (Paul Monash, ABC, September 1964–June 1969) showcased the expression of female sexuality, leading to its controversial reception as part of the new "single girl" phenomenon. Concerned with self-fulfillment rather than altruistic domestic duties, the single girl was not content merely to enter the "men's world" but wanted to remodel it in accordance with her desires. Along with *Sex and the Single Girl* and the revamped *Cosmopolitan*, *Peyton Place* focused on female sexuality *outside* marriage and its role in defining women's identity and selfhood. Its narratives were thus widely interpreted as propaganda for the era's fundamental social reorganization and critiqued for their role in the erosion of moral propriety.

Peyton Place was loosely based on Grace Metalious's scandalous 1956 novel about sex and intrigue in a small New England town. Plots primarily revolved around the sexual adventures of three families (the Mackenzies, Andersons, and Harringtons). Both the younger generation's publicly known sexual escapades and their parents' secret pre- and extramarital liaisons continually disrupted this small community. Together, these narratives positioned the present as a new era, one remodeled by confessions of past misdemeanors and the flaunting of sexual transgressions. This new era was most clearly evidenced in the show's focus on irreparably broken homes, a move that departed from prime-time dramatic conventions. During its first season, for instance, the Andersons were the only one of the eight featured families to live together, and this unit soon disintegrated. This example suggests that modernity was not simply celebrated in *Peyton Place;* new "liberated" values threatened the stability of this small town even as they unmasked the amnesia, guilt, secrecy, and deceit buried in its past.

As befits a "literary" adaptation, *Peyton Place* was highly influenced by the period's publishing trends. Like Helen Gurley Brown's *Sex and the Single Girl* (1962) and, under her editorship, the revamped *Cosmopolitan,* (July 1965–), it helped question taboos about the expression of female sexuality outside marriage. Like Betty Friedan's *The Feminine Mystique* (1963), it exposed women's domestic frustrations and called for more feminine involvement in public life. As part of a larger attack on the cold war doctrines that positioned women within the private sphere and strove to contain their sexual and ambitious desires within marriage, it was popular with the young women educated during the Sputnik crisis who had been led to expect a greater involvement in public life.[1]

Grace Metalious's *Peyton Place* (reportedly the fastest-selling novel ever printed and, as late as 1969, the biggest-selling work of fiction) and her 1959 sequel, *Return to Peyton Place,* were in many ways the precursors of this trend, suggesting that there were women readers who were dissatisfied with sanitized romance and domestic treatises.[2] These novels met with immediate popularity and scandalous acclaim, becoming particularly popular among teenage girls, who saw them as a store of hidden sexual secrets. By the mid-1960s, their success spawned a subgenre of sexual fiction designed for women. Best-sellers like Mary McCarthy's *The Group* (1963) and Jacqueline Susann's *Valley of the Dolls* (1966) focused on ensemble casts of women who did not assume marriage as their inevitable and fixed destination. Drawing on their multiple protagonists' often lewd and dramatic experiences, they revealed how different events might mold alternative identities for women, revealing the multiple possibilities inherent in femininity. Their immense popularity suggested that conventional representations of female characters as serene, self-sacrificing homemakers, dutiful daughters, or one-dimensional sex symbols were out of touch with contemporary women's fantasies. They also drew on women's pleasurable investments in female camaraderie, indicating that these narratives might play a pivotal role in fantasies of feminine sexual liberation.

Unlike Hollywood cinema, which had customarily traded on the sexuality of its young female stars, television had long created an image of itself as the domestic medium, drawing on a repertory of more "traditional" images.[3] Prime-time television, in particular, had typically represented heroines as homemakers, associating them with the moral rectitude of private space.[4] *Peyton Place* purposefully departed from these norms; its repertoire of "new" women, its salacious narratives, and its prime-time slot were all calculated to snare young female viewers, particularly working women who no longer watched soap operas on daytime television.

With *Peyton Place*, ABC hoped to copy the success of England's top-rated soap, *Coronation Street* (Granada Television, 1961–), which had demonstrated that the format could be successful in prime time.[5] Producer Paul Monash had loftier ambitions and hoped to use the novel as the springboard for a high-class anthology drama.[6] He held this belief throughout the show's run, proclaiming that "soap opera is a pejorative term. . . . We're using the novel form on television."[7] His unaired pilot, which adhered closely to the movie, suggested his desire to produce a "quality" serial, but this vision did not mesh with network plans. Without his consent, ABC appointed soap queen Irna Phillips (the woman often credited with "inventing" soap opera and creator of *The Guiding Light* [CBS, 1952–], *As the World Turns* [CBS, 1956–], and *Days of Our Lives* [NBC, 1965–]) as series consultant.[8] Edgar J. Scherick, head of ABC's Program Department, summarized the conflict, observing that "Paul wanted to make the show a view of Americana, microcosmically presented. . . . Miss Phillips was brought in as a consultant to teach the West Coast boys how to churn up a real sudsy soaper."[9]

Disagreements between Monash, Phillips, Twentieth Century–Fox, and ABC lasted a year, delaying the show's appearance until the fall of 1964.[10] The final version dropped the film's, novel's, and pilot's pivotal Cross family, claiming they were "too sordid for television"; transformed Michael Rossi from a schoolteacher into a medical doctor (a more "soapish" occupation designed, according to Scherick, "to get him onto the square, into the center of action"); and started the story with teen siren Betty Anderson single and pregnant. These changes illustrated how *Peyton Place* tried to engage with modern morality and female sexuality while avoiding the novel's more sensational aspects, like incest. Nevertheless, the changes were hardly progressive. The recasting of Rossi's profession recalled traditional melodramatic images of masculine power while leaving off-screen the events leading up to Betty's pregnancy. Despite its notoriety, the show was structured throughout its run around a similar balance between traditional and modern sexual morality.

Peyton Place was an instant hit, despite the network's chancy decision to show two 30-minute episodes a week (Tuesdays and Thursdays at 9:30 P.M. EST)—also a strategy borrowed from *Coronation Street*. By June 1965, ABC had added a third show (at 9:30 P.M. on Fridays). Without much competition, the show dominated the summer schedule. As *Time* noted in August 1965, "Ever since, even the laggard in the entry was never out of the Top 15 and, at one point, the whole trio was bunched into the first five."[11] The network had hit gold: *Peyton Place* was cheap—at about $60,000 an episode, it was the cheapest half-hour on prime time, prompting sardonic writers to comment that "the production is . . . sometimes barely distinguishable from the commercials."[12] To ensure against interruptions, producers stockpiled 30 finished episodes, resulting in an uninterrupted run of 514 episodes.[13]

This popularity did not last. By September 1966, *Peyton Place* was cut to two episodes a week (Tuesday and Thursday) as ratings fell. The show was hurt by Mia Farrow's departure during the summer of 1966 (she played the central role of Allison) and, most significantly, by the pace of social change during the late 1960s, which rendered its representation of sin and scandals quite outmoded. By 1969, with the show nestling at around 82 in the Nielsen ratings, even *Life* called it dated:

> The program—and before it the book—that exploded upon a nation's uptight Puritan consciousness like a nitroblast has, in sophisticated '69, all the sizzle of a wet birthday candle. With lesbian lovers playing show-and-tell in the movies, and nudes on Broadway, and *Candy* and *Portnoy's Complaint*, what chance is there for square, middle-class, heterosexual hanky-panky that has to be all talk and reduced to a 19-inch screen and prefaced by toothpaste spiel?[14]

In September 1968, at the beginning of what would be its final "season," Twentieth Century–Fox announced that its show would "deal with electrifying subjects. The war, the draft, riots, music, God, and godlessness."[15] A wandering priest and a rock group were added to pep up the old combination of adultery, premarital sex, betrayal, and murder, but the most notable change involved the addition of a black family headed by a neurosurgeon, Dr. Harry Miles. This change was particularly desperate, as, evidently, the Miles family had always lived in Peyton Place but had never been mentioned before. Once considered "the first TV series delivered in a plain wrapper" and "television's first situation orgy," *Peyton Place* aired its last original episode on June 2, 1969, a casualty of the social changes it documented and arguably helped bring about.[16] Thus, the show's first two years represent its period of greatest cultural vitality, the years when it contributed to social debates, particularly those centering on female sexuality.

When *Peyton Place* debuted in 1964, widespread hostile criticism charged that television had betrayed its trust by transmitting images of sexual and social depravity into the American home. In 1964, *Time* called *Peyton Place* "a concentration of sex and adventurism such as no network had ever risked before"; *Life*'s correspondent noted that it presented "an avalanche of teen-age trauma and illicit love . . . a huge mass-audience dirty joke"; and *Look* suggested that "it . . . has enough sex and sin in it to worry parents whose children are likely to be . . . watching."[17] Even *Cosmopolitan* described it as "a bowdlerized version of [Grace Metalious's] tarnished little New England township . . . a labyrinth of intermarriages, chain-reaction disasters, adultery, and murder."[18] This notoriety was compounded by its position on the prime-time schedule, which brought the program greater visibility than its daytime counterparts, which were experimenting with similar topics without the same widespread criticism. The relationship between scheduling, visibility, and possible influence underlies Billy Graham's criticism of the show: "I don't doubt that some of the things in *Peyton Place* do go on in small towns. But I'm not sure how much of it we ought to bring out in public. For instance, I don't have the right to have a bath in public. I don't have the freedom to run an open sewer down the middle of the street. I don't think we should take all this dirt and throw it to the public and into the home."[19] Like other voices protesting (and celebrating) the show's "new" morality, Graham ignores the popularity of the book, suggesting that it is the medium that matters, that the more profound sin was committed in the translation into small-screen prime-time images.

Much of this press and public interest centered on the show's two teenage heroines—blond, virtuous Allison Mackenzie (Mia Farrow) and dark-haired siren Betty Anderson (Barbara Parkins). These iconic representations both summoned up and undermined the traditional virgin/whore dichotomy around which femininity has conventionally been disciplined and judged. *Peyton Place* used these contradictions to suggest the broader, more complex scope of modern femininity. Betty's errant sexual behavior, for example, ironically resulted from her hunger for a traditional marriage, whereas Allison's fragility belied her desire to become a successful professional writer.[20] Rather than exploring representation around the axis of sexual difference, across masculine/feminine and male/female binaries, *Peyton Place* shifted the terrain to examine the equally pivotal differences involved in the period's struggle over definitions of femininity. This shift is, as we shall see, perhaps its most "progressive" quality.

Like much mid-1960s popular feminism, *Peyton Place* drew on the new images of single working girls popularized by Helen Gurley Brown. In her first editorial for *Cosmopolitan,* dated July 1965, she promised readers a monthly share of her intimate thoughts and secrets (her column was titled "Step into My Parlor"). Using her own biography as the basis of her quasi feminist/self-help philosophy, Brown instructed readers to be "grown-up girl[s], interested in whatever can give you a more exciting, fun-filled, *friend-filled,* man-loved kind of life!" (emphasis mine).[21] Under her direction, *Cosmopolitan* left behind its previous identity as a traditional women's service magazine to become an icon of the sexual revolution. Although its career hints and fashion/beauty advice seemed to revolve around the all-important issue of seducing men, most of the images it offered were of women as individuals, friends, and, sometimes, lovers of men. Unlike most of its competitors, *Cosmopolitan* placed the single woman first, focusing on ways to maximize her pleasure at work, with her man, or in the more narcissistic and ultimately, perhaps, most significant realm of her relationship with her own body.

Hilary Radner has argued that Gurley Brown's work constitutes a moment of departure, "a cultural reworking of femininity" that produces "a connection between 'doing it' à la heterosexual and the narcissistic involvement that produces the moment of *pleasure* [Gurley] Brown extols —a pleasure generated outside the scene of heterosexuality."[22] This pleasure was centered on self-(re)creation, the transformation of the "mouseburger" into the "glamour puss" that Gurley Brown herself embodied. She was born to a poor Arkansas "hillbilly" family and, as she often noted, was neither beautiful nor educated. After completing secretarial school at age eighteen, she landed her first job as secretary to an announcer at

Los Angeles radio station KHJ. She was neither motivated, hardworking, nor skilled and went through seventeen secretarial jobs in seven years. Her last position was for an advertising executive. After three years, her boss's wife noticed that she composed good letters and persuaded him to let Gurley Brown write Sunlight radio commercials at Christmastime. For the next two years she completed these annual campaigns in conjunction with her secretarial duties until, at age thirty-one, she was finally promoted to copywriter.

Having established a career, she started improving her private life. At thirty-seven, her self-beautification efforts resulted in her marriage to handsome film producer David Brown. As part of her consistent efforts for self-betterment, she entered thousands of magazine writing contests, finally winning *Glamour* magazine's "Ten Girls with Taste Contest." Aged thirty-nine and bored with advertising, she wrote *Sex and the Single Girl*, which was based on her husband's idea. After its publication, she received lots of mail from lovelorn women, prompting him to suggest that she should edit a magazine. Several publishers rejected her prospectus before Hearst invited her to take over and retool their failing title, *Cosmopolitan*. In the meantime, she published another book, *Sex and the Office*.[23] In September 1967, capitalizing on *Cosmo*'s success, she began hosting her own syndicated half-hour talk show, *Outrageous Opinions* (1967). Each of its five weekly episodes featured a celebrity discussing his or her sex life and ideas about sexuality. Her guests, who included Woody Allen, Norman Mailer, and Bishop James Pike, were predominantly male, but it seemed that Gurley Brown had problems relating to them, and the show was one of her rare failures.[24]

Gurley Brown believed that engagement with public life enhanced femininity, that the single girl was more glamorous than her married counterparts, who dealt with the dirty work of cleaning homes and raising children.[25] In contrast to domestic labor, she extolled the more productive hard work and pleasure of beauty rituals. For Gurley Brown, being beautiful, elegant, graceful, *and* successful in public life was an active and aggressive act.

Dismissing reproduction and largely ignoring children throughout her magazine, Gurley Brown's work positioned the beautiful, improved woman as the object of her own creation.[26] At the same time, as Radner suggests, she posited heterosexual relationships as the guarantee of this success, suggesting that romance was a reward for, but secondary to, this investment in self.[27] The *Cosmo* girl also displaced (or foreclosed) the maternal by positioning herself as self-made, erasing her own mother's role in her birth.[28] This disavowal of the maternal plays a key role in her articulation of self throughout her work and suggests her incomplete and fragmented understanding of the interrelationship between gender, power, self, and the social sphere. Significantly, the popularity of her work indicates that this investment might be a pivotal and widespread female fantasy, showing a widespread resistance to conventional gendered expectations and women's very different understanding of their own feminine identity.

Nonetheless, contradictions mark Gurley Brown's biography and the theories that she derives from her own experiences. Her narrative of feminine power and self-advancement is marked by her reliance on her husband, who plays a pivotal role in her greatest successes. Her narrative suggests a more conventional understanding of marriage and sexual difference—albeit one that is rendered unstable by her refiguration of women's relationship to the maternal. Her earliest promotion is the direct result of intervention by her boss's wife, but this other woman remains at the margins, in the home, her own abilities remaining overlooked. This recalls earlier beliefs that women exert power and influence through their husband—the same myth that helped deny women suffrage—but here it is another (single) woman who benefits. Brown's early secretarial career is unremarkable and traditionally feminine (she has a low rank, no resilience, is itinerant, and takes on a "woman's job"). The long tenure of her years in the workforce support her confessions of homeliness, but promotion, along with her careful use of diet, cosmetics, and clothing, helps her become a more viable candidate for marriage. Her boredom after two years of wedlock and her "advanced" age at marriage also seem interrelated—she has no children to distract her and so she needs a career change. Writing a successful book and editing a magazine based on self-re-creation enable her to displace maternal interests onto herself and others. As the maintenance of a youthful beauty is a never-ending process, she can continually involve herself with the question of reinventing the self and passing this knowledge onto her disciples, rechanneling her maternal drives.

Still, Gurley Brown's gospel was not solely driven by sublimated maternal instincts. In her biography—as in all her writings—the central figure of desire is the female self. Despite all the publicity *Cosmopolitan* received in the late 1960s for publishing a male-centerfold of a naked (but self-covered) Burt Reynolds, it was really more interested in promoting a "fun-filled, friend-filled, man-loved kind of life" that largely seemed to center on women and their image.[29] *Peyton Place* similarly offered female viewers the pleasure of consuming images of sexual women, a move that both encouraged identification with figures at the center of the narrative world and mobilized desire away from the female figure as a masculine object of desire to create an image of femininity as self-validating for women. Although this strategy is/was not uncommon in women's fiction or magazines, it had not been as publicly broadcast on American prime-time television before *Peyton Place,* which suggests one reason why the program became renowned as a liberatory or scandalous text, despite its often moralistic recuperation of feminine desire.[30] As befits a serial drama, *Peyton Place*'s heroines were soon free to sin again, as the narrative structure mitigated against any form of closure and thus against any ultimate morality.

Nonetheless, sexual, forceful women were at the center of most disasters that hit the community, indicating that they had to be contained before peace and order could be reestablished. The serial structure of the narrative and its reliance on further transgressions reinforced the impossibility of such containment. Both the show and the novel started with the premise that women's misbehavior had disrupted the town's social order, yoking narrative to unbridled female sexuality. Twenty years earlier, Catherine Harrington, wife of the wealthiest man in town, had murdered Elizabeth, the flighty wife of Elliot Carson, for having an affair with Harrington's husband, Leslie. Rather than confessing, she let Elliot go to jail and took the secret to her grave. The consequences of her sin remained, contaminating the social and moral order through another generation of wayward, repeatedly transgressive women.

Peyton Place struggles with the issue of how to represent the modern girl, suggesting larger crises over gender and sexual difference. Even its attempts to anchor femininity through more traditional icons of virginity like Allison Mackenzie are fraught and overdetermined. Described by Monash as the show's "Little Nell," Allison was supposedly a symbol of untarnished innocence.[31] The camera repeatedly explored her physical delicacy, framing her slight, blond figure next to her pet caged birds, against small white flowers, or in the act of drawing a smile on a snowman in an exaggerated attempt to reinscribe virtue on the feminine body. As befits an updated "Little Nell," she was often associated with the past, particularly Victorianism, partly through her consumption of nineteenth-century fiction and partly through her respectful friendship with the town's older residents. Her mother, Constance, protects her from society because of her illegitimate birth, fearing a destructive public reaction.[32] As she tells Dr. Rossi, "If it weren't for Allison I wouldn't feel the way I do about a lot of things. But she has to be protected." This attitude has potentially harmful consequences, suggesting that there is no way to preserve virtuous femininity. As Allison tells Elliot Carson, she has given up writing poetry, because she "lack[s] any experience." He reminds her that Emily Dickinson was also isolated, a consoling and seemingly encouraging remark that initially suggests traditional patriarchal wisdom. However, some viewers (and certainly, Allison, the voracious reader) would be aware of Dickinson's mental illness and its relationship to both her writing and her very seclusion, producing a subtext about the dangers of not allowing women to engage in public life.

Efforts to distance Allison from the show's sexual intrigue and locate her outside corporeal sexuality are repeatedly undermined. Her illegitimate birth means that her very presence incarnates her mother's fall and her unbounded sexuality. Extratextually, too, viewers could not avoid the stories of Farrow's off-screen romance with the much older Frank Sinatra, which culminated in her sudden seven-week absence from the screen while she dallied on Sinatra's yacht. In a desperate attempt to preserve Allison's morality in the face of Farrow's depravity, this absence was inscribed in the text as a twenty-one-episode-long coma caused by a hit-and-run driver.[33]

More significantly, however, the show's narratives between 1964 and 1966 are largely structured around Allison's and Betty's desire. Although the narratives attempt to elevate Allison's preferred virginal sexuality over Betty's transgressions, they problematize issues of feminine sexuality in ways similar to Helen Gurley Brown's. Like Betty, Allison desires Rod Harrington, but she separates herself from him and tries to repress their love because of his failed marriage to Betty. She is not vengeful, remaining on good terms with both her friend and her former suitor. She refuses to get involved with Rod more because she cares about Betty and respects her emotions, despite Betty's betrayal. Instead, Allison displaces her desires into dates with safe men like Norman, Rod's younger brother.

But none of Allison's romances are particularly convincing. Even when she is with Rod, her true love, she grabs her books to her chest, looks down, and tries to maintain physical distance. More convincing is her desire for herself, articulated through beauty and costume à la Helen Gurley Brown. Her purchase of a bright lipstick, despite the druggist's disapprobation, signifies her investment in her own body. The show suggests, furthermore, that Allison is re-creating herself for the approving glance of a primarily female audience. When she descends the staircase at home in her new skirt, ostensibly to protest a stuck zipper, she repeatedly asks her mother and Mrs. Anderson (and, presumably, the female viewers) to reassure her that she is pretty.

If Allison suggests the impossibility of establishing a stable, nontransgressive heterosexuality, then the character of Betty foregrounds the problems of narrativizing the new image of the 1960s single girl—especially in a serial form that resists closure. Some of these difficulties are highlighted during the first season in a sequence of episodes featuring Betty's adventures in New York—the city she escapes to after the collapse of her marriage. Rather than self-imposed exile brought on by shame, Betty's temporary relocation corresponds to the mise-en-scène of the period's single-girl myth, in which the big city stands for freedom, choice, possibilities, and adventures unfettered by social and moral restrictions. In *Valley of the Dolls* (Mark Robson, Twentieth Century–Fox, 1967), for example, Anne Welles (also played by Barbara Parkins) leaves her Connecticut home for New York; in *That Girl* (Pensky-Deneroff, ABC, 1966–71) the credit sequences recall the journey of Anne Marie (Marlo Thomas) from her home in rural upstate New York to New York City.[34]

Because of its size, the city represented a space without moral boundaries, offering single women opportunities to display themselves and gain widespread recognition and admiration. During the mid-1960s, women flocked to large metropolitan areas seeking alternatives to early marriage and domestic confinement. Between 1961 and 1964, for instance, New York employment agencies estimated a 15 percent increase in out-of-town clients.[35] At the same time, women often found it difficult to negotiate the city's anonymity. Articles lamented the lack of suitable men in the modern city, and even *Cosmopolitan* warned readers about crime with horrifying stories of young women murdered as they slept.[36] Perhaps most significantly, all these stories point to one major problem women often faced in the big city—the loss of the female camaraderie that facilitated dating and finding work and produced a certain sense of safety.

This isolation is foregrounded as one of the major problems Betty might face in the city. As the announcer for the first episode exploring her life in the city grimly intoned, "To some, New York City is a place of excitement, of glamour. To Betty Harrington, fleeing from a life that has become intolerable, it is a place of refuge, a place to start afresh. Betty has little real hope and virtually no money." This statement clearly denotes the tension between her fantasies and the cold reality of urban poverty and isolation. It is this space—created by desire and bordered by social limitations—that the single girl inhabits in *Peyton Place,* making her position both precarious and liminal. This tension contrasts with the city of the single-girl fantasy, in which women enjoy their bodies and gain social standing through controlling their display—whether as models or as courtesans. The female perspective is emphasized through Betty's look and the power and pleasure she derives from her newly unrestrained vision, a perspective and pleasure the viewer shares. Her viewpoint contrasts with the male voice of God, whose more somber predictions frame the narrative.

Significantly, Betty's life improves once she finds herself a female friend, which she accomplishes remarkably quickly. From the moment Sharon liberates Betty from her concerns about survival, most of the city scenes are captured in images full of feminine visual pleasure and feature shots of these girls looking at their bodies, their reflections, or surveying each other's appearance. In all the scenes with Sharon, the camera focuses on the details of her lifestyle—her work as a model, her isometric exercises, her wardrobe, her apartment decor, and her movements across the screen. This focus is combined with an emphasis on Betty's gaze at her own body in the mirror while dressed in Sharon's clothes, admiring her own body as she dances to Sharon's jazz records, or looking at Sharon as she models designer furs, exercises, rolls around on her bed, or flirts with her married lover Phil. The viewer identifies with Betty's gaze and desire for this life, an identification reinforced by cutting back and forth between the beauty of Sharon's New York and the restricted landscape of Peyton Place.

The pleasure and power that these women gain from looking at the female body is perhaps best demonstrated in a scene at a designer boutique. It opens with an establishing shot of a New York street covered with snow. Betty looks into the window of a designer store as she holds her thin coat close to her neck to protect herself from the cold. Somber, melodramatic music underlines her longing to participate in a luxurious urban lifestyle. But the image in which she is immersed also includes her own reflection. Once Betty enters the store, the space of her fantasies, a clerk asks if she needs help and then leads her to Sharon, who is trying on "a heavenly sheath." Throughout the sequence, Betty's gaze is emphasized. As the music swells, the camera slowly moves in to a close-up as Betty opens her mouth in amazement. The shot ends the segment, building suspense.

After an appropriately placed commercial break, the close-up of the transfixed Betty returns, accompanied by different music—a love theme. Subsequent shots reveal the object of Betty's desiring look: Sharon trying on a selection of furs. She walks toward a full-length mirror in order to admire her reflection while Betty looks on. As a gesture of friendship, Sharon offers Betty the chance to try on the fur, and, as Betty moves to the center of the room, the camera tracks in to reframe the two women in medium shot beside the mirror. The bond between them is expressed not just in terms of a shared love of clothes but in the way they both move in front of the mirror, exchanging reflections. As Betty strokes the fur across her face, Sharon alludes to the secrets of her success, noting that a girl has to be "smart" to survive the city. Accepting this new role, Betty drapes herself in fur and walks seductively toward the mirror.

"Getting smart," as Sharon called it, was one solution to this dilemma, albeit one that involved abandoning the world of work in favor of a new career, the ancient role of the courtesan. As *Peyton Place* showed in its New York scenes, single women might be tempted to depend financially on older men because of women's low salaries. As Sharon repeatedly tells Betty, one cannot live in a reasonable apartment and eat well, let alone buy clothes on a $75 weekly wage. Instead, single women could only manage "salads at the automat . . . and nights with good books," confining them economically. Certainly, Betty is more restricted in New York than in Peyton Place. In the big city, she is framed inside buildings (employment agencies, the shop, Sharon's apartment) or gazing at herself in front of a mirror, whereas in Peyton Place she roams across the town square and through public buildings. This spatial restriction might have been cautionary, suggesting that young viewers had better stay at home if they want some form of freedom.

Rather than placing women on display and facilitating their explorations of the public sphere, working life in the city probably restricted many young women to their cheap apartments or rooms, where they might indulge in the relatively affordable—and private—pleasures of reading a novel or magazine or, possibly, watching television. This restriction points to a larger trend—the rise in media designed primarily for domestic consumption that centers on narratives and images of young women engaging in adventures in the public sphere—just like *Peyton Place* and *Cosmopolitan*. These new consumer products, then, simultaneously point to the *poverty* of many working women and the limitations that economic inequalities placed on their lifestyles, as well as suggesting their increasing importance as a demographic group for advertisers.

Within new single-girl texts like *Cosmopolitan* and *Peyton Place,* young women could vicariously consume images of their more affluent counterparts experiencing the city. At the same time, the subtext of both these fantasies and their lived experiences suggested that marriage was still the preferred resolution, given the "real world" possibilities. Even Helen Gurley Brown saw single life as a way to prepare for marriage. Despite her assertion that *Sex and the Single Girl* "is not a study on how to get married but how to stay single in style," she opens with the story of winning her movie-director husband.[37] In her rewriting of the *Playboy* lifestyle for women, she argued that she was responding to women's economic dependence and general disempowerment. In *Cosmopolitan*'s 1966 interview with Hugh Hefner, the reporter chastises Hef for promoting an unattainable lifestyle based on expensive material goods that is only accessible to the wealthy few.[38] In contrast, Gurley Brown based much of her advice on women's general lack of power and economic control, believing the two to be interrelated. As she stated in her 1963 *Playboy* interview,

> If all things were equal, if we really did have a single standard, if men and women held the same jobs and got the same things out of being married, then I think it would be very wrong [to use sex to manipulate men]. As things stand, there aren't enough men. It is desirable to get married in most people's view. *A husband is a priceless commodity.* Whatever means you use to get a husband, outside of blackmail and

> things that are illegal, I think is all right. . . . *A woman desperately needs to be married more than a man does. She wants and needs the baby.* So to get what she wants, she uses every available weapon. Sex is one of them.[39] (emphasis mine)

Ironically, then, *Sex and the Single Girl* was not a tract against wedlock, but, avowedly, an illustration of an interim phase between adolescence and marriage where women could follow Gurley Brown's steps and devote themselves to their own bodies, careers, and leisure in order to become better wives. But given her derogatory tales of domestic life and unhappy wives, her glamorous images of dates, the office, and single-girl life, it appears that Gurley Brown is either being disingenuous, is responding to the restrictions placed on representing women's sexuality, or is caught articulating an impossible paradox of feminine sexuality.

Peyton Place similarly illustrated the abuses and failures of wedlock as it strived to assert marriage as the best solution for women's sexual fulfillment. Betty—perhaps *Peyton Place*'s nearest approximation to Gurley Brown's ideal—confesses that she would give up the thrills of New York and her desire to "be someone on my own, as Betty Anderson," and return to Peyton Place for Rod.[40] Yet, like Gurley Brown's emphasis on marriage as the best solution, *Peyton Place*'s images of Betty favoring an upper-middle-class New England home over the excitement of the big city are far from convincing—especially given the visual pleasure the audience has also shared through Betty's gaze. Similarly, her relationship with Sharon seems more sincere, open, and certainly more fun than any life she might have with Rod.

But this unmarried, sexual single girl undermined the contract of marriage itself, and with it the established organization of sexual difference. As the outcry over *Peyton Place* suggests, the image of female sexuality outside marriage, particularly one unleashed by the self-made, self-admiring *feminine* woman, harbors radical implications, ones that cannot be erased by punishing Betty once again and sending her back home. Although working mothers could at least argue that their incomes helped support the family unit, the economy of the single girl was centered solely on the female self. Yet the viewers' elevation of Allison and Betty above Constance—the intended lead, sacrificial mother, and repentant sinner—suggests that Allison and Betty's struggles against accepted gender roles and practices conformed more closely to women's fantasies and social realities.

Although girls like Betty might be punished for their sexual transgressions, *Peyton Place*'s organization around this feminine look also invited more "radical" readings. Images of feminine self-absorption structure *Peyton Place*'s New York scenes, and these patterns are repeated at home in small-town Peyton Place. Sharon and Betty's interest in each other, each evaluating themselves against the other, is paralleled on a larger scale in the relationship between Allison and Betty. Although their involvement ostensibly pivots around Rod, the real drama and interest rests in the way both girls handle themselves and their relationship with each other. As a safe, pale, feminized, passive male, Rod acts as a cipher for feminine desire, a mechanism to produce feminine intrigue. In this way, he acts as a fashion accessory—complementing both Allison and Betty's appearance and suggesting their social success. Thus he differs very little from *Cosmopolitan*'s one-dimensional images of male escorts. The question of "who will win Rod?" encourages viewers to compare and evaluate Allison and Betty, focusing their attention on these girls and their relationship with each other. Press reports reinforced this focus by encouraging readers to contrast both girls—not just in terms of their on-screen images, but with a comparison of their off-screen behaviors and a study of the contradictions between the personas of Allison/Mia and Betty/Barbara, which invited confusion between various combinations of on- and off-screen images.[41]

This comparison seemed to underline a particularly feminine way of engaging with the self and with the pleasure of looking at other women. As Hugh Hefner noted in a 1966 interview with *Cosmopolitan*, these images in women's magazines were not the kind that interested men, suggesting a dichotomy between male and female pleasure in representations of the female body:

> But particularly symptomatic, I think, are the schizophrenic conflicts of feminine beauty that have evolved in the men's and women's magazines. I think, for example, that some interesting conclusions can be drawn from a comparison of *Playboy*'s Playmate of the Month and the typical high-fashion models in *Vogue* and other fashion magazines. Female beauty, as it is projected in the high-fashion women's magazines, is flat-chested, angular, hip-less and almost as tall as the average

> American man. It is not, quite honestly, a heterosexual concept. *It is a projection of the female that is competitive and in conflict*, rather than the complementary counterpart.[42] (emphasis mine)

Given his self-appointed role as sexual libertine, it is interesting to find Hefner condemning these images for disturbing gendered hierarchies. This homosocial desire—which Hefner too easily dismisses—is arguably a component of heterosexual femininity, shaping much of the pleasures of women's magazines, which let the reader evaluate incarnations of the self alongside multiple images of the day's celebrities and models. It is, however, as he suggests, outwardly oriented, producing a very different type of sexuality and pleasure.

Hefner's comments not only point to different gendered ways of looking at and desiring women, they also suggest that the mechanisms by which Gurley Brown advocated self-improvement would not be successful in attracting men. Given that his observations were reported in *Cosmopolitan,* over which she maintained tight editorial control, she would have been aware that he found her prescriptions for feminine beauty and success unconvincing. In a similar vein, the failure of her chat show reinforces her strange inability to tap into male desire, suggesting that very different economies of desire—furnished by a remarkably different mise-en-scène and way of looking—operated across the sexes at this time. Furthermore, given the public forums in which these debates took place, it is likely that the *Cosmo* girl would also be aware that Gurley Brown's vision of beauty and her attendant advice were oriented not toward making oneself more attractive to men but rather toward the self and other women. As in *Peyton Place,* Gurley Brown's promises of pleasure in the beautiful female body are primarily for feminine consumption, be it one's own or that of a model or actress.

This feminine look at the female body suggests another level at which these representations operate and posits another reason why *Peyton Place* provoked such a scandal during its first years but lost the public's interest by the late 1960s. Without Allison's presence, Betty's scandalous acts lost their power to fascinate the viewer, indicating that without this homosocial subtext, the show could not engage as powerfully with heterosexual feminine desire. But the departure of Allison also suggested a more significant change in representations of female sexuality, one that

Gurley Brown would later address in her 1970 rewrite, *Sex and the New Single Girl.* Discussing the changes that have occurred in the last eight years, she dismisses some of the external trappings of femininity (like hairpieces), rejoices that women are no longer contemplating what their identities might be, and tells them to divert their interest to themselves, without external causes.[43] Perhaps more significantly, she opens her new introduction with a discussion of the internal feelings produced by sex.[44] Rather than dealing with sexuality from an external perspective, filtering it through the experiences of multiple women, Brown considers the internal mechanisms of desire through a single protagonist. Brown's introduction points to a clear shift in representational practices, moving toward more explicit investigations of internal, individual desire that were less suited to the kinds of group-oriented serial narrative characteristic of *Peyton Place.*

Notes

1 Ira Mothner, "TV's *Peyton Place:* Sweet Virtue's Country Seat," *Look* 29, no. 21 (19 October 1965): 83; Deborah Haber, "Television à Go Go," *Television* 22, no. 6 (June 1965): 50; Jack Star, "Where We Stand: The Senior Class," *Look* 27, no. 1 (15 January 1963): 51–53; Lynn Spigel, "From Domestic Space to Outer Space: The 1960s Fantastic Family Sitcom," in *Close Encounters: Film, Feminism, and Science Fiction,* ed. Constance Penley, Elisabeth Lyon, Lynn Spigel, and Janet Bergstrom (Minneapolis: University of Minnesota Press, 1991), 205–35. By January 1964, even the leading teen magazine, *Seventeen,* was predicting that Equal Rights would become the latest craze, as teenage girls contemplated whether to follow careers as doctors, photographers, or join the Peace Corps ("The Teen Scene," *Seventeen* 231 [January 1964]: 92).

2 Joan Barthel, "Requiem for a TV Town," *Life* 66, no. 16 (25 April 1969): 48.

3 See, for example, Lynn Spigel, *Make Room for TV: Television and the Family Ideal in Postwar America* (Chicago: University of Chicago Press, 1992), 36–98.

4 For further discussion of the articulation of gender and the home see Mary Beth Haralovich, "Sitcoms and Suburbs: Positioning the 1950s Homemaker," in *Private Screenings: Television and the Female Consumer,* ed. Lynn Spigel and Denise Mann (Minneapolis: University of Minnesota Press, 1992), 111–42.

5 See "The Month In Focus," *Television* 21, no. 11 (November 1964): 7; Deborah Haber, "The Studio That Came In from the Cold," *Television* 22, no. 9 (September 1965): 61; and Barthel, "Requiem for a TV Town," 49.

6 Ibid.

7 Mothner, "TV's *Peyton Place*," 83.

8 Robert C. Allen, *Speaking of Soap Operas* (Chapel Hill: University of North Carolina Press, 1985), 110–14, 164–69; Mothner, "TV's *Peyton Place*," 83–84.

9 Quoted in Mothner, "TV's *Peyton Place*," 83.

10 Barthel, "Requiem for a TV Town," 49.

11 "Triple Jeopardy," *Time*, 20 August 1965, 65.

12 Mothner, "TV's *Peyton Place*," 86; "Triple Jeopardy," 65.

13 Ibid.; Barthel, "Requiem for a TV Town," 48.

14 Ibid., 47.

15 Ibid.

16 Quotations from Johnny Carson and Jack Paar cited in Barthel, "Requiem for a TV Town," 48; Tim Brooks and Earl Marsh, *The Complete Directory to Prime Time Network TV Shows, 1946–Present* (New York: Ballantine Books, 1981), 596.

17 Gail Cameron, "Soapy Sex Moves to Prime Time," *Life* 57, no. 23 (4 December 1964): 17; Stanley Gordon, "Mia Farrow: An Actress in Search of a Character," *Look* 28, no. 24 (1 December 1964): 76; "Triple Jeopardy," 65.

18 "Triple Jeopardy," 65; Vernon Scott, "Pandemonium in *Peyton Place*," *Cosmopolitan* 160, no. 3 (March 1966): 73.

19 Matt Fessier, "Billy Graham Discusses: Love, Sin, and *Peyton Place*," *Photoplay* 68, no. 6 (December 1965): 48.

20 Ironically, she accomplished this desire in Metalious's 1959 sequel, *Return to Peyton Place* (New York: Dell, 1960), but never on the television show.

21 Helen Gurley Brown, "Step into My Parlor," *Cosmopolitan* 159, no. 1 (July 1965): 4.

22 Hilary Radner, *Shopping Around: Feminine Culture and the Pursuit of Pleasure* (New York: Routledge, 1995), xi.

23 Helen Gurley Brown, *Having It All* (New York: Pocket Books, 1982), 2, 12–13, 16–17, 25, 36–39, 115–58, 247–48, 368–69.

24 "How Now, Brown Wren?" *Time*, 20 October 1967, 74.

25 See Barbara Ehrenreich, *For Her Own Good: 150 Years of the Experts' Advice to Women* (Garden City, N.Y.: Anchor Books, 1978), 286–92.

26 As former *Cosmopolitan* writer Harris Dienstfrey observes, "There are never any articles [in *Cosmopolitan*] on children, except how to be nice to those of a divorced man. Helen has no interest in children, and probably does not care for them. Work is what a woman should do" (Dienstfrey, "That *Cosmopolitan* Girl," *Antioch Review* 41, no. 4 [fall 1984]: 434–35).

27 Radner, *Shopping Around*, xi–xiv.

28 This seemingly self-generated being arguably constituted a "third sex," the

single or *Cosmo* girl. As Marjorie Garber notes in relation to the cross-dresser, another term that confounds the stability of male-female sexual difference, "the 'third term' is *not* a *term*. Much less is it a *sex*, certainly not an instantiated 'blurred' sex as signified by a term like 'androgyne' or 'hermaphrodite,' . . . The 'third' is a mode of articulation, a way of describing a space of possibility." Although this possibility might be empowering (as is intended throughout Gurley Brown's advice manuals, recordings, and, of course, *Cosmopolitan*), Garber notes that it also signifies a more general "category crisis," suggesting the disturbance of other socially constructed binaries (e.g., self/other, black/white, public/private) (Garber, *Vested Interests: Cross Dressing and Cultural Anxiety* [New York: Routledge, 1992], 16–17).

29 Gurley Brown, "Step into My Parlor," 4.

30 During the mid-1960s, representation of even the consequences of illicit sexual activity was completely taboo. In 1964, for instance, a proposed episode of *Dr. Kildare* (NBC, 1961–66) dealing with syphilis was curtailed by NBC's Broadcast Standards Department on the grounds that "it would be inappropriate for family viewing." Although the producers and the American Medical Association protested on the grounds that the show could "have made a significant contribution, in the public interest, to the fight against VD," the project was killed. Interestingly, the producers emphasized in support of their project that "nowhere in [the] script is the phrase 'sexual intercourse' used, and writer [E. Jack] Neuman obviously went out of his way to maintain decorum. There are few references to how VD is contracted." Because VD had been mentioned in the previous season in an episode of *The Nurses* (CBS, 1962–67), NBC's decision was seen as a step backward in terms of television's representation of sexuality. Institutional constraints also prohibited explicit representations of female sexual activity outside marriage in a prime-time show; complete endorsement of feminism might alienate some audiences ("VD on TV?" *Newsweek*, 30 November 1964, 62).

31 Mothner, "TV's *Peyton Place*," 84.

32 Using Allison and Constance, an illegitimate child and unwed mother, to represent the forces of "good" was also a radical step for 1960s television, one that threatened to dissolve the traditional family structure, as their lives seemed to flourish without any paternal presence. Nevertheless, this model family unit was not simply endorsed. In a move deemed necessary to protect herself and her child from social ostracism, Constance hid her unmarried status, signifying her shame by masquerading as a widow. This fiction allowed her to keep her child and her dignity, masked her past "immorality," and simultaneously justified her career as her sole means of supporting her family. Her career and participation in the town's public life

were not challenged, largely because motherhood was placed as her first priority, her most well-defined trait, and the hallmark of her interaction with all members of the community.

Nevertheless, Constance still represented the show's most stable articulation of femininity. Because she is an older woman, she is represented as having lost some of the potentially dangerous power of youthful ambition, beauty, and sexuality. Her marriage at the end of the first season further secured and legitimized her place in society, erasing the stigma of her affair with Elliot. As *Photoplay* observed, this wedding "was so right . . . Constance Mackenzie and Elliot Carson . . . eventually made it right by getting married" (Polly Terry, "The Next Wedding on *Peyton Place!* Who Will Marry Whom and Why," *Photoplay* 68, no. 2 [August 1965]: 50–51).

33 Lyn Randall, "Mia Farrow's Marriage to Sinatra!" *Photoplay* 68, no. 4 (October 1965): 30, 32–33, 97–98.

34 See, for example, "Cities and the Single Girl," *Newsweek*, 15 November 1965, 120; "The Girl Ghetto," *Cosmopolitan* 161, no. 3 (September 1966): 106–10; "New Rules for the Singles Game," *Life* 63, no. 7 (18 August 1967): 60–65.

35 Martin Abramson, "Single Girls in New York City," *Cosmopolitan* 158, no. 2 (February 1965): 48.

36 See, for example, "Cities and the Single Girl," 120; Linda Rosenkrantz, "20 Tips on Making Friends . . . in the Big City," *Cosmopolitan* 161, no. 3 (September 1966): 28–30; Lee Israel, "Violence. How Does a Career Girl Cope?" *Cosmopolitan* 164, no. 2 (February 1968): 81–85.

37 "*Playboy* Interview with Helen Gurley Brown," reprinted in Hugh M. Hefner, *The Bedside Playboy* (Chicago: Playboy Press, 1968), 363; Helen Gurley Brown, *Sex and the Single Girl* (New York: Random House, 1962), 11.

38 Theodore Irwin, "*Cosmopolitan* Interviews Hugh M. Hefner, *Playboy*'s Controversial Editor," *Cosmopolitan* 160, no. 5 (May 1966): 77–78.

39 "*Playboy* Interview with Helen Gurley Brown," 372–73.

40 This endorsement of marriage is especially significant, given that many texts promoting the pleasures of single life, such as *Peyton Place* and *Cosmopolitan*, were actually consumed by a greater number of *married* women, as Barbara Ehrenreich has shown, suggesting that discourses on the single girl did not simply mirror a new social reality but rather addressed a popular feminine fantasy. In 1967, for example, *Cosmopolitan* published an article entitled, "Is Marriage Dying?" Although at first sight, this essay appeared to be just another tribute to the virtues of single life, it was actually written by an Episcopalian minister, Earl Brill, to promote marriage. Rather than adhering to the cold war family ideals found in journals like *Good Housekeeping* and *McCall's*, however, Brill acknowledged that marriage was no longer neces-

sary given women's more active role in society; nonetheless, he argued that this development provided the strongest justification for its survival:

> Space age girls are playing it cool. Few of them reject the idea of marriage the way their feminist grandmothers did, but even fewer assume the superiority of home and hearth the way their mothers did. Talking with today's youth gives the impression that they are willing to consider marriage, but that they are going to require real persuasion. . . . When marriage becomes a matter of *genuine* choice . . . then they will get married for only one reason: They really want to. . . . There's no real danger that marriage will disappear; even with the pressure off, most young people will probably decide to marry. If we can ever reach the point where they can do it as an act of real freedom, then we will have made the act more meaningful.

Indeed, evidence suggests that the sixties single-girl phenomenon was not that widespread, despite all the media attention it received; rather, it tended to be mobilized in order to redefine marriage as a more equitable union. As Elaine Tyler May has shown, there was actually only a slight growth in the single population during this time, with people only postponing marriage, on average, by a matter of months. Between 1964 and 1969, the median age at first marriage only increased from 20.5 to 20.8 years for women; during the same period, men married at an average age of 22.4 (1964), escalating to 22.7 (1965–1967), only to return abruptly to 22.4 years (1968). Marriage was still an overwhelmingly popular choice for most women, suggesting that the single-girl lifestyle represented more of an expanded dating period than a permanent refutation of commitment. Ironically enough, the rise in single life ultimately revealed a greater affirmation of marriage. In the face of rising divorce rates, many women and men postponed marriage in favor of a prolonged period of dating because they took the responsibility of finding a lifelong partner more seriously, often turning to the city to avail themselves of its greater choice when choosing a lifelong partner. As Gurley Brown observed, "A marriage should be for life if you can possibly get it to be, and I do not see how you can know someone in every way without participating [in sex]." The continued respect for marriage was arguably one reason behind the lifting of taboos on premarital sex—earlier documents like *The Kinsey Report* had revealed the stress that chaste dating practices had placed on subsequent marriages as well as the problems that arose from couples rushing into early marriages (Ehrenreich, *For Her Own Good*, 287–92; Earl H. Brill, "Is Marriage Dying?" *Cosmopolitan* 163, no. 2 [August 1967]: 36; Elaine Tyler May, *Homeward Bound: American Families in the Cold War Era* [New

York: Basic Books, 1988], 6–7, 120–22; "*Playboy* Interview with Helen Gurley Brown," 379).

41 See, for example, Alice P. York, "What Mia Farrow Does for Love That Barbara Parkins Doesn't Have To," *Photoplay* 68, no. 5 (November 1965): 52–57, 73; Matt Fessier, "I'm Going to Have an Affair After I'm Married," *Photoplay* 68, no. 1 (July 1965): 44–45, 92–93; Terry, "The Next Wedding on *Peyton Place!*" 49–52, 80–81.

42 Irwin, "*Cosmopolitan* Interviews Hugh Hefner," 78–79.

43 Helen Gurley Brown, *Sex and the New Single Girl* (Greenwich, Conn.: Fawcett Crest, 1970), 12–13.

44 Ibid., 9–10.

I Spy's "Living Postcards"

The Geo-Politics of Civil Rights

Mary Beth Haralovich

> The network and producer Sheldon Leonard have, with more guts than ordinary observers could imagine, cast Negro comedian Bill Cosby in a feature role, then turned about in the premiere . . . and racked another ethnic group, the Chinese. . . . But the Chinese commies are bound to be the new heavies of pulp fiction.
>
> —review of *I Spy*'s first episode, *Variety*, 22 September 1965

I Spy (NBC, 1965–68) represents the first visible result of civil rights pressures on the television industry.[1] An hour-long weekly drama, *I Spy* served up racial integration with a team of U.S. intelligence agents (Robert Culp as Kelly Robinson and Bill Cosby as Alexander Scott) who travel the world undercover as a professional tennis player and his trainer. *I Spy*'s cultural significance lies not only in its embrace of racial integration through cast and characters but also in its representation of the value of civil rights for the U.S. position in the Cold War. In their dealings with Communists and Soviet agents, *I Spy*'s agents use advances in civil rights as a weapon in the Cold War, asserting progress in U.S. race relations and defending against charges that the United States is a racist country.

I Spy's foreign locations add dimension and spectacle to television spy fiction. In their travels, the spies enact the global politics of the Cold War. But as tourists, they enjoy the sights and sounds of other countries, embrace cultural if not political difference, and celebrate humanist similarities. As a travelogue, *I Spy* uses color cinematography and locations to provide a form of what Cynthia Enloe calls "living postcards . . . natives in their exotic environment." Even as it reveals the terrain of the Cold War, *I Spy* demonstrates the ease and pleasures of foreign travel, including "sex tourism," the sexual availability of local women for the white male tourist.[2]

Television historians have applauded *I Spy*'s efforts at racial equality, which they credit to a series design that allowed a black character most of the flexibility and opportunities afforded white characters. In *Blacks and White TV*, J. Fred MacDonald argues that because "it affected the history of blacks in American television, the most crucial series in the latter half of the 1960s was *I Spy*." MacDonald appreciates the "bold decision" to cast an integrated partnership, one that "broke the color line as had no series in TV history," providing opportunities for other African American performers as well as for Cosby. Historians Allen Woll and Randall Miller welcome "a sympathetic, realistic black character in a lead role," and Eric Barnouw values the "feeling of equality and warm friendship" revealed in the performances. MacDonald applauds *I Spy* for providing audiences with the "educational experience [of seeing] an Afro-American hero operating constructively abroad in the service of the United States." He takes pleasure in Cosby/Scott's very presence in European locations and finds that Scott was "able to feel and express emotions historically forbidden to black characters in mainstream entertainment media . . . [including] physical expressions of inter-racial romance." In "Televisual Representation and the Claims of 'The Black Experience,'" Phillip Brian Harper discusses Cosby's "belief in the unique contributions that the show could make to improved U.S. race relations and his sense of solidarity with other blacks involved in the civil rights struggle."[3]

Despite the attempted equality of the partners, *I Spy* opens with a credits sequence dominated by Robinson/Culp. A tennis player in silhouette swings his racket as names of world cities move by, ending with "USA" (in red, white, and blue).[4] The racket becomes a gun as the tennis player becomes a crouched man in a suit. He shoots offscreen three times. The exploding bullets become the series name: *I Spy*. This title dissolves to a cool and collected Robinson/Culp, wearing a suit and tie. He uses a lighter to ignite a cigarette and then a bomb, which he casually tosses offscreen. After the explosion, his eyes look down from the top of a split screen onto a series of scenes taken primarily from the episode to come. Aside from his name above the title—and depending on the episode—Scott/Cosby might make only one appearance in the credits sequence. However, as if to underscore the integrated partnership, the credits of *I Spy*'s first episode pair Scott/Cosby with Robinson/Culp in various action scenes. One shot is a close-up of two hands—one black and one white—each pointing a gun in the same direction.

Like other TV spies of the period, Robinson is derived from James Bond, by 1965 a staple of spy fiction. Scott, however, has a more complex etiology that attempts to explain how an African American came to occupy his position. *The Cold War File,* a compendium of spy fiction, describes Robinson as "a major contender at Wimbledon . . . a romantic and an adventurer . . . equally proficient in the arts of seduction and assassination." *The Cold War File* describes Scott's up-by-the-bootstraps super achievements: despite "racial barriers and an impoverished childhood," Scott became a college football star, champion tennis player, graduate of Temple University [as is Cosby], Rhodes scholar, and fluent in eleven languages.[5] Repressing the pointed race commentary of 1960s social issue comedians such as Lenny Bruce and Dick Gregory, Scott's character design takes on attributes of two heroic figures—Moe Berg (the multilingual athlete-spy of World War II) and Arthur Ashe (the African American tennis champion who won the first U.S. Open in 1968).[6]

Although exhibition tennis and espionage are motivations for setting the series in foreign lands, *I Spy*'s travelogue is also a register of its verisimilitude as spy fiction. Foreign countries are contested territory in the Cold War, and they are also accessible sites for tourism. *I Spy*'s espionage is visually grounded in NBC's first prime-time season of color programming in 1965.[7] The action takes place against the vistas and skylines of foreign locations. The spies often function as tour guides, particularly in Mexico, which is presented as our friendly neighbor to the south, a haven for U.S. spies on vacation.

I Spy is one among many films and TV shows connected with 1960s espionage culture, but its recombination of spy fiction and travelogue makes it different from the others. Although *I Spy*'s spies can be suave and witty, the series engages the 1960s world of espionage not through parody but through realism. In *Get Smart* (NBC, 1965–69; CBS 1969–70), *Mission: Impossible* (CBS, 1966–73; ABC, 1988–90), *The Man from U.N.C.L.E.* (NBC, 1964–68), and *The Avengers* (ABC, 1966–69), agents typically take on one specific mission at a time to fight fantastic or ambiguous Soviet bloc villains. *I Spy*'s agents are deployed worldwide to observe and interfere with Communist activities. Robinson and Scott behave in many ways like "real" CIA agents—as they have been described in intelligence histories.[8] They do not reveal their actual identities to civilians, but other spies know them to be spies—and vice versa. Not reliant on gimmicks or gunplay, Robinson and Scott often work without weapons and try to convince people of the wisdom of rejecting Communism.[9]

One source of *I Spy*'s verisimilitude and ideological positioning in the 1960s is public awareness of intelligence and its role in state security. In the early 1960s, there were several highly visible Cold War incidents—the missile gap, the U-2 spy mission, the Cuban missile crisis. In addition, the period has been described as the "Cult of the Defector" for the way defections were announced in "government-sponsored press conference[s]." Although such public events raised questions about the autonomy of the CIA and the legality of its actions, espionage remained central to the U.S. struggle with the Soviet bloc for world domination. Barnouw suggests that 1960s TV spy fiction may have contributed to "public acceptance of a foreign policy based on good guy/bad guy premises [and] clandestine warfare" and helped Americans get used to the covert actions of the CIA.[10] *I Spy* adopts the Cold War attitude prevalent in the CIA and State Department of the time: that Communism is pernicious and pervasive, that Communists are dupes who follow Party-line directions from Moscow.

Although *I Spy* was produced in the mid-1960s—in the wake of the 1963 March on Washington, Freedom Summer, and the Civil Rights Act of 1964—one can look at the series (and at civil rights law) as a solution to the State Department's public relations problems of the 1950s. In her study of U.S. race relations and foreign policy during the Cold War, Mary Dudziak shows how race discrimination became "a critical cultural and ideological weak point" for U.S. foreign policy during the 1950s.

> Voting rights abuses, lynchings, school segregation, and antimiscegenation laws were discussed at length in newspapers around the world, and the international media continually questioned whether race discrimination made American democracy a hypocrisy. How can democracy be attractive to Third World countries when the U.S. abuses its citizens of color? This situation was exacerbated by "African Americans [such as entertainer Josephine Baker, actor-singer Paul Robeson, and writer W. E. B. DuBois who] criticized race discrimination in the United States before an international audience."[11]

I Spy resembles an official response to the U.S. Cold War predicament of the 1950s. At a time when both the Cold War and civil rights are hot, *I Spy* reassures audiences that U.S. intelligence is working to protect U.S. interests abroad, and it affirms the value of civil rights for the United States by showing an integrated partnership that is friendly, color-blind, and patriotic. Traveling the world, Robinson and Scott represent racial harmony both in their relationship and in dialogue with Communists. Robinson and Scott occupy the discursive role the State Department searched for in the 1950s: African Americans who would travel overseas and say "the right thing" about race relations in the United States. Dudziak notes, "Patriots were supposed to close ranks" when overseas. One could be critical in the United States but, "when sent abroad [one should] emphasize racial progress in the United States and argue that persons of color had nothing to gain from communism."[12] Emerging from an environment that compressed civil rights activism and Cold War vigilance, *I Spy* presented analogues to 1950s black activists such as Baker and Robeson.

The first episode of *I Spy* pointedly announces the series's stance on civil rights and the Cold War. Written by Robert Culp, whose personal commitment to racial integration was important to the series,[13] "So Long, Patrick Henry" (first season, 1965) deals with an African American Olympic medalist who defects to the People's Republic of China for $250,000 in a Swiss bank account (more than he would earn as a professional athlete in the United States at the time). Suspecting that the defector may be unhappy with his situation, the U.S. government assigns Robinson and Scott to determine whether he wants to return to the United States.

As with the public parade of actual defectors, the athlete and his Chinese handlers appear together in several press conferences. When they announce his defection, the athlete rejects a speech prepared by the Chinese ("Who wrote this thing, huh?") to credit himself with his successful rise in spite of racism ("I'm the best, see, because I worked like a slave—if you'll pardon the expression—to get that way"). At the press conference that concludes the episode, the athlete denounces Chinese attempts to control the Afro-Asian games (described by Mr. Tsung, the main Chinese heavy, as a means for China to "be firmly entrenched in Africa"). The athlete leaves the press conference to a standing ovation from the assembled group of Africans and Asians after he states: "They'll poison it for you. . . . So have your games, but you do it yourselves. I'll help you if I can, but right now I just want to go home."[14]

Robinson and Scott's contact with the defector is an opportunity for the agents to explain—to the defector and thus to the viewing audience—current race conditions in the United States and the need for commitment to racial integration. Throughout, Robinson and Scott visually express their disgust with the defector. In a key conversation in a bar, Scott explains the dual struggle for international and domestic civil rights. The United States is "trying to make the law of the land stick, holding the world together with one hand and trying to clean their own house with the other—yeah, something no country's ever done before in the history of the world." Scott declares, "The whole world is trying to keep bloody fools like you from selling themselves back into slavery." The word "slavery" gets the defector's attention.

Yet *I Spy* is not a didactic tract. The series also presents its messages through hip banter between Robinson and Scott.[15] In this episode's epilogue, a summary joke merges integration, espionage, and sex tourism. A bellboy whom Scott enlists to help the agents refers to himself as "007." Scott wants to reward the bellboy by taking him to "an English movie" about "the adventures of 007." When Robinson resists, Scott implores, "Don't knock the competition. . . . You may learn something. Not only does he get the women, but he gets them painted all the different colors of the rainbow. It's called widescreen integration." Open discussion of race relations is important to *I Spy*. In addition to dialogue and narrative logic, *I Spy* relies on visual confirmation of racial equality in the way Robinson and Scott exercise their partnership, living and working together.

In "Tonia" (second season, 1967), Robinson and Scott again confront a black American who has been duped by Communists, this time in Italy. Scott figures centrally—as an African American, as a heterosexual lover, and as a patriot.[16] "Tonia" takes place in Rome, where anti-U.S. actions are widespread: Uncle Sam hangs in effigy from a building; a bartender at the U.S. Officers' Club reports to a Communist cell leader; Communists look at Robinson and Scott with distaste; the hammer-and-sickle graces a street poster; other street posters announce demonstrations against the war in Vietnam; a Communist cell leader attempts to destroy Robinson and Scott's integrated partnership.[17]

The daughter of a black USO performer, Tonia is an American who moved to Italy when she was a child. Now involved with the Communist Party, she confronts Scott about racism and poverty in the United States. As Tonia and Scott walk through a side street in Rome, they pass children playing in cardboard boxes. Scott remarks, "Apart from the fact that it's Italy, it's no different from my old neighborhood" in Philadelphia. Tonia counters this humanist observation ("Americans think that poor people are morally inferior") and accuses the United States of "ruthless exploitation of racial minorities." Scott offers a good-natured reply, one that deflects discussion of race relations with wry recitations of Marxist theory: "I see. And capitalist warmongers and their Wall Street lackeys." Their ideological difference is a motif of the episode. Scott accuses Tonia of living in a "political dream world" and of spouting "cliches" and "assumptions." She charges him with being an "agent of American militarism." When Scott asks her to go on a picnic, Tonia prefers that their meeting be a "seminar, a discussion period."

But Tonia makes one remark that hits home. She reproaches Scott for being Robinson's servant, for "carrying the white man's rackets." Unable to reveal his actual identity as a U.S. agent and Robinson's partner, Scott is disturbed by this accusation. Later, Scott complains to Robinson ("People think I'm your servant") as, dressed in formal attire en route to the officers' club, the two men leave their hotel room. Robinson is at once sympathetic ("She's been brought up on propaganda") and a good-natured joker ("You get a good salary and every other Sunday off"). Although their spy partnership cannot be publicly spoken of, Robinson and Scott's joint destination, easy camaraderie, similar formal wear, and shared sleeping quarters visually underscore their equality.

In "Tonia," both the Soviets and the Americans justify their counterespionage strategies. Blair, a representative of the U.S. State Department, wants Scott to "go after that girl," since "Washington has been on my back for weeks to make contact among these extreme left-wingers." The United States is "dying for information" about leftist activities in Rome ("how well are they organized, what are their immediate plans") to avoid disturbances such as the "riot last month at a NATO base [in which] three people [were] killed . . . any excuse for a good noisy anti-American demonstration." Blair explains that young people are duped by Communists: "The direction comes from [the Party]. Regardless of what these kids say, they are not independent."

Cold War realism: Robinson (Robert Culp) flanked by anti-U.S. posters in Rome, *I Spy*.

Racial equality: *I Spy* visually underscores the integrated partnership of Scott (Bill Cosby) and Robinson.

On the other side of the Cold War, Zugman, the Communist cell leader, explains to Tonia the need to break up the Robinson-Scott partnership. They are "doubly effective. Not only are they engaged in espionage, but their mere presence is always a source of constant propaganda." Zugman shows Tonia newspaper clippings—photos of Robinson and Scott together in cities around the world: Tokyo, Hong Kong, Acapulco, Mexico City, Rome. Robinson and Scott are "the very picture of harmony, equality, racial equality. They destroy one of our most important propaganda points." Zugman rips a photo of Robinson and Scott in half to illustrate the effect he wants from Tonia—to create jealousy in order to "set them at each other's throats." Tonia refuses and Zugman kills her, setting up Robinson as the murderer.

The episode concludes by establishing a parallel romantic effectiveness between Robinson and Scott in that both have enticed Communist women to the West. Zugman had once been a high-level agent in Latin America but lost his position when his daughter defected to the United States. Robinson denies accountability: "She thought she was in love with a tennis player [but] she was in love with freedom." Like Robinson, Scott wooed a woman to freedom, as Tonia came to believe in him. In the epilogue, Scott continues to reach out to people of color. Strolling down a street in Rome, the agents see a young black girl sitting on a stoop. Scott gives the girl two gelatos saying, "mia sorella" (my sister). In "Tonia" and "Goodbye, Patrick Henry," Scott's interactions with black characters suggest an essential bond through race.

In *I Spy*'s Mexico episodes, race is not as politically inflected as it is in Europe or Asia. Mexico is not contested territory in the Cold War but our friendly neighbor to the south. Although Soviet agents travel easily in Mexico, Communism does not have the pernicious presence it can have in Europe or Asia. In Mexico, spies from both sides find respite from espionage life. *I Spy*'s Mexico episodes typically begin with Robinson and Scott on vacation—relaxing, shopping, fishing, enjoying the attractions of city and country, including (for the white agent) the sexuality of local women.

I Spy uses sounds and images to articulate Mexico as a beautiful, comfortable, and exotic site for tourism. "Return to Glory" (first season, 1966) illustrates how *I Spy* combines the Mexican travelogue with geopolitics, weaving tourism with intelligence gathering. Robinson and Scott are assigned to evaluate a Latin American general living in exile in Mexico. Deposed by revolutionary forces, the general plans to launch an invasion to regain his country. Robinson and Scott are in Taxco (shopping for a silver chafing dish for Scott's mother) when they are contacted by a Mexican national who is a U.S. agent working undercover (in serape and som-

Mexico: an appealing site for tourism and shared culture, *I Spy*.

brero) as a street photographer. Robinson and Scott are ordered to contact the general and recommend action to the United States, but they are told to take no position because "the State Department cannot officially be involved . . . in military adventures . . . especially if they are frivolous." At the same time that the United States was building its forces in Vietnam, *I Spy* adopts a familiar government discourse of disavowal: the United States is aware of international actions but does not become involved in them.

I Spy positions characters in a mise-en-scène and sound calculated to reveal indigenous musical arts of Mexico. In a club with several performance spaces, Robinson and Scott meet the general's wife and adviser (whose past service includes working for the French at Dien Bien Phu and Algiers—"all losers," Scott observes pessimistically). As they talk, the group moves from room to room, pausing to witness Indian acrobats, a drummer, a mariachi band. Later, the agents encounter street musicians who dance and play before an appreciative crowd. *I Spy* typically shows Robinson and Scott in long shot, leisurely driving along roads that display the vistas of the Mexican countryside.

The agents often have a native guide—a woman or a boy whom Robinson has charmed—who explains Mexican history and customs. These conversations are a significant motif in *I Spy*'s Mexican episodes. The series is didactic in its explanations of customs and its assertions of commonalities between the peoples of the United States and Mexico.

Although they can draw on stereotypes, these conversations are an effort to celebrate Mexican culture and to appreciate cultural differences between the United States and Mexico.

"Happy Birthday . . . Everybody" (third season, 1968) opens with Robinson and Scott at a site overlooking Guanajuato. They enjoy the view and identify the site as a monument to the Mexican Revolution. Rosie (this episode's guide and Robinson's sex interest) tells Robinson that bargaining with vendors is expected when shopping in Mexico. As Robinson buys a toy from a boy for three pesos (down from five), he explains that one peso is worth 20 cents. Later, at the historic Teatro Juarez, a long take tracks with strolling mariachis into a town square where Robinson regales a group of rapt children with the story of "mama burro, papa burro, and baby burro" as Rosie translates.

"Bet Me a Dollar" (first season, 1966) uses a wager to motivate tours of Mexico City and the countryside. The episode opens with generic signifiers of Latin America: a flamenco guitarist and dancer. Robinson intervenes as two men beat up a third against a wall scrawled with "Viva El Presidente" graffiti.[18] In the scuffle, Robinson is scratched by a knife infected with anthrax. Unaware of the impending danger from his wound, Robinson and Scott alleviate their boredom between missions by playing "hide-and-seek"—Robinson takes a 24-hour headstart and Scott tries to find him. The chase passes through diverse places that illustrate the range of Mexican life accessible to tourists: a river boat fiesta in Xochimilco; in Mexico City, the grounds of the university with its Diego Rivera mural; a bus ride to the country. Rustic spectacle—a cottage with a religious shrine, a peasant driving a burro-drawn cart along a country road—converges with the modern world, illustrated here by a village pharmacy where a young woman welcomes the chance to speak English. The *I Spy* Mexican travelogues depict Mexico as a synthesis of rural and modern life.

Enloe observes that "tourism [is a] motor for global integration . . . drawing previously 'remote' societies into the international system, usually on unequal terms."[19] To a degree this is the case in *I Spy,* in which emulating the greater economic privilege of the United States is assumed to be a natural and attractive goal for Mexico. In "Bet Me a Dollar," Robinson enlists Ramon, a boy who earns money shining shoes, to help him elude Scott. Introducing Ramon to credit cards ("very progressive, no?") and expense accounts, Robinson interpellates Ramon into modern corporate business practices, situating the man (the U.S. present) and the boy (Mexico's future) in what Dean MacCannell describes as "mutual complicity . . . the interaction between the postmodern tourist and the ex-primitive."[20] However, the episode avoids making an easy distinction between modern urban progress and rural underdevelopment. When Robinson needs emergency medical aid, for example, a villager provides alternative medicine—herbs that effectively reduce his fever and save his life.

In the Mexico episodes, *I Spy* appreciates cultural differences, suppresses politics, and naturalizes a humanistic unity between the peoples of the United States and Mexico. The fight that begins "Bet Me a Dollar" takes place in front of political graffiti. Lest a causal connection be drawn between bacterial warfare and presidential politics, a Mexican doctor explains that the fight was caused by "machisismo—who is the better man." Robinson understands: "We call it the same thing." At the university, Ramon confidently points to an optimistic future through education, explaining that "there are many students here ready to serve Mexico." Mexico's Left, which might have played a narrative role the way Italy's did in "Tonia," is repressed in favor of tourism and humanism.[21]

The Mexico episodes often have little directly to do with the Cold War, and the Mexican people are not implicated in a Communist conspiracy for world domination. Instead, Mexico provides an opportunity for *I Spy* to assert friendly relations and cultural similarity with a foreign country situated at the U.S. border. Yet, Soviet presence in the Mexico episodes is a reminder of the Cold War in Latin America and Cuba. However, instead of emphasizing Cold War vigilance in Mexico, *I Spy* presents a collegial fraternity between Soviet and U.S. spies. This relationship lowers the international stakes: even as they work against each other on opposite sides, the spies share mutual understanding and respect. Mexico is a haven from the stresses of espionage work for the Soviet agents as much as it is for the Americans.

In "A Day Called 4 Jaguar" (first season, 1966), a Soviet air force officer (Dimitri, a "people's hero" who wears the Order of Lenin) finds refuge from a goodwill tour of Latin America by hiding out in a remote Mexican village that retains Aztec rituals. This episode introduces Mexico's Aztec past through the living history museum of the village. The interpretation of Aztec culture is delivered through both the Soviet and American tourist-spies. Scott reads from a book about Mexico, describing Quetzalcoatl and his place in Aztec lore—twice, as if it were too complex to understand one time through. He works to pronounce the god's name correctly.

Dimitri bears a physical resemblance to Quetzalcoatl, a "bearded blue-eyed man." A student of anthropology and Aztec culture before his military service, Dimitri is attracted to the village for its "timelessness and innocence, purity." He explains that the villagers know that he is not actually Quetzalcoatl, but they use him as a reminder of Aztec life. The villagers serve meals ("cooked in this exact manner for 2,000 years") and prepare baths (Scott squirms in the hot tub as comic relief while Robinson negotiates with Dimitri). However, the U.S. spies observe that the Aztec villagers do not live completely in the past. As Robinson and Scott pass a man working with an acetylene torch, they comment on the "ancient and modern mix" and "overlapping cultures." The Aztec villagers have no dialogue and express themselves only through their actions. Aztec identity is defined by the U.S. and Soviet tourist-agents, who merge anthropological observations with nostalgia for a bucolic past.

Unlike the Aztec villagers, other rural Mexicans in the episode vocally resent and resist the U.S. presence in Mexico. In *I Spy*, economic difference tends to be suppressed, but occasionally tensions emerge from the imperialist advantages that make Mexico available for U.S. tourism. As Scott and Robinson search for Dimitri in villages, they offer money ("$15 . . . $20 . . . name your own price") for guides into the jungle. In one village, Robinson and Scott are surrounded by threatening male peasants: "You Americans come here waving your dollars and we, like hungry dogs, are expected to do tricks for that. What do you know of a man's pride, his honor? No man in this village will accept your insulting offer." Although *I Spy* episodes regularly include opportunities for the agents to counter anti-U.S. sentiments, here their only response is to flee from these peasants, whose animosity is grounded in the unequal economic and political relationship between the United States and Mexico.

Robinson is the lead signifier of the pleasures and freedoms of U.S. economic and patriarchal imperialism: he is a guide to the benefits of corporate capitalism and to sex tourism; he is the hip white American male tourist, free to travel and free to engage in sexual relations with native

Scott watches from a distance while . . . , *I Spy*.

The white agent (Robinson) enjoys the pleasures of "sex tourism," *I Spy*.

women. As Enloe explains, "[The] male tourist . . . is freed from standards of behavior imposed by respectable women back home. . . . Local women are welcoming and available in their femininity."[22] Part of Robinson's attractiveness is the assumption that he holds an income that can contribute to personal and local economies. *I Spy* adopts a well-known argument about tourism: "There is *no* difference between [the locals] and Europeans, with the single exception that the Europeans have money and [the locals] don't."[23]

In "Happy Birthday . . . Everybody," Rosie wants Robinson to buy her things: "I want one" (a pinata), "Can I have this?" (a primitive statue), "I want it" (a huge vase). When Robinson resists, saying that the vase is too large for her apartment, Rosie replies, "It was big enough for you wasn't it? And you're taller." Although Rosie is probably not a prostitute and does not appear impoverished, Enloe observes that "sex tourism requires Third World women to be economically desperate enough to enter prostitution."[24] Part of the attraction of the white male tourist is that he is backed with first world capital.

On one level, *I Spy* offers a world that is apparently "color blind" in that the agents travel without anyone (except Communists) noticing that Scott is black or that the partnership is interracial. However, the spies are not equal in terms of their sexual activity. Although their mission benefits from the attractiveness of both men to women,[25] *I Spy* tends to suppress the black man's sexuality. Although some television historians claim that Scott had equal access to romance, in *I Spy* sex tourism is more available for the white man. Robinson is presented as irresistible to women: he is a sexually available and attractive American version of James Bond. Women ogle Robinson as he walks by. In "Bet Me a Dollar," two women compete over the quality of the repair to Robinson's pants, torn in the knife fight ("I could do it better." "No, you couldn't."), and a nurse asks him for a date. "A Day Called 4 Jaguar" opens with Robinson and a Mexican woman making out among lush foliage.

Although he has his share of body display and shirtless screentime, Scott's sexuality is marginalized relative to Robinson's. "Bet Me a Dollar" ends in Acapulco, where Robinson enjoys a backrub from a Mexican woman while Scott sits under an umbrella with the boy, Ramon. In "A Day Called 4 Jaguar," Robinson banters with a woman from a synchronized swim team while Scott comically flaps around in goggles and swim fins. In "It's All Done with Mirrors" (first season, 1966), Scott quietly steps aside and waits for his more adventuresome partner to return from a tryst. In all of these examples, the black male tourist-spy functions as a sidekick to the more sexually active white male tourist-spy.

Richard Dyer observes in *White*, "The point of seeing the racing of whites is to dislodge them/us from the position of power, with all the inequities, oppression, privileges and sufferings in its train, dislodging them/us by undercutting the authority with which they/we speak and act in and on the world." Despite inequalities in the actions available to Robinson and to Scott, *I Spy* boldly sustained an argument for racial equality for three seasons on prime-time television. Its discourses on domestic civil rights and geopolitics echo those offered by John F. Kennedy in his inaugural address on January 20, 1961:

> [We are] unwilling to witness or permit the slow undoing of those human rights to which this Nation has always been committed, and to which we are committed today at home and around the world. . . . Let every nation know . . . that we shall pay any price, bear any burden, meet any hardship, support any friend, oppose any foe, in order to assure the survival and the success of liberty.

Each week, *I Spy* dramatized this effort to create harmony between two seemingly incongruous goals: social justice and global hegemony. Through its interracial partners and its insistence that state security is enhanced by racial equality, *I Spy* affirms the value of civil rights for the United States, at home and overseas.[26]

Notes

1 Advocacy groups had pressured U.S. television to improve its representation of blacks since the early 1950s when *Amos 'n' Andy* (CBS, 1951–53) was on the air, but it was not until the widespread civil rights activism of the 1960s that the television industry responded. See Kathryn C. Montgomery, *Target Prime Time: Advocacy Groups and the Struggle over Entertainment Television* (New York: Oxford University Press, 1989). Although they credit civil rights activism for influencing the networks, Woll and Miller also recognize that 1960s television advertising practices allowed African Americans to become identified as a demographic group with disposable income. See Allen L. Woll and Randall M. Miller, *Ethnic and Racial Images in American Film and Television: Historical Essays and Bibliography* (New York: Garland Publishing, 1987), 72–77.

2 Cynthia Enloe, *Bananas, Beaches, and Bases: Making Feminist Sense of Inter-*

national Politics (Berkeley: University of California Press, 1989), 26, 35–40. Enloe derives the term "living postcards" from world's fair displays of other cultures.

From the start, Sheldon Leonard's conception of the series integrated the travelogue: "The spy genre would yield opportunities for action and adventure and would give us the mobility I wanted. It could take us into obscure, picturesque corners of the world" (Leonard, *And the Show Goes On: Broadway and Hollywood Adventures* [New York: Limelight Editions, 1995], 144).

3 J. Fred MacDonald, *Blacks and White TV: Afro-Americans in Television since 1948* (Chicago: Nelson-Hall Publishers, 1983), 109–12; Woll and Miller, *Ethnic and Racial Images in American Film and Television,* 72; Eric Barnouw, *Tube of Plenty: The Evolution of American Television,* 2d rev. ed. (New York: Oxford University Press, 1990), 370–72. Cosby crossed over into white-dominated television as guest host for *The Tonight Show* and host of a television documentary about African American history (Woll and Miller, *Ethnic and Racial Images in American Film and Television,* 77). Phillip Brian Harper, "Televisual Representation and the Claims of 'the Black Experience,'" *Living Color: Race and Television in the United States,* ed. Sasha Torres (Durham: Duke University Press, 1998), 67–68. Despite reports of interracial romances (see ibid., 77), Scott was usually reserved for African American women characters such as those played by Barbara McNair in "Night Train to Madrid" (second season, 1967) or Lesley Uggams in "Tonia."

4 Several people have told me that they remember *I Spy* opening with the silhouettes of *two* men holding tennis rackets that become guns. However, available videotapes of *I Spy* present only one man in silhouette.

5 Andy East, *The Cold War File* (Metuchen, N.J.: Scarecrow Press, 1983), 299–300. For a discussion of James Bond's cultural location, including his transformation from book to film, see Tony Bennett and Janet Woollacott, *Bond and Beyond: The Political Career of a Popular Hero* (New York: Methuen, 1987).

6 I am grateful to Tim Anderson for telling me about Moe Berg. See Nicholas Dawidoff, *The Catcher Was a Spy: The Mysterious Life of Moe Berg* (New York: Pantheon, 1994). The Olympic games have long been caught up in international affairs, and this theme is developed in *I Spy*'s first episode, discussed in this essay.

Exhibition tennis forms part of the verisimilitude of *I Spy,* as does the increasing visibility of tennis champions of color. In *Off the Court,* Arthur Ashe deliberates on race and tennis: how the class status of tennis makes it difficult for nonwhites to become tennis players; how Ashe coped with being the "first black" to win tennis competitions; the awareness of race among Third World tennis players (described by Pancho Segura as "brown bodies"); the black-power salute from the winners' platform at the 1968 Olympics in Mexico City. See Arthur Ashe with Neil Amdur, *Off the Court* (New York: New American Library, 1981). For a history of tennis, see United States Lawn Tennis Association, *Official Encyclopedia of Tennis* (New York: Harper and Row, 1972), 1–68.

For examples of 1960s political comedy, see Frank Kofsky, *Lenny Bruce: The Comedian as Social Critic and Secular Moralist* (New York, Monad Press, 1974); and Dick Gregory, *From the Back of the Bus* (New York: E. P. Dutton, 1962).

7 By the mid-1960s, television was well on the way to a complete conversion to color. The major manufacturer in the TV industry, RCA, joined its broadcast partner, NBC, to open the television market to color. See Brad Chisholm, "Red, Blue, and Lots of Green: The Impact of Color Television on Feature Film Production," in *Hollywood in the Age of Television*, ed. Tino Balio (Boston: Unwin Hyman, 1990), 227.

Despite a production budget that invested in foreign locations as well as color, *I Spy* had to overcome equipment problems before it hit its stride as a travelogue. *Variety*'s review of the first episode was critical: "The location work in Hong Kong was a dishevelled patchwork." Indeed, Leonard describes the difficulties the crew encountered with rental equipment in Hong Kong (Leonard, *And the Show Goes On*, 148–49). Yet, transporting production equipment was extremely expensive. Leonard credits *I Spy* cinematographer Fouad Said with designing the solution: the Cinemobile, a location van outfitted with compact production gear and small enough to be loaded into a cargo plane (ibid., 153–55).

Variety was more pleased with the quality of *I Spy*'s second-season opener: "Producer Sheldon Leonard has learned to gain maximum production values from exteriors [in Palm Springs]." At the beginning of *I Spy*'s third season, *Variety* glowed that *I Spy* holds the "distinction as one of video's better travelogs . . . even on the smallscreen those 35mm vistas panned beautifully in color" (reviews of *I Spy* in *Variety*, 22 September 1965, 21 September 1966, 13 September 1967).

Shooting on location also supplied grist for *I Spy*'s publicity (see Sheldon Leonard, "Having a wonderful time—except, of course, for that typhoon and a few other mishaps," *TV Guide*, 24 July 1965, 6–9; Dick Hobson, "The Ptomaine in Spain Came Mainly on the Plane," *TV Guide*, 25 March 1967, 15–18).

I Spy's location work also circumvented unions and "Model T techniques" in Hollywood. *TV Guide* reported that Said practiced techniques so "incendiary . . . that for many years his own union barred him from shooting in the U.S. It feared that, were his practices to be adopted, whole complexes of studios, soundstages and backlots would be obsolete overnight; vast inventories of archaic cameras, lights, arcs, generators, dollies and microphones would be relegated to the junkpiles; and armies of super-annuated technicians would be mercifully released to retirement" (Dick Hobson, "Little Fou's Big Revolution," *TV Guide,* 23 March 1968, 22–27).

I Spy was not the first Sheldon Leonard television show to use foreign locations. Producer Leonard took *Make Room for Daddy/The Danny Thomas Show* (ABC, 1953–57; CBS 1957–65) to England, Ireland, France, and Italy "to get it away from the confines of Stage Five and open it up." He found the creative challenges of "working on foreign locations immensely stimulating" (see Leonard, *And the Show Goes On,* 97–98). The *I Spy* chapters of Leonard's autobiography are replete with anecdotes about shooting on location in Asia, Europe, and Mexico.

8 James Der Derian's poststructuralist analysis of international relations describes the "collective alienation" in which countries become "dependent on a common diplomatic culture *as well as* a collective estrangement" from other state systems. In the "modern panopticism" of espionage, Robinson and Scott are HUMINT—human intelligence operatives. Although still important to state security, HUMINT "lacks the ubiquity, resolution, and pantoscopic power of the technical intelligence system" (TECHINT, COMINT, ELINT, RADINT, TELINT, PHOTOINT) (Der Derian, *Antidiplomacy: Spies, Terror, Speed, and War* [Cambridge, Mass.: Blackwell, 1992], 30–31).

For insider descriptions of espionage work see Jock Haswell, *Spies and Spymasters: A Concise History of Intelligence* (London: Thames and Hudson, 1977); Joachim Joesten, *They Call It Intelligence: Spies and Spy Techniques since World War II* (New York: Abelard-Schuman, 1963); Sir Kenneth Strong, *Men of Intelligence: A Study of the Roles and Decisions of Chiefs of Intelligence from World War I to the Present Day* (London: Cassell, 1970); Nigel West, *Games of Intelligence: The Classified Conflict of International Espionage* (London: Weidenfeld and Nicolson, 1989).

Allen Dulles, the first director of the CIA, who served until the Bay of Pigs failure, "saw the whole world as an area of conflict, in which the prime duty of an Intelligence service was to provide its government with warning of hostile or provocative acts wherever they might occur. . . . [Dulles believed that] a close-knit and coordinated Intelligence community, constantly on the alert, should be able to report accurately and quickly on developments in any part of the globe" (Strong, *Men of Intelligence,* 128). Indeed, one can ponder the role television journalists might have played in Cold War espionage and the verisimilitude of *I Spy*. In *I Spy*'s first episode, the end credits thank NBC's Far Eastern news staff for their cooperation.

9 *I Spy* does not set up a simple opposition between Communism and democracy. "It's All Done with Mirrors" (first season, 1966) ends with some cynicism about Cold War alliances and U.S. state power. Dr. Zoltan Karolyi is a Soviet brainwashing expert ("hate me . . . love me . . . obey me") who has set up a laboratory in Acapulco to create "a universe of pain" from which Robinson will "do anything, believe anything, to escape." Karolyi attempts to condition Robinson to kill Scott in public and thereby embarrass the United States. In a finale set against the ocean harbors of Acapulco, Scott relies on his three-year friendship with Robinson to break Karolyi's conditioning. Unlike the Soviet agent in "A Day 4 Jaguar," who killed his lifelong friend out of loyalty to the state, Robinson withstands the urge to assassinate Scott. Captured, Karolyi defects to the United States ("I am corrupt") and asks to continue his brainwashing experiments for the United States in Mexico. Robinson mutters that the United States will probably take the offer and then assign Robinson and Scott to be Karolyi's bodyguards. Although Robinson and Scott are certainly loyal to the United States, they occasionally express a weariness about government authority and the exigencies of spywork.

10 Barnouw, *Tube of Plenty*, 367; Joesten, *They Call It Intelligence*, 226; see also intelligence histories cited above.

11 Dudziak argues that "the Soviet Union increased its use of race in anti-American propaganda; by 1949, American race relations were a 'principle Soviet propaganda theme.'" With race discrimination giving a propaganda advantage to the Soviet bloc, the U.S. government "came to realize that if [it] wished to save Third World countries for democracy, [it] would have to improve the image of American race relations" (Dudziak, "Josephine Baker, Racial Protest, and the Cold War," *Journal of American History*, 81, no. 2 [September 1994]: 543–46).

12 Ibid., 568. She explains that Baker, Robeson, and DuBois "angered [U.S.] government officials" who "attempt[ed] to counter the influence of such critics . . . by sending speakers around the world who would say the right things about American race relations. The 'right thing' was: yes, there are racial problems in the United States, but it was through democratic processes (not communism) that optimal social change for African Americans would occur" (ibid., 546). An exemplar of this position was New York Representative and "staunch civil rights advocate [Adam Clayton] Powell [who] refused to criticize the United States before a foreign audience" (ibid., 557). As Herman Gray observes, "For all of their limits and contradictions, commercial network television's representations of blackness are socially and

culturally rooted someplace and are in dialogue with very real issues" (Gray, *Watching Race: Television and the Struggle for "Blackness"* [Minneapolis: University of Minnesota Press, 1995], 55).

13 See Dick Hobson, "He bears witness to his beliefs," *TV Guide,* 15 January 1966, 10–12. In this story, Cosby comments, "We don't have any race jokes in the scripts. Even in real life, race jokes would be embarrassing to Bobby and embarrassing to me."

14 In the 1960s, the People's Republic of China organized the Games of the New Emerging Forces (GANEFA) during the debate over whether Taiwan or China would be the official Chinese representative to the Olympics (see Jonathan Kolatch, *Sports, Politics, and Ideology in China* [New York: Jonathan David Publishers, 1972]). Awam Amkpa, Phebe Chao, and Roger Sorkin have all shared with me anecdotal accounts of the China-Africa relationship during this period. In the late 1960s, the People's Republic of China built stadia and theaters across Africa as gifts of friendship.

15 Culp came to *I Spy* as an experienced television lead actor; Cosby came from stand-up comedy (including three record albums and a Grammy) with television exposure mostly on *The Tonight Show* (NBC, 1954–) (MacDonald, *Blacks and White TV,* 100; and Robert de Roos, "The Spy Who Came in for the Gold," *TV Guide,* 23 October 1965, 17). De Roos explains that Culp and Cosby developed "a language of their own." The combination of Culp's 1960s hipster word play and Cosby's facility with stand-up contributed to the verbal style of the show, what *Variety* described as "good voice overlap form, though this bit gets a bit strained after a time" (review of *I Spy, Variety,* 13 September 1967). Leonard found that the banter became a problem: "It's easy to be amused by a witty ad lib and to overlook the damage it's doing to the structure of the tale you're telling. . . . What had started as harmless interjections became increasingly intrusive ad-libs, often inconsistent with the story line" (see Leonard, *And the Show Goes On,* 171–73).

16 Scott/Cosby appears in nearly every scene in the credits sequence of this episode.

17 This strategy appears in other *I Spy* episodes. See discussion of "It's All Done with Mirrors" in note 10. Considering the series's Cold War attitude, it is interesting to note that Leonard attempted to coproduce *I Spy* "stories that emphasized the benefits of cooperation between the great powers" with the Soviet Union. Negotiations broke down when Leonard determined that it would take more than twice the time to film an episode in the Soviet Union (Leonard, *And the Show Goes On,* 193–95).

18 *I Spy* often uses posters and graffiti to identify a country and its politics.

19 Enloe, *Bananas, Beaches, and Bases,* 31.

20 Dean MacCannell, *Empty Meeting Grounds: The Tourist Papers* (New York: Routledge, 1992), 30.

21 Mexico has long had an open door for travel by Soviets. Filmmaker Sergei Eisenstein traveled and worked in Mexico in the early 1930s. Guidebooks direct tourists to the house in Coyoacan, near Mexico City, where Leon Trotsky was assassinated in 1940. For a survey of Cold War struggles over Latin America see George Black, *The Good Neighbor: How the United States Wrote the History of Central America and the Caribbean* (New York: Pantheon, 1988). For discussion of the 1968 student rebellion in Mexico City see James M. Goodsell, "Mexico: Why the Students Rioted," *Essays on the Student Movement*, ed. Patrick Gleeson (Columbus, Ohio: Charles E. Merrill, 1970), 91–99

22 Enloe, *Bananas, Beaches, and Bases*, 28, 32.

23 MacCannell, *Empty Meeting Grounds*, 41.

24 Enloe, *Bananas, Beaches, and Bases*, 36.

25 Although the sexually available agent is part of the pleasure of spy fiction, MacCannell argues that the unattached agent is also important to maintaining the security of the state: "Heterosexual arrangements . . . disrupt the individual's attachment to 'higher' orders of organization: for example, the gang, the state, the corporation. . . . A man who can be entirely satisfied by the love and companionship of a woman is lost to the state" (MacCannell, *Empty Meeting Grounds*, 60).

"Happy Birthday . . . Everybody" illustrates this point. An explosives expert has escaped from prison and seeks to kill the U.S. agent who "red dogged" him. The agent, now retired, lives peacefully with his young American wife and their son outside Guanajuato. The criminal places explosives in a piñata, intending to blow up the family during the boy's birthday party. The agent's age and his devotion to family separate him from effective action, compelling Robinson and Scott to watch over the family's safety.

26 Richard Dyer, *White* (London: Routledge, 1997), 2.

Leading Up to *Roe v. Wade*

Television Documentaries in the Abortion Debate

Julie D'Acci

Social upheavals, legal battles, and judicial rulings involving abortion have shaken the United States since abortion was decriminalized in 1973; rather than abating, such tumult has intensified, culminating in the brutal murders of health care professionals and aides at U.S. clinics.[1] Recent Supreme Court decisions and legislative amendments have curtailed women's access to abortions in public hospitals, constrained publicly employed doctors from performing the procedure, promoted the recognition of fetuses as persons, and declared that neither federal nor state governments must pay for abortions (even if medically necessary) for women on welfare.[2] It seems astonishing that the fury over abortion rages more heatedly now than it did in 1973, when the Supreme Court handed down the *Roe v. Wade* decision decriminalizing abortion in the United States. But a closer look at the vested interests and pressures that helped shape the decision (as well as the decriminalization of abortion in seventeen states prior to *Roe*) makes it clear that fury and mounting struggle would be its most certain legacies.[3] The medical and legal establishments, the women's movement (including proabortion black feminist groups and individuals), and population-control organizations (some with clear histories of racist, sexist, and imperialist policies) were among the odd allies that actively struggled for liberalized abortion during the late 1960s and early 1970s. They formed the coalitions that advocated decriminalization. But the muting of feminist voices and women's movement demands, in both these coalitions and in the final legislation, contributed to a public policy that situated abortion not as a woman's *absolute* right but one contained under the right to privacy, governed by a physician's discretion, and subject to state intervention after the first trimester.[4] This muting is all the more troubling because, as Linda Gordon and Rosalind Petchesky demonstrate, it was these feminist voices that by and large forced the issue onto the U.S. public scene.[5]

Struggles over abortion in the United States during the years leading up to *Roe* involved four television documentaries that illuminate the medium's role in establishing the terms of the abortion debate and its "officially" legitimated players. These programs raise several crucial questions: How did TV's attempts to achieve "balance" shape the abortion debate?[6] How did institutional conceptions of television news and documentary film cast the debate as a "democratic" struggle among "legitimate" competing voices? How did the combination of participants and pressures intersect with the conventions of television documentaries to help frame abortion policy? How did TV participate in defining abortion as a government—and medically—controlled practice, and a moral, ethical, and medical quandary, rather than as an unequivocal and socially based right of women?

Television's imperative to produce "balance"—to present what it deemed as "both" sides of a controversial public issue—had grave political consequences for the women's movement and for feminist objectives regarding abortion. Its effacement of the women's movement and ultimate framing of the "pro" side within the discourses of population control clarifies (in retrospect) but obfuscated (at the time) the racism, classism, and sexism that undergirded part of the reform movement and helped make *Roe* a possibility. On the one hand, the documentaries and their production histories show how television brought a controversial social issue to a mass audience of diverse classes, races, and ages. In some ways this fulfilled TV's stated ideals of educating and informing. On the other hand, television distorted the terms in which abortion was discussed, maintaining social hegemony and constraining the medium's more emancipatory possibilities. The first two television documentaries on abortion illustrate how "balance" was determined, how particular spokespeople in the abortion debate were invested with authority and approbation and others—specifically women and feminists (both white and women of color)—were not. The second two documentaries make eminently clear how national policy on abortion was ushered in under the auspices of population control instead of a feminist vision of reproductive rights.

Each of the documentaries coincided with turning points in the history of abortion debates in the United States and brought out and defined the opposing sides as never before.

The Historical Context

Abortions in the United States (following British Common Law) were by and large legal until the later 1800s. However, between 1850 and 1890, physicians agitated for bans on the practice, and by 1900 every state in the union had passed antiabortion laws. For various reasons, the medical and legal establishments tried to relax these laws during the 1950s, and in the second half of that decade, continuing into the 1960s, public exposés of abortion rackets and unsafe illegal procedures were common.[7]

Linda Gordon and Rosalind Petchesky have documented the ways that the women's movement of the late 1960s forced the abortion issue onto the stage of public policy and have analyzed the many complications involved in battling over legislation. Although Gordon specifies that she is not diagnosing a failure of tactics, she does describe how some segments of the women's movement retreated from the early "abortion on demand" slogan to one of an individual's "right to choose." This shift occurred amid fierce oppositional pressures, a philosophy of individualism that underpinned much of the women's movement, and a lack of focus on the *social* aspects of abortion.[8] Furthermore, Gordon attributes important influence to the population control movements and traces how they "clouded the vision" of reproductive freedom that feminism upheld.[9] Under the aegis of population control, public policy on abortion became increasingly dissociated from the women's movement. For Petchesky,

> The state—and the population policy establishment that had become the architect of state policy on fertility—carefully avoided concessions to feminist ideology about reproductive freedom. To accommodate popular pressures without legitimating feminism—or acknowledging the true causes of the need for abortion—state and population planners subsumed abortion politics under the rubric of population control.[10]

The slogan "right to choose," in sharp contrast to "abortion on demand," better fitted the rhetoric of population control and the growing desire to situate abortion policy within the individual's right to privacy.

Prime-Time Abortion

The first U.S. television program on abortion was a 15-minute dramatic re-creation titled "Abortions: A Look into the Illegal Abortion Racket," on the 1955 syndicated program *Confidential File*. But the first actual *network* documentary appeared ten years later on the critically acclaimed *CBS Reports*. Called "Abortion and the Law," it was written and produced by progressive journalist/filmmaker David Lowe and narrated by newsman Walter Cronkite. In 1969 ABC filmed the second documentary, "Abortion," written and produced by the equally progressive, though less well-known, Ernest Pendrell and broadcast on the *Summer Focus* series.

There is no question that each of these documentaries strongly advocated legalization. There is also little doubt that the networks and producers were willing to put themselves on the line to do the programs.[11] (The 1965 *CBS Reports* team, however, had the benefit of working during the Johnson administration, which was itself urging at least the widespread dissemination of birth control information, while the Pendrell team faced a more restrictive Nixon White House.)[12] But despite the producers' and networks' support of decriminalization, it was the way the dimensions of the struggle were *defined* and its participants determined that has proven so problematic for U.S. abortion policy. These first two documentaries established the groundwork for how the debate would be framed and handled on American television and for deciding which players would be selected for airtime and which ones would be shunted to the sidelines. The notion of "balance" that grounded these decisions was tied to the liberalism that marginalized and muffled feminist and female spokespeople.

In "Abortion and the Law," most of the legitimated players were enumerated in Cronkite's opening statement: "Only recently have our abortion laws been openly questioned, has a dialogue begun among *doctors, lawyers and clergymen*" (emphasis mine).[13] Indeed, the documentary, which presented a complex and well-researched case for decriminalization, included an array of *male* experts in favor of liberalizing the law (nine physicians, a lawyer, an Episcopal priest, and a state legislator); and four speaking against liberalization, a physician (speaking from a religious position), an attorney (representing the U.S. Catholic bishops), and two Catholic priests.

In the course of the documentary, five women tell stories of traumatic illegal abortions obtained in the United States or by traveling to Puerto Rico or Mexico; another tells of qualifying for a legal U.S. procedure because she had contracted rubella; another (who currently wants to terminate her pregnancy) speaks of the fear of a "back alley" abortion; and a final one (the mother of a young woman who endured an illegal and badly executed treatment without telling her parents) speaks about the horrors her daughter faced.[14] Although their testimonies provided the ground for the documentary's discussion—giving bodily evidence to the need for legal reform—the women were not seen as legitimate participants in the "dialogue" that had begun among those openly questioning abortion laws. The women were taking enormous risks and displaying personal and political courage, yet, they were not afforded positions in the debate per se, were not cast as active subjects of the documentary's argument. Instead, they were presented as its cause and its objects, its victims, and, on some level, its physical spectacle.

Four years later, in "Abortion," the sanctioned players included two male physicians and a Catholic priest. However, mothers of rubella babies and politicians also became "rightful" participants in the dialogue. In this documentary, two white, middle-class women who had contracted rubella speak out for abortion—one was able to terminate her pregnancy legally, and the other gave birth to a child with multiple and severe disabilities. The president of the borough of Manhattan speaks fervently about the class injustices in the present situation, and seven New York state legislators (six male and one female) debate the New York bill for decriminalization. In "Abortion," therefore, a few women emerge as more active participants in the debate. But they draw their authority primarily from their status as mothers, presenting cases for legal abortions in the face of potential "birth defects." Two other white, middle-class women who give personal testimonies of abortions (one illegal in the United States and one in Puerto Rico), are handled in ways similar to the women in "Abortion and the Law"—not as active players but as objects and the ground of the controversy.

The Quest for "Balance"

The production files of producer-writer Ernest Pendrell for "Abortion" offer a fascinating glimpse into how the various participants and positions in the documentary were actually determined and selected, and how the "balance" required by the network was adjudicated and achieved. At the project's outset, ABC's lawyers advised,

> While we can argue for a liberalization of existing laws, we should not advocate that anybody deliberately violate existing state statutes, no matter how outmoded they be. And if we do take a "position" on a controversial subject like this, should we not outline conflicting attitudes in this self-same program—so as to avoid "fairness" problems to the network and to each of its affiliates?[15]

As the research and writing went forward, network executives grew increasingly worried about the achievement of this fairness and the exercise of "balance."[16] The show's executive producer, Lester Cooper, wrote to Pendrell calling for script revisions and admonishing him about the "danger in the point-of-view. The slant is so obvious; the sympathies so definite. It ceases to be a report and becomes a tract. . . . I feel this shouldn't be a 'horror' story but a *balanced* report on the issue, the problem and the various attitudes toward them" (emphasis mine).[17]

The network's vice president for news and public affairs, Thomas Wolf, although supportive of the documentary's "slant" and "sympathies," began firing off memos urging Pendrell to achieve balance by incorporating particular spokespeople and opposing positions. Attached to one memo was a copy of a letter to ABC President Elton Rule from a fundamentalist anti-abortion attorney, Robert Sassone:

> I am a member of a Right to Life committee interested in protecting the rights of infants and unborn babies. I would like to insure that you have access to all of our committee's arguments favoring strict abortion laws. If you wish, I will send you a six page summary of the medical, psychological, and sociological arguments favoring strict abortion laws.[18]

Wolf notes on the letter's margin that Pendrell should "be sure to get his material."[19] But Pendrell's response to Wolf, while stopping short of insubordination, suggests that he had adequate representation of that perspective: "re: Your note on the letter from Robert Sassone of the Right to Life Committee sent you from Mr. Rule. We have done an extensive sound piece on Mrs. Valerie Dillon, spokesman for this committee in New Jersey at her home in Somerset. . . . This was the lead you had sent me, if you recall. I will, of course, write him [Sassone] and get his material."[20]

Vice President Wolf also solicited material from the women's movement. A letter to Wolf from Joanna Martin of the Chicago National Organization for Women (NOW) reads: "Enclosed is a tape of the keynote address which Betty Friedan delivered at the recent national conference on abortion laws. Mrs. Friedan told me that you had asked for tapes of her speech."[21] The final documentary, however, included no spokespeople from *either* the women's movement (not even its reform-oriented, rather than radical, wing, represented by Friedan) or fundamentalist antiabortion groups.[22]

So in 1969, a couple of years before the voices of the population control movement would come to exert a truly widespread discursive authority over the pro side of U.S. abortion debates, a network documentary declined to offer representation to women's movement spokespeople. It appears that at the time *both* the women's movement and the fundamentalist antiabortion groups were too far outside the mainstream—outside the hegemony of officially warranted interests—to be included in the television debate. Even after seeking out Friedan's speech and directing Pendrell's attention to fundamentalist antiabortionists, the network ultimately allowed the documentary's "fairness" and "balance" to be achieved without their representation.

Prime Time and the Path to Roe

On the heels of "Abortion," in July 1969, President Nixon appointed a commission to examine population growth and its impact on the country. Chaired by John D. Rockefeller III, the Commission on Population Growth and the American Future included twenty-three other participants from medicine, academia, the corporate and religious worlds, elite foundations, Congress, students, and members listed as "housewife-volunteers."[23] The commission's work also spawned the next two television documentaries about abortion.

A number of contextual factors must be foregrounded at this point:

Rockefeller and the Rockefeller Foundation had a long history of work in eugenics and population control, some of which involved attempts to control Third World populations during the height of the cold war, as well as African Americans, other U.S. people of color, and the poor during the 1950s and 1960s.[24] As Petchesky demonstrates, in 1968 Rockefeller had laid out a rationale for a proabortion consensus among population groups, family planners, medical organizations, and government officials. This rationale underscored the growing need for medically controlled and medically adjudicated abortions, the fact that women were skirting the law, and the belief that children had the right to be born into families that wanted them.[25] The rationale never mentioned the needs or rights of women. However, it was the actions of the women's movement that provoked the issue and the very need for consensus: women in large numbers were refusing to abide by federal and state laws, were continuing to terminate pregnancies illegally, and setting up women-run services that provided safe, inexpensive abortions.[26]

Nixon certainly knew Rockefeller's background in the population control movement, as well as his position on abortion, when he appointed Rockefeller to chair the commission.[27] But Nixon always took a *public* position against abortion and supported the Catholic Church, which, in the late 1960s and early 1970s, was abortion's most outspoken opponent.[28] Petchesky argues that Nixon wished to *appear* to oppose abortion in order to preserve the political support of the Church but, at the same time, wanted to go along with the corporate-backed population control movement that by the late 1960s favored not only government-sponsored family planning but legalized abortion as well.[29] All these factors contributed to shaping the work of the Nixon-appointed commission, its report, its aftermath, and the next two documentaries dealing with abortion.[30]

In March 1972, almost three years after its establishment, the commission issued a 186-page, $1.6 million report called "Population and the American Future." It delineated forty-seven recommendations for sex education, abortion, voluntary sterilization, family planning, immigration, racial minorities and the poor, and equal rights for women—which included advocating the passage of the Equal Rights Amendment (ERA). Several members of the commission issued separate dissenting statements that repudiated the report's sections on abortion and reproductive control.[31] In May, Nixon reacted to the document publicly and unequivocally rejected the recommendations for liberalized abortion and birth control education for minors. The report, followed by the president's remarks, touched off the first major mobilization of the newly configured fundamentalist and Catholic right-to-life coalitions. The *New York Times* reported that letters were five to one against the commission's findings; many came from organized religious groups, and at least one letter writer told of sample protest forms being handed out to congregations from church pulpits.[32]

The commission itself, unwilling to let its work be rebuffed and go unimplemented, was spurred by Rockefeller to form what it called the Citizens' Committee on Population and the American Future.[33] The committee was funded by private foundations and cochaired by former *Today* host Hugh Downs and the African American feminist lawyer-activist—now congressional delegate from Washington, D.C.—Eleanor Holmes Norton. (That Holmes Norton and John D. Rockefeller III were working together graphically underscores the contradictory character of some of the movement's coalitions at the time.) The committee's main tasks were to complete a filmed documentary of the commission's report, to get it aired on television, and to circulate it throughout the nation's high schools with accompanying teaching materials. A corporation called Population Education, Inc., also financed by private corporate money, was formed to produce the film.

This documentary was conceived as a straightforward filmed version of the commission's report, and shooting was begun as the commission was completing its work. Once Nixon nixed what many commission members considered their most important recommendations, the completion and broadcast of the documentary became urgent. What the president rejected was, in fact, the most important section for the committee; as the committee's executive director put it, human reproduction "is the subject which we feel is the key."[34]

The Importance of Television

Rockefeller, many of the original commission members, and the newly formed committee saw television as the medium that would bring their message to those they most wanted to reach. They spoke of the power of TV to achieve for this commission report what no other report ever had—

the widespread dissemination of its ideas to the American public.[35] The committee took the film to the three major networks and tried to buy airtime. The various players, of course, had mixed and conflicting investments in pursuing television so wholeheartedly.

Part of the motivation for Rockefeller and some of the other population control–oriented members of the commission was at least to some degree rooted in their belief that TV was one of the best ways to reach people of color and the poor with birth control and abortion information. Although the commission's report attempted to defuse what had become widely publicized worries about the eugenics and racist undertones of population control, racist and classist discourses were nonetheless evident. For example, although the report explicitly stated that "despite their high fertility rates, minorities—precisely because of their smaller numbers—contribute less to population growth than does the rest of the population," it also repeatedly, and somewhat contradictorily, linked "high fertility" and even "excess fertility" to families of color and poor people.[36]

Progressives on both the commission and the committee may have considered television as simply the best way to reach the greatest number of people, especially women and teenage girls, with alternative views on reproductive technologies and issues.[37] For many of the medical doctors involved, it might have been a way to go broadly public with a view of abortion that would guarantee not only the procedure's safety and respectability but also its control by the medical establishment. For the Nixon White House, it may have been a way to allow the views of the corporate-backed and administration-friendly population movement—views that Nixon himself explicitly opposed to get widespread airing.[38]

For an African American feminist such as Eleanor Holmes Norton, co-chairing the committee and pushing for the television documentary most likely involved a number of intricate negotiations. Many African American leaders at the time were speaking out against government-sponsored reproductive control and family planning policies as disguised attempts to weaken and contain the black population; they were urging black women to produce more, not fewer, children.[39] Despite this, African American feminists such as Toni Cade Bambara, Shirley Chisholm, and the Black Women's Liberation Group of Mt. Vernon, New York, were publicly opposing *both* population control and the notion that black women should produce more children. They supported legal abortions for women of color and birth control education.[40]

Eleanor Holmes Norton's advocacy for a televised version of the commission's report seems to have been rooted in a unique combination of positions. She vociferously championed the belief that women of color and poor women should have the same exposure to reproductive control options as white and middle-class women. However, in an article on reproductive rights for women of color, she also invoked the need for population control and so seems to have forged a position in which advocacy for both population control and birth control (including abortion) was a possibility for African Americans at the time.[41]

With these numerous and sometimes conflicting motivations tacitly churning within its own membership, the committee approached all three networks with the proposed documentary.[42] According to Craig Fisher, the film's producer/director, Rockefeller was convinced that CBS would air the film because of his friendship with network president William Paley and because, as Rockefeller said to Fisher, "Paley got whatever he wanted."[43] After a lunch with Paley, however, Rockefeller reported that CBS, like the other networks, retained complete control over its editorial material and would not broadcast the film because it had been produced by an out-of-house filmmaker—one not part of the CBS staff.[44] The other two networks, ABC and NBC, declined the project for the same reasons.[45] Most articles in the mainstream press claimed that the networks had rejected the film because they did not want to touch such a politically and socially controversial package; some reporters even speculated that the networks were afraid of the power of the Catholic Church.[46] Fisher, who had been hired away from NBC by Rockefeller to work on the project, truly believed the networks would not take news or documentary material that did not originate with their own news divisions. He states he had warned Rockefeller about this policy at the outset.[47] The Public Broadcasting Service (PBS), however, agreed to broadcast the film. Several months later, ABC, under the supervision of producer Marlene Sanders, began production on its own self-generated documentary of the commission's report.[48]

"Population and the American Future"

The commission's official 1-hour documentary, called "Population and the American Future" (bearing the same name as the commission's report), was produced by Craig Fisher, cowritten and codirected by Fisher and John Martin, narrated by Hugh Downs, and broadcast from PBS station WGBH Boston on November 29, 1972. Prior to its airing, Catholic and fundamentalist right-to-life groups (considerably more organized than when "Abortion" was broadcast in 1969) protested about the film to Congress, the Federal Communication Commission (FCC), PBS, and the Xerox Corporation, which had contributed $250,000 to its production. The executive director of the U.S. Coalition for Life threatened to take PBS to court and to seek an injunction that would delay the program.[49] The public affairs coordinator for PBS fired back: "Population control, regardless of how you feel about it, is a burning national issue and deserves an airing on national television."[50]

The 57-minute film comprises footage with voice-over or on-screen narration by Hugh Downs. Unlike the first two television documentaries dealing with abortion, there are no interviews or spokespeople for different sides of the issues. In addition, this documentary, and the Marlene Sanders one after it, is not only about abortion. The first half of "Population and the American Future" reviews population statistics and their effects on the economy, the environment, housing, transportation, poverty, cities, and national security. It also deals briefly with the commission's recommendations on immigration. The second half focuses on human reproduction, recommending a range of progressive social policies, such as comprehensive health care for mothers and children, day care, widespread sex education, freedom of choice in all reproductive matters, and the elimination of laws restricting access to contraceptive information and services by adults and teenagers.

The 7-minute section on abortion reviews the different options considered by the commission, ranging from fairly strict prohibition to the repeal of all restrictions, without ever mentioning the women's movement. It discusses the commission's choice of middle ground: that abortions up to the twenty-fourth week should be left to the "conscience of the woman concerned in consultation with her physician" and that abortion should be liberalized along the lines of the 1971 New York state law. One segment opens with a large banner that is difficult to read in the shot: "Stop religious oppression! Abortion . . . freedom of choice!" But that image is quickly followed with shots that make clearly legible more than twenty signs carrying such slogans as "Christ was a fetus," "I love life," "Forgive Them Father for They Know not What They Do," and "What if you had been aborted?" Other signs also bear drawings of fetuses, and footage includes shots of large antiabortion rallies with clerics and lay people praying on the steps of public buildings and picketing in front of clinics. At the end of the documentary, there is a 1-minute segment urging the passage of the Equal Rights Amendment that includes footage of a women's movement march replete with signs declaring, "Equal Rights" and "Sisterhood is Powerful." But at no point is feminism, or any feminist spokesperson, tied to the documentary's advocacy of abortion or other reproductive rights.

Furthermore, like the report before it, the film is troubling with regard to issues of race and class. Although it takes care to report that 70 percent of the growth in the American population comes from white middle-class families, it also reproduces subtle and not-so-subtle stereotypes and innuendos. In the section in which it ties poverty to overpopulation, virtually all the shots are of African Americans or other people of color. The section on sex education also claims, "Couples in all age and socio-economic groups experience unwanted pregnancy but they *occur most often and have the most serious effects among the low income couples*" (emphasis mine). The image at this point is a shot of a young African American woman. Finally and most disturbing, a segment recommending surgical sterilization for contraception focuses and lingers on a young black woman, an image that overwhelms the following quick shots of two white men and a white woman.[51]

In regard to abortion and birth control matters, PBS deemed that "balance" was missing from the documentary. To provide a forum for opposing views, it scheduled an hour following the documentary for people to challenge the documentary's proabortion stance. The Reverend Jesse Jackson spoke against abortion and population control as racist. Marjory Mecklenberg, president of Minnesota Citizens for Life, displayed slides of fetuses and played a recording of a fourteen-week-old heartbeat. Valerie Dillon of the Respect for Life Committee quipped, "Shall we sell [contraceptive technologies to teenagers] in school vending machines?" Conservative Ben Wattenberg argued for *more* births. After the program, at least one newspaper article remarked that this hour was significantly more effective television than the documentary itself.[52] The discussion touched off a huge letter-writing campaign coordinated by fundamentalist groups and the Catholic Church that resulted in the shelving of the documentary, which was to have been distributed to schools and colleges by the U.S. Office of Education.[53]

Feminist representatives, who would have articulated proabortion arguments associated with women's rights and distinct from those of population control, were not included in the group of invited challengers or in the documentary. Because particular spokespeople were ordained and others were not, because women's movement voices were so completely silenced, the terms in which the proabortion position could be cast were severely limited.

"Population: Boom or Doom"

Two weeks before *Roe v. Wade,* on January 6, 1973, Marlene Sanders's ABC documentary "Population: Boom or Doom" was broadcast. Like the Fisher film, it was intended to be a documentary version of the commission's report, but Sanders included interviews with many commission members as well as with numerous others. The documentary was divided into three parts: a short introduction to population statistics and issues, a long segment on reproductive matters, and a short segment on immigration. The segment on reproduction included sections on birth control technologies, sex education, and abortion. The only participants speaking against the commission's recommendations on these matters were commission member Paul Cornely (an African American physician) and James T. McHugh (a priest from the U.S. Catholic Conference), both of whom opposed the recommendations on contraceptives for minors and on abortion. (Dr. Paul Cornely's objections, it should be noted, were articulated in religious rather than race-based arguments.)

In the section on sex education, the racist implications of population control surface momentarily. During a question-and-answer session at the University of North Carolina, an African American male student asks Rockefeller, "How do you rationalize with a black person that for them to stop having a certain number of kids is not genocide but is indeed helping their race as well as helping society as a whole?" Rockefeller replies that he believes in "voluntarism" and "freedom of choice" and that "every citizen should have the same knowledge and availability of services."

The 7-minute section on abortion includes footage at a Planned Parenthood clinic where abortions were performed and an interview with the clinic's director, Cornely and McHugh objecting to the commission's stand, and commission member Carol Foreman defending the report's conclusions. As in the Fisher documentary, no women's movement spokesperson is presented. The sole feminist-oriented statement—"women should have the freedom to control their own fertility and the freedom from the burdens of unwanted childbearing"—is framed and embedded within almost an hour of population-control discourse.[54]

Prior to the airing of the documentary, ABC encountered active protest, and it received much pro and con correspondence after the broadcast. As with the 1969 "Abortion," many letters from fundamentalist spokespeople complained that the documentary misled viewers by having a Catholic priest articulate the only opposing view. (While preparing the documentary, Sanders had inquired of her bosses if having a "Protestant" spokesperson was necessary for "fairness" considerations. Obviously, she and ABC ultimately decided—as did Pendrell and the network in 1969—that it was not.)[55] Other letters congratulated ABC and the documentary for living up to television's responsibility to inform and educate.[56] Rockefeller wrote to ABC president Elton Rule, praising the film. The executive director of the committee wrote that three people had called her office "wondering why we wasted time making an independent film of the Commission Report when you were obviously able to do it so much better. Ah, that hurts."[57]

Considering the Ramifications

The struggle over these two abortion documentaries prior to the *Roe v. Wade* decision illuminates how the original feminist perspective—abortion as a woman's unequivocal right, which has nothing to do with population control—was silenced in what became official public policy. Television's quest for "balance," more fervidly enacted as the FCC began to crack down on documentaries that they felt provided a biased view of topics under discussion, shaped the public debate by giving recognition to what it deemed the *legitimated* voices struggling over abortion.[58]

Television allowed population control advocates (some with legacies of blatant racism and classism) and the medical establishment to speak the proabortion view. This turned a complex, multifaceted battle into a two-sided contest—those who were *for* and those who were *against* legalized abortion. Those against were the Catholic Church, the having-it-both-ways Nixon White House, the fundamentalist New Right, African American abortion and birth control opponents, and individual politicians. Those for were the population-control groups, the medical and legal establishments, and other politicians. The women's movement, including African American feminist groups, was totally suppressed.

This suppression happened at various levels of the fight, and the shift of part of the women's movement to a "choice" framework for abortion rights—a framework that was commensurate with that of the population-control movement—ended up exacerbating the dilemma. For example, Sarah Weddington, the young liberal feminist lawyer who argued *Roe*, has discussed the ways she received help from the population-control establishment in researching the case and how she welcomed the commission's report "Population and the American Future" as a support and groundwork for her own preparation of *Roe*.[59]

My aim here is not to assign "blame" to abortion proponents such as David Lowe, Ernest Pendrell, Marlene Sanders, Craig Fisher, Thomas Wolf, or even ABC and CBS for not attending to how they chose to apportion "balance"; or to players like Sarah Weddington for pleading the case within the terms of privacy—as opposed, for example, to those of equal rights and protections; or to feminists who moved the terms from "abortion on demand" to "freedom to choose." I am simply arguing that trouble followed for this coalition on abortion rights, which included liberal views in its legitimated "pro" position, but which strategically decided to ignore, minimize, or subsume radical (delegitimated) views in order to secure its goals—goals that were inflected with many different meanings for different "pro" participants. That this is the case seems abundantly clear not only from the aftermath of *Roe* but from the ways TV documentaries with generally liberal and progressive viewpoints on abortion played out the struggles over these rights.

For television, the ideology of documentary production practices was inflected repeatedly by how "balance" was conceived.[60] In this case, U.S. TV documentary's conception and enactment of "balance" shored up the notion of liberal pluralism—that competing voices contribute equally to fashioning public policy on difficult social issues. What gets repressed is the incontrovertible fact that some voices are given legitimacy through representation and others are not, some get airtime and others get stifled. The documentaries reduced the complexities of the abortion debate to a particular "pro" and "con" binary and then went on to situate the terms of public discourse around that binary. Decisions about "balance" had the effect of pulling the "pro" sides of the debate into the vortex of the population-control discourses on abortion, rather than into those of feminism, because that became the rational, sanctioned position in favor of liberalizing the law.

Among many other things, this analysis reveals the ongoing and remarkable disparities between the lived social and the officially represented—represented in terms of having sanctioned and recognized positions from which to speak, and in terms of gaining places on U.S. documentary television. The vast array of women who participated in the battle for legal abortions, who marched and protested, argued the issue, spoke out in state legislatures, worked as physicians, nurses, and lawyers, performed abortions, and secured for themselves illegal and sometimes traumatic treatment, found very few opportunities to be active subjects in America's home-screen documentaries. This lack of opportunity contrasts to the way antiabortion groups and individuals (as we saw with the PBS forum) ultimately gained representation in the pre-*Roe* period.

The policy that ensued in *Roe v. Wade* fell short of situating abortion as an absolute right conceived in terms of women's socially constructed and socially situated position. It therefore invited an array of other opposing rights to rise up and challenge women's abilities to secure legal abortions. The rights of the fetus (pitted, in fact, more and more, in the 1980s and 1990s, against the selfish and immoral mother), the rights of the husband, of the father, the rights of the state, the rights of a pregnant teenager's parents, were some of the many challengers that sought to erode the permanence of the 1973 decision.

Although Celeste Condit has argued, in a rhetorical study of abortion discourse, that it was not the essentially liberal social system but the barrage of competing voices that resulted in a compromising of the women's movement's full goals, I am arguing that U.S. television documentaries' liberal democratic character contributed to shaping a troubled U.S. abortion policy that will most likely be up for renegotiation in the not too distant future.[61] The history presented here makes plain that feminist abortion supporters should be prepared to articulate clearly formulated demands for judicially protected abortion rights that, in my opinion, should be reframed around terms of equal rights and protections rather than privacy, and around the *social* rather than the individualistic dimensions of abortion.[62]

Notes

Thanks to Charlotte Brunsdon, Mary Beth Haralovich, Michele Hilmes, Laura Stempel Mumford, Lauren Rabinovitz, and Jane Schacter for many astute suggestions on various drafts of this chapter.

1 For articles on abortion and reproductive politics, see Sarah Franklin, Celia Lury, and Jackie Stacey, eds., "Part 3. Science and Technology," in *Off-Centre: Feminism and Cultural Studies* (London: Harper Collins Academic, 1991), 129–218. See also Linda Gordon, *Woman's Body, Woman's Right: Birth Control in America* (New York: Penguin, 1990); Rosalind Petchesky, *Abortion and Woman's Choice: The State, Sexuality, and Reproductive Freedom,* rev. ed. (Boston: Northeastern University Press, 1990); Kristin Luker, *Abortion and the Politics of Motherhood* (Berkeley: University of California Press, 1984); Marlene Gerber Fried, ed., *From Abortion to Reproductive Freedom: Transforming a Movement* (Boston: South End Press, 1990); Sarah Weddington, *A Question of Choice* (New York: Penguin, 1993); Ruth Bader Ginsburg, "Some Thoughts on Autonomy and Equality in Relation to *Roe v. Wade,*" *North Carolina Law Review* 63 (January 1985): 375–86; Dawn E. Johnsen, "The Creation of Fetal Rights: Conflicts with Women's Constitutional Rights to Liberty, Privacy, and Equal Protection," *Yale Law Journal* 95 (January 1986): 599–625; Wendy Brown, "Reproductive Freedom and the Right to Privacy: A Paradox for Feminists," in *Families, Politics, and Public Policy,* ed. Irene Diamond (New York: Longman, 1983), 311–88; Meera Worth, "Spousal Notification and the Right of Privacy," *Chicago Kent Law Review* 59 (fall 1983): 1129–51; Laura Grindstaff, "Abortion and the Popular Press: Mapping Media Discourse from *Roe* to *Webster*" (paper presented at Console-ing Passions: Television, Video, and Feminism Conference, Los Angeles, April 1993).

2 See Gordon, *Woman's Body, Woman's Right,* 397–488; Petchesky, *Abortion and Woman's Choice,* 241–329; Weddington, *A Question of Choice,* 197, 211–25.

3 Gordon, *Woman's Body, Woman's Right,* 403.

4 Ibid., 405. As Rhoda Copelon points out, it was not until 1977 that the court

actually extended the right to decide about abortion to the woman herself—*Roe* had technically assigned it to physicians (see Copelon, "From Privacy to Autonomy: The Conditions for Sexual and Reproductive Freedom," in Fried, *From Abortion to Reproductive Freedom,* 35).

5 Gordon, *Woman's Body, Woman's Right,* 397–426; Petchesky, *Abortion and Woman's Choice,* 125–32.

6 The issue of "balance" that is so central to the history of the television documentaries presented here pivots on what came to be called the U.S. Federal Communication Commission's "Fairness Doctrine." At the time of the documentaries under discussion, the Fairness Doctrine stated that the public had the right to an "uninhibited marketplace of ideas" and that broadcasters were obliged to "afford reasonable opportunity for the discussion of conflicting views on issues of public importance." Achieving representations of "conflicting views" led to the many struggles over the notions of "balance" and "balanced programming." The Fairness Doctrine was abandoned with the deregulation of U.S. broadcasting in the 1980s. See Christopher H. Sterling and John M. Kitross, *Stay Tuned: A Concise History of American Broadcasting,* 2d ed. (Belmont, Calif.: Wadsworth, 1990), 426–27.

7 Gordon, *Woman's Body, Woman's Right,* 34–40, 400–416; Petchesky, *Abortion and Woman's Choice,* 49–137; Luker, *Abortion and the Politics of Motherhood,* 11–15.

8 Gordon, *Woman's Body, Woman's Right,* 396–400.

9 Ibid., 396.

10 Petchesky, *Abortion and Woman's Choice,* 117.

11 "This series [about ABC's *Summer Focus*] is being undertaken with or without the support of sponsors, as part of our continuing obligation to bring to the American people the major concerns of the day—many of them involving considerable difference of opinion" (Thomas Wolf to Martin Rubenstein, ABC Interdepartment Correspondence, 6 February 1969, Ernest Pendrell collection, box 7, folder 2, Wisconsin Center for Film and Theater Research, State Historical Society of Wisconsin, Madison).

12 Untitled clipping, *Business Week,* 13 February 1965, David Lowe collection, box 1, folder 6, Wisconsin Center for Film and Theater Research, State Historical Society of Wisconsin, Madison. This clipping describes President Lyndon Johnson's State of the Union message that urged that birth control information should be made available to more people.

13 Unpublished script, "Abortion and the Law," David Lowe collection, box 1, folder 5.

14 Since with "Abortion and the Law," I am working from a script only (rather

than the film itself or a videotape), I am unable to specify the races or classes of the women presented.

15 Vernon L. Wilkinson, McKenna & Wilkinson Law Offices, to Martin Rubenstein, ABC, 20 February 1969, Ernest Pendrell collection, box 7, folder 2.

16 This was the case even though ABC, through its owned and operated New York station, had already taken a publicly televised stand in favor of liberalizing existing laws: on 3, 4, and 5 February 1969, WABC-TV, New York, broadcast an editorial urging such liberalization. See "WABC-TV Editorial Favors Proposals for More Moderate Abortion Law in New York," Ernest Pendrell collection, box 7, folder 2. This was rebutted by Mrs. Valerie Dillon for the Respect for Life Committee (see "WABC-TV Editorial Rebuttal," Ernest Pendrell collection, box 7, folder 3).

17 Lester Cooper to Ernest Pendrell, ABC Interdepartment Correspondence, 17 March 1969, "Subject: Abortion," Ernest Pendrell collection, box 7, folder 2.

18 Robert Sassone to Elton Rule, 2 April 1969, Ernest Pendrell collection, box 7, folder 2.

19 Ibid. It is clear from Thomas Wolf's letters, memos, and actions dealing with this and the Marlene Sanders documentary in 1973 that he was supporting liberalization of abortion laws.

20 Ernest Pendrell to Tom Wolf, typed note, 14 April 1969, Ernest Pendrell collection, box 7, folder 2.

21 (Mrs.) Joanna Martin, Public Relations, Chicago NOW to Thomas Wolf, ABC, 10 March 1969, Ernest Pendrell collection, box 7, folder 2.

22 The omission of non-Catholic antiabortion spokespeople raised ire in both the religious press and viewer responses to the program (Russell Faist, "ABC's of Abortion," *Catholic Universe Bulletin* [paper of the Cleveland Catholic diocese], Ernest Pendrell collection, box 7, folder 2; Russell Faist, letter to *Catholic Universe Bulletin*, 13 June 1969, Ernest Pendrell collection, box 7, folder 2).

Although Betty Friedan and NOW's position were not included, the documentary itself opened with a strong analysis and *implicitly* feminist indictment of the antiabortion position from a young, white, middle-class woman identified simply as "Mary": "I do feel that on a level maybe that isn't conscious that most people, that society in general feels that girls who get themselves pregnant are bad girls, they aren't nice girls, and they've been careless and wayward, and promiscuous, and that they should get punished. You know, this is the only way to teach them, because if you let girls get abortions, then they're going to run around and have sex all the time, and the whole society will fall apart" (*Abortion* script, Ernest Pendrell collection, box 7, folder 3. See also the film *Abortion,* Ernest Pendrell collection, Film Archives of the Wisconsin Center for Film and Theater Research, State Historical Society of Wisconsin, Madison).

23 "Population and the American Future," *Report of the Commission on Population Growth and the American Future* (Washington, D.C.: U.S. Government Printing Office, 1972), 5.

24 Gordon, *Woman's Body, Woman's Right,* 386–96; Petchesky, *Abortion and Woman's Choice,* 116–25; Angela Davis, "Racism, Birth Control, and Reproductive Rights," in Fried, *From Abortion to Reproductive Freedom,* 15–26. Linda Gordon warns that we must be careful to recognize that not all participants in the population control movement were working with a racist or imperialist agenda (*Woman's Body, Woman's Right,* 389).

25 Petchesky, *Abortion and Woman's Choice,* 122–23.

26 Gordon, *Woman's Body, Woman's Right,* 400–409; Petchesky, *Abortion and Woman's Choice,* 122–32.

27 It is worth noting that Nixon's own message while creating the commission spoke of the specific need to get reproductive information to lower-income women. See Production Research Document, 18 July 1969, Marlene Sanders collection, box 2, folder 1, Wisconsin Center for Film and Theater Research, State Historical Society of Wisconsin, Madison.

28 Petchesky, *Abortion and Woman's Choice,* 122.

29 Ibid. It is also important to note here that the population control movement shifted from not advocating abortions (favoring instead sterilization) to supporting them when it became clear that women would continue to obtain them illegally (ibid., 118–25).

30 Ibid., 120.

31 "Population and the American Future," 141–69.

32 "Pro Abortion Policy of Population Panel Opposed 5-1 in Mail," *New York Times,* 11 May 1972.

33 See "ABC Report on the Population Show," undated, Marlene Sanders collection, box 1, folder 1, 3, 4. It states that in order to avoid oblivion, John D. Rockefeller III insisted on establishing a Citizen's Committee on Population and the American Future, which would be privately funded and exist for a year to push the commission's findings.

34 Carol Foreman, Executive Director of the Citizens' Committee on Population and the American Future, to Marlene Sanders, 9 January 1973, Marlene Sanders collection, box 2, folder 5.

35 David K. Lelewar of Rockefeller's office to ABC President Elton Rule, 29 July 1971, Marlene Sanders collection, box 1, folder 1. Lelewar writes, "Because

of the report's importance and its wide interest to Americans generally, we feel that it should be presented not only as a written document but via TV as well." See also Jeannette Smyth, "Getting It Down on Film," *Washington Post,* 22 November 1972. Such reports are known for falling into oblivion.

36 "Population and the American Future," 72–73.

37 Articles in family planning pamphlets were describing the success of TV spots in generating, for example, "a 7-fold increase in calls to family planning information services." See "The Family Planner," May 1970, Marlene Sanders collection, box 2, folder 1.

38 According to the film's producer, Craig Fisher, Nixon had asked Rockefeller to put a halt to the filming very early on, but Rockefeller threatened to resign from the commission, and Nixon backed down, agreeing that shooting could continue (Craig Fisher, telephone interview by author, August 1992).

39 Petchesky, *Abortion and Woman's Choice,* 130. Gordon writes, "Birth control and abortion advocates were insensitive to black fears about population control—51 per cent of black women surveyed in the early 1970s believed that the survival of black people depended on increasing black births, and 37 per cent believed that birth-control programs were genocidal in intent. (Black men were even more suspicious.) Indeed, throughout the 1960s and 1970s, fears of genocide were prominent in black commentary on all forms of birth control" (Gordon, *Woman's Body, Woman's Right,* 441)

40 Ibid., 441–42. See also Petchesky, *Abortion and Woman's Choice,* 130; Toni Cade, "The Pill: Genocide or Liberation?" in *The Black Woman,* ed. Toni Cade (New York: Signet, 1970), 162–69; Shirley Chisholm, "Facing the Abortion Question," in *Black Women in White America: A Documentary History,* ed. Gerda Lerner (New York: Vintage 1972), 602–6; Black Women's Liberation Group, Mt. Vernon, N.Y., "Statement on Birth Control," in *Sisterhood Is Powerful,* ed. Robin Morgan (New York: Random House, 1970), 360–61.

41 Eleanor Holmes Norton, "For Sadie and Maud," in Morgan, *Sisterhood Is Powerful,* 353–59.

42 Frank Getlein, "Television Report with Bite," *Evening Star News,* 29 November 1972; David K. Lelewar to Elton Rule, 29 July 1971, Marlene Sanders collection, box 1, folder 1.

43 Craig Fisher, telephone interview by author, August 1992.

44 Ibid.; Getlein, "Television Report with Bite."

45 Ibid.

46 Getlein, "Television Report with Bite"; John Carmody, "PBS: Focus on Overpopulation," *Washington Post,* 29 November 1972.

47 Craig Fisher, telephone interview by author, August 1992; Jeannette Smyth, "Getting It Down on Film."

48 Marlene Sanders to Tom Wolf, memo, 6 July 1972, Marlene Sanders collection, box 1, folder 1. Sanders tells Wolf about the Fisher film that is well under way, and an unnamed ABC executive writes back on the margins telling Sanders to "go ahead . . . try to break some new ground"; Tom Wolf writes in the margins, "It's important to us for reasons you know."

It is important to consider the institutional conditions that accompanied the undertaking of these potentially incendiary documentaries at this particular time. As Charles Hammond points out in his book on television documentary, during the late 1960s and early 1970s TV had become the primary U.S. news source. The air was glutted with news from civil rights to black power coverage, and the networks began increasingly to conceive of this information function as part of their corporate mission. Although there was a drop-off in traditional news and theme documentaries between 1968 and 1975, the documentaries actually produced during this time became fairly bold and hard-hitting (ABC's "Abørtion" falls within this category). By 1972 and 1973, such documentaries began to come under attack by the FCC for alleged lack of fairness and balance. See Charles Hammond, *The Image Decade: Television Documentary, 1965–1975* (New York: Hastings House, 1981), 70, 106–7, 224–27.

Each of these conditions is evident in the ways that PBS and ABC proceeded with their programs. Both networks seemed to conceive of their efforts under the aegis of providing the country at large with what it needed to know. Furthermore, the documents in Marlene Sanders's production files indicate that, as with the Pendrell film a few years earlier, ABC's news division (where Tom Wolf was still vice president of news and public affairs) wanted to take what it considered to be an aggressive approach to the subject matter. The division was, in fact, both angry yet unshaken by what was reported as lack of cooperation, an implied threat, and intimidation from the White House. But at the same time both PBS and ABC, as we saw with ABC in 1969, tried to present what they determined to be the sanctioned opposing sides and "balanced" presentations (Marlene Sanders to Tom Wolf, memo, undated, Marlene Sanders collection, box 1, folder 1).

49 Jack Rosenthal, "TV Film of Population Report Fought by Anti-Abortion Groups," *New York Times*, 28 November 1972.

50 Ibid.

51 The film is in the possession of the author on loan from Fisher.

52 John Archibald, "More-People People Steal Population Show," *St. Louis Post Dispatch*, 1 December 1972.

53 Nancy Ross, "Television: Shelving a Film," *Washington Post*, 11 January 1973.

54 L. Clare Bratten's research has shown that in 1970, the three major television

networks' nightly news programs presented stories on the fifty-year celebration of the beginning of women's suffrage, and, in these stories, they explicitly linked abortion to women's movement demands. Each of the networks reported that the women's movement was demanding free child care centers, free abortions, and equal rights. Both NBC and CBS aired stories on the day of the celebration, August 26, 1970. The day before, August 25, ABC ran its story (L. Clare Bratten, "And That's the Way It Is: Second Wave Feminism and Network News" [paper presented at Console-ing Passions: Television, Video, and Feminism conference, Montreal, 1 May 1997]).

55 See Marlene Sanders, "ABC Report on the 'Population Show,'" undated, Marlene Sanders collection, box 1, folder 1. Sanders inquires, "If we interview McHugh [the Catholic priest] does fairness dictate that a Protestant leader who supports the proposal be included? Please advise."

56 Examples of letters may be found in the Marlene Sanders collection, box 2, folder 5.

57 Carol Foreman, Executive Director of the Citizens' Committee on Population and the American Future, to Marlene Sanders, 9 January 1973, Marlene Sanders collection, box 2, folder 5.

58 Hammond, *The Image Decade*, 224–27.

59 Weddington, *A Question of Choice*, 91–93, 135.

60 Stuart Hall, Ian Connell, and Lidia Curti wrote in 1976 that although political news programs in Great Britain may have offered different "party sides" to issues, they essentially worked to buttress and fortify the very notion of parliamentary democracy (Stuart Hall, Ian Connell, and Lidia Curti, "The 'Unity' of Current Affairs Television," in *Cultural Studies 9: Working Papers in Cultural Studies* [Birmingham, U.K.: Centre for Contemporary Cultural Studies, 1976], 51–93).

61 Celeste Michelle Condit, *Decoding Abortion Rhetoric: Communicating Social Change* (Urbana: University of Illinois Press, 1990).

62 For a delineation of the equal rights and protection versus the privacy justifications for abortion law, see Frances Olsen, "Unraveling Compromise," *Harvard Law Review* 103 (1989): 105–35; Reva Siegel, "Reasoning from the Body: A Historical Perspective on Abortion Regulation and Questions of Equal Protection," *Stanford Law Review* 44 (1992): 261–381; Catharine MacKinnon, "Privacy v. Equality: Beyond *Roe v. Wade*," in Catharine MacKinnon, *Feminism Unmodified* (Cambridge, Mass.: Harvard University Press, 1987), 93; Ginsburg, "Some Thoughts on Autonomy and Equality in Relation to *Roe v. Wade*," 375–86; Johnsen, "The Creation of Fetal Rights," 599–625; Brown, "Reproductive Freedom and the Right to Privacy," 322–88; Copelon, "From Privacy to Autonomy," 27–43.

Ms.-Representation

The Politics of Feminist Sitcoms

Lauren Rabinovitz

Murphy Brown's (CBS, 1988–97) last first-run episode of the 1991–92 season ended with its eponymous star (Candice Bergen) giving birth as a single parent. Two days later, Vice President Dan Quayle delivered his now famous speech in California in which he blamed the "lawless social anarchy" of the Los Angeles riots on the "poverty of values" represented and encouraged by such things as Murphy's single parenthood on *Murphy Brown:* "It doesn't help matters when prime-time TV has Murphy Brown, a character who supposedly epitomizes today's intelligent, highly paid, professional woman, mocking the importance of fathers by bearing a child and calling it 'just another lifestyle choice.'"[1] In one move, Quayle exchanged the real-life material poverty in Los Angeles for an ideological poverty of popular entertainment and, in particular, made a woman's body and her reproductive rights the central problem. One of the chief consequences, however, of the Republican party crusade that he launched is the degree to which the "family values" debate put forward a definition of feminism as simple matters of personal choice in women's issues. Quayle disqualified feminism both as a doctrine of equal rights for women and as an ideology of social transformation by reducing it to its liberal manifestation as a theory of individual freedom.

What Quayle objected to was not simply that unwed Murphy had become pregnant but that she *chose* to remain both a mother and unmarried. Unlike women characters in melodrama, who have long been dealing with unplanned pregnancies, Murphy offended the vice president because as a comic heroine she was neither punished nor chastised by the narrative.[2] At least, this was how Dan Quayle understood her. Murphy's actions suggested a sexual autonomy of choice and a mockery of the law of the Father by refusing marriage and conservative morality. She flaunted herself as a rebellious, insurgent woman and as a feminist because her identity was not fixed in relation to either a father or a husband. In this way, Murphy's self-identified stance offers a critique of patriarchal culture and values. Indeed, Quayle's response was, "Marriage is probably the best anti-poverty program there is."[3]

But by emphasizing Murphy's situation as one of "lifestyle choices," Quayle was only thinking in terms of individual morality. His terms ignored the constraints of class, racial, and gendered contexts on sexual politics. Quayle, however, was upholding a definition of feminism that has dominated television programming. Feminism's capacity to disrupt and upset cultural categories has always been so ambiguously presented on television that it lends itself to a range of political interpretations. Although television consistently articulates feminism as reformist, liberal, and progressive, it simultaneously disavows any racial or class determinants. Television allows for the expression of a feminist critique but represses feminism's potential for radical social change.

The situation comedy, in particular, has been the television genre most consistently associated with feminist heroines and with advocating a progressive politics of liberal feminism. From *The Mary Tyler Moore Show* (CBS, 1970–77) to *Murphy Brown*, from *Laverne & Shirley* (ABC, 1976–83) to *Kate & Allie* (CBS, 1984–89), from *Rhoda* (CBS, 1974–78) to *Roseanne* (ABC, 1988–97), from *The Golden Girls* (NBC, 1985–94) to *Designing Women* (CBS, 1986–93), the feminist sitcom helps construct powerful everyday knowledge about political and cultural feminism. Although the boundaries for woman-centered topics have expanded considerably over two and a half decades, feminist sitcoms' strategies for defining feminism have remained structurally the same.

Network programming executives initially became interested in "feminist programming" in the early 1970s because it was good business. New marketing data, organized according to a greater number of demographic categories, suggested an important national shift in audience. A more independently minded female generation was coming of age (the baby boomers), and advertising agencies began earmarking greater portions of their budgets to address the swelling numbers of female consumers under fifty.[4] Fewer customers could be valuable if they earned more and spent more. Daytime television had for years organized its fiction, formats, and commercial advertisements around a homogeneous group defined as female, married, and house bound. But now prime-time products (the shows) attempted to address the "demographic" products (the audience) for which the advertisers were looking by merely inscribing liberal politics and values as well as younger, urban characters increasingly marked by gender, race, or ethnicity.[5] The extent to which such strategies became thoroughly internalized policies by the 1980s was best summarized by CBS broadcast Vice President for Research David Poltrack in 1986: "The affluent, upscale woman between twenty-five and fifty-four is [now] the primary target of advertisers."[6] A generic address of "feminism" became an important strategy because it served the needs of American television executives who could cultivate programming that could be identified with target audiences whom they wanted to measure and deliver to advertising agencies.

In the first decade of feminist sitcoms, shows like *The Mary Tyler Moore Show*, *Rhoda*, and *Maude* (CBS, 1972–78) broached the narrative premise of the new implicitly feminist woman coping with her everyday world (*Mary Tyler Moore*'s theme song "You Can Make It After All" has become emblematic of this focus). The overwhelming success of this new heroine quickly made her a staple in feminist sitcoms, defining her liberation in relation to woman's traditional place within the nuclear family or the surrogate family of the workplace.[7] In no fewer than ten feminist sitcoms between 1975 and 1985, white, middle-class women who were divorced or widowed became single moms and attempted to cope with the tensions between self-fulfillment and selfless mothering.[8] Although the father was erased or marginalized in all these cases, the nuclear family was maintained through the regular reinscription of symbolic fathers, patriarchal figures who, although not the legal or biological father of the families, served to authorize the women's positions as simultaneously unmarried/married.[9]

Indeed, this very situation is perpetuated in recent feminist sitcoms like *Murphy Brown* that include an adult male as a regular part of the family household, such as Murphy's live-in painter-turned-nanny Eldin (1988–94). He and Murphy have effected a gender role reversal in the 1990s, since he stays at home and nurtures the child while she is the breadwinner. Eldin (Robert Pastorelli) is a privileged character in the show because he inhabits her domestic space and regularly articulates the boundaries for acceptable moral behavior, frequently providing common sense stability when Murphy strays too far. Eldin demonstrates that, within a static structure of a symbolic nuclear family, the postfeminist man can also be a mom. Indeed, one has to question Murphy's status as a model for American single parenthood at all: her class position and ability to afford a live-in nanny hardly mirror that of most working single mothers, and her relationship to Eldin represses all aspects of employer-employee labor relations and refigures them as equals coparenting the child. This situation was the same in *The Two of Us* (CBS, 1981–82), *Who's the Boss* (ABC, 1984–94), *Charles in Charge* (CBS, 1984–85; syndicated, 1987–90), and *The Phenom* (ABC, 1994–95), in which single-mom breadwinners and their household employees or tutors share domestic space, and the males frequently represent a new nurturing masculinity. This arrangement allowed for the construction of symbolic nuclear families, of power and class relations reconfigured as gender role reversals and cultural stereotyping, or of a romantic battle of the sexes, or sometimes all three.

For years, prime-time TV has defined feminism and responded to a "family values" argument by coding women's identities in relationship to figurations of family and by masking and effacing women's economic and material conditions.[10] This historically static definition was already at work in *Kate & Allie,* the feminist sitcom that best demonstrated in the 1980s how political conflict is rerouted into individual "lifestyle choices."[11] In an episode initially broadcast in 1986–87, college student activists invite new older student Allie (Jane Curtin) to a demonstration against toxic-waste dumping after she expresses her interest in and commitment to their goals because she is a concerned mother. The initial invitation poses a possible narrative trajectory: will motherhood motivate political action? Set in the college classroom, the scene ends with Allie's indecision about whether or not to join the demonstrators.

Once she expresses ambivalence, however, a spatial and narrative shift occurs. The next scene occurs in the domestic space that Allie shares with another single parent, Kate (Susan St. James), where their discussion about the demonstration redefines the problem as *both* Kate's and Allie's. Allie expresses her uncertainty to Kate because she has never been to a demonstration—"not even in the sixties. . . . I was the only one in my class that thought SDS was a chain of florists." Allie becomes humorously realigned with a naive position about politics, giving new narrative emphasis to her uncertainty.

Such signifiers as "SDS" and "the sixties" draw on the target audience's extratextual associations. The words denote opposition while eliciting nostalgia. The "nostalgia theme" becomes a topic in and of itself for Kate. Remembering her past as a college campus radical, Kate persuades Allie to go with *her* to the demonstration. Rather than advance a resolution of the initial questions posed by the narrative, the scene reorganizes Allie in relationship to Kate while the political subject becomes personal.

Such a movement from problems of social to individual fulfillment continues at the protest itself. Kate turns the protest into a friendly trivia game of sixties song titles. When Kate and Allie are arrested, Kate makes a date with the handsome cop. Thus the narrative abdicates its initial political questions as well as any model of problem solving through collective action in favor of nostalgia and romance. If anything, the episode suggests that political protests are a good place for single women to meet eligible bachelor policemen.

Picking up both chronologically and thematically where female friends Kate and Allie leave off, *Designing Women* (CBS, 1986–93) is an even better example of how the feminist sitcom represents women interacting with women. *Designing Women* is both feminist and contradicts feminism through its racism and homophobia. On Monday nights, *Designing Women* followed *Murphy Brown* during the years in which they were both in production. It was consistently ranked in the top twenty and often in the top ten in the A.C. Nielsen ratings.[12] *Designing Women*'s contribution to the genre is its engagement with femininity as a site of female excess.

Feminine excess as comic is a regular practice in feminist sitcoms (e.g., Sandra in 227 [NBC, 1985–90], Blanche [Rue McClanahan] in *The Golden Girls*, Suzanne Sugarbaker in *Designing Women*, Corky Sherwood Forest in *Murphy Brown*).[13] These characters wear fashionable, bright, soft, and often form-fitting clothes over figures dressed and molded to emphasize female anatomical difference. (This is modified and complicated somewhat by Delta Burke's weight gains, and the producers of *Designing Women* increasingly clothed her in dresses that attempted to mask her size. But this representation itself became, through star discourse and the evolving text, a self-reflexive issue regarding fat and femininity.) Their performances invoke narcissism. In an exemplary moment on 227, Sandra (Jackee Harry) tells the others, "When I look in the mirror, I love what I see." In *Murphy Brown*, Corky (Faith Ford) tells Murphy's baby a fairy tale about a princess clearly marked as herself. This narcissistic pleasure in her princess-like femininity and the traditionally feminine trajectory of her life culminating in romance and marriage is treated ironically, however, as the scene depends on Corky's poignant and unfunny revelation that she did not "live happily ever after" with her prince, from whom she has recently gotten a divorce.

Both Corky Sherwood and Suzanne Sugarbaker are former beauty queens, an identity repeatedly defined by other characters as the epitome of culturally objectified, commodified femininity. Suzanne, Corky, Blanche, and Sandra frequently serve as the object or butt of jokes made by characters from a range of other positions. Such shifts of jesting humor make possible feminist criticism about the female body as a commodity.

But it is important not to situate feminine excess as expressed solely by a single body. Feminine excess becomes central to the feminist sitcom only because feminism, too, is presented as an opposite extreme. They are set up in relationship to each other as structuring binary oppositions. *Designing Women*'s humor as a feminist sitcom, for example, relies on the ways in which it centrally treats relationships between femininity and feminism in the program. The notion that femininity and feminism are in a mutual relationship in the feminist sitcom depends on two important assumptions about femininity. First, femininity is not an essential property of women; it is an image that is usually correlated with women's appearances. Second, the function of femininity, as elaborated by numerous feminist critics, is to provide cover for the female's Otherness and to distance the female spectator from finding fullness in self-identification.[14]

The majority of *Designing Women*'s narratives are about the ways in which the site of feminine excess may be displaced from Suzanne Sugarbaker (Delta Burke) onto other characters. For example, as the feminist opposite of her ultrafeminine sister Suzanne, Julia Sugarbaker (Dixie Carter) sometimes becomes transformed into the site of feminine excess, such as when she gets her head stuck in between two banister rails at the governor's mansion or when she gets drunk at her son's wedding and does an on-stage burlesque. In these instances, Julia is spectacularized as the object for other characters' as well as our visual consumption and is rendered comic through the course of her objectification. In one episode, Julia even assumes a double life as a flirtatious, sexy lounge singer. When her shocked coworkers discover her performing both for on-screen and offscreen (at-home) spectators, she explains that she was tired of being so proper and was literally trying on the role for fun. Unlike Suzanne, Julia shows (usually through spectacle) how femininity is an *assumed* masquerade of sexualized behavior, costuming, and performance. What is most striking, however, is the program's repetitive argument that such a political, albeit sexualized, displacement is itself a product of feminist desire, since this is a world where feminism signifies women's limitless individual choices, and Julia may just as easily choose to be coy and feminine as assertive and independent.

Thus, Suzanne may also assume the *feminist* position. In an episode in which she discovers that her girlfriend Eugenia Weeks is a lesbian, Suzanne becomes the unlikely site for transformation from feminine excess to feminist when she alone among her women coworkers and friends confronts her homophobic fears. On the one hand, the function of such feminist displacement to Suzanne serves up a comic portrayal of white liberal feminism. In a scene where the other designing women accompany outspokenly homophobic Suzanne to a lesbian bar to meet her friend, "ethical" positions become reversed, since Suzanne's consistent acceptance of her homophobia contrasts with her friends' mounting nervousness and hypocrisy over being recognized or approached by anyone at the bar. When the group learns that this is, indeed, not a lesbian bar at all, the joke is not on Suzanne but on her liberal coworkers, who are comically unmasked as equally homophobic. On the other hand, such a transferral also serves a more conservative function by providing an opportunity to dissociate feminism from lesbianism. Viewers who identify with the nervousness of the designing women may be reassured that, like the designing women, they can be both feminist and homophobic.

In the episode's climax, Suzanne runs into her friend at a health club sauna, where their conversation occurs while their bodies and heads are wrapped only in towels. Suzanne's friend reassures Suzanne that she "is not [her] type." First visibly relieved and then registering dismay that *anyone* might not find her sexually attractive, Suzanne does a slow double-take and responds, "You don't have to get insulting," rendering comic the imagined threat of lesbian "difference." When the sole woman witness to their conversation runs out of the sauna in disgust, Suzanne opens the door and yells after her, "Lady, who cares what you think? You got more problems than lesbians in your sauna." The naming of *lesbian* and women desiring women—the repressed aspect of female friendship throughout these programs—as well as Suzanne's verbal incorporation of herself as a lesbian (the plural "lesbians") shift Suzanne to a position of political resistance. It is a highly significant textual movement that yields feminist pleasure.

Yet, two things mitigate this pleasure, since Suzanne is only exceptionally feminist at this moment. Because she is otherwise available as an example of feminine excess, Suzanne is a complicated figure for identification.[15] Second, the scene's concluding punch line ultimately shuts down or at least confounds the political progressivism otherwise articulated. The last line is Suzanne's: "We can put a man on top of the moon. Why can't we put a man on top of you? I say we can do it." Suzanne's moment of woman-identified politics is ruptured through a denial of her friend's articulated desire for women, thereby ensuring that in future episodes Suzanne may be returned safely to the realm of heterosexual feminine excess. The lesbian (herself unthreateningly marked physically as feminine, conventionally pretty, thin, and well dressed) disappears altogether from *Designing Women*, since she cannot be integrated into the group of female friends. Her sexuality remains Other, inexplicable, only partially representable and beyond rational understanding.[16] This example demonstrates that, even though discursively claiming both feminist rhetoric and a feminist subject, such dissociation of lesbianism from feminism compromises any feminist commitment to social transformation and identification with gay, lesbian, and bisexualities.

Designing Women's troublesome feminism is problematic not only for its homophobia but also for its racism. It is not the *body* of Suzanne that most often provides the means for renegotiating feminine excess. Rather, Suzanne's feminine excess is transferred onto Anthony (Meshach Taylor), the decorating firm's African American male employee (and, in later years, partner). In "The Bachelor Auction" episode, Anthony even becomes a "beauty queen" in tight shorts and a tank top, coached by Suzanne on how to become a sexualized object. He is then ogled by on-screen female spectators. He assumes the position of the Other, here grafting gender and racial differences onto the position of to-be-looked-at.

The literal process of Anthony's bodily "feminization" at the hands of Suzanne is a frequent subject for the narrative.[17] In one such exemplary

Designing Women: "lesbians in your sauna."

instance, Anthony has thrown his back out at the interior decorator living room and, because of a snag in his insurance policy, allows Suzanne to take him to her house. The narrative's chief scene is structured around Anthony lying helplessly in Suzanne's bed while she feeds and treats him like a living doll. He is an immobilized, passive, male body encased in or wrapped in silks and soft fabrics. Suzanne further sculpts his appearance through clothes, nails, skin treatments, and hair. This process identifies Anthony as the imperfect body that requires work, fixing, molding into an object—becoming feminized. By the end of the episode, Anthony's only recourse is infantile regression as he attempts to crawl away on all fours. *Designing Women* promotes comic pleasure in its reversal of class relations by showing a white upper-class Southern woman waiting on a black working-class man. It also reproduces racist relations by infantilizing the black man through feminine excess administered at the hands of the Southern belle.

In another episode, Suzanne convinces Anthony to portray her Afra-Caribbean maid Consuela for the immigration authorities. The narrative stalls during a lengthy scene in which Suzanne puts Anthony in a dress and wig, applies make-up to his face, and flourishes hair bows as his crown. The comedy centers on Suzanne's desire to feminize Anthony and Anthony's capacity to be a visual signifier of femininity. This scene reverses gendered power relations while maintaining class and racial ones. On the one hand, it may seem "refreshing" to see the realm of the femi-

Designing Women: Suzanne (Delta Burke) dresses Anthony (Meshach Taylor) in drag so that he can impersonate her maid.

nine so gender-confused or dispersed. On the other hand, one must also acknowledge how this process represses the Southern racist myth underlying the show, that black men pose a sexual threat to white women and thus to society generally. *Designing Women* does not confront the myth but instead effaces Anthony's capacity to pose male sexual desire at all.

In one exceptional episode, however (which bears striking similarities to Suzanne's confrontation of homophobia), Suzanne and Anthony confront the possibility of their desire for each other. In "The Bachelor Auction," Suzanne inadvertently wins a date with Anthony. After prolonged suspension of their goodnight at Suzanne's door through comic verbal play, Anthony steps toward Suzanne as if to kiss her. She steps back, and they both fall off the porch into a wet garden. The pratfall, the use of physical comedy, literally breaks the tension and displaces any sexual desire onto slapstick-styled camaraderie.

However, in the final scene back at the decorators' living room, a giggling Suzanne and Anthony go to an offscreen storage room. Mary Jo and Charlene are on-screen eavesdroppers to Suzanne's and Anthony's offscreen double entendres and innuendos about the removal and return of Anthony's (wet) clothing. Mary Jo's and Charlene's reaction shots stand in for the lost promise that the couple's sexual desire for each other would be expressed. Their mistaken assumption about Anthony's and Suzanne's sexual union provides an opportunity for a spectator to replace the lost kiss with a fetish.

Star and popular discourses beyond the text of the episodes themselves also exercise this relational axis between feminine and feminist. *Designing Women* became feminist through its reception and then compromised its feminist status through a series of public production disputes. *Designing Women* was initially broadcast for half a season on Monday, switched to Thursday, then was taken off the air. At this point, women's magazines claimed the show as a *feminist* sitcom, the brainchild of a female producer-creator, Linda Bloodworth Thomason (with her husband). As a result of such publicity and a massive letter-writing campaign spearheaded by the organization Viewers for Quality Television (50,000 letters), the network brought back the show.[18] Thus, both before and after some viewers directly encountered the program, it was known as a feminist sitcom because women's magazines had foregrounded it as feminist and because the activity of women's viewer resistance to get the show back on the air was deemed a feminist activity.

But, the show's feminist status became compromised in the 1990–91 season when significant publicity about troubled labor relations among the female stars and the show's producers disrupted *Designing Women*'s political cachet as a progressive feminist site. In supermarket tabloids, *TV Guide,* women's magazines, and in interviews with the stars on television talk shows, *Designing Women* became singularly famous for actress Delta Burke's public accusations and tearful confession on *The Barbara Walters Special* (itself a site of feminized expression) that the producers locked her in a room and verbally abused her, threatened to fire her if she did not lose weight, and imposed a series of disciplinary strictures on the actresses.[19] The cast publicly disagreed about making these problems public.[20] The show's troubled labor relations overwhelmed its fictional inscriptions of "feminism in the workplace" at Sugarbakers.

It is not coincidental then that much of the strife about *Designing Women*'s production became displaced onto a woman's body—that of actress Delta Burke. Stories about the show and the stars quickly shifted from discussions about employee-employer relations to the fetishization of her weight as both a site of feminine excess and a signifier that she was out of control and undisciplined. Burke was ultimately fired from *Designing Women* on June 7, 1991. An announcement of this "ending," however, ran alongside a story that Burke and her actor-husband Gerald McRaney would renew their wedding vows to prove that he still loved her despite her increased weight.[21]

However, her excessive femininity was revised a year later. One set of stories suggests that McRaney was the real villain and that Burke was the unwitting victim of a domineering husband who repeatedly interfered in her career and threatened her bosses. This narrative rewrites Delta in line with a feminine country-western character she was set to play on her new but short-lived show *Delta* (1992–93).[22] Another set of stories claims that Delta's mood swings, tears, and bizarre behavior during the production controversy were a consequence of her recent admission that she had been molested as a child.[23] In this scenario, Delta becomes a different kind of topically trendy, highly feminized victim-survivor. A last round of stories that circulated within the entertainment industry portray a different Delta Burke, still highly feminized but less a stereotype for a women's magazine audience than for Hollywood businessmen. In this scenario, Delta is an aggressive feminine shrew who attempts to wield power in a Hollywood club of male executives but is successfully blocked and checked by none other than presidential candidate Bill Clinton, a personal friend of the Thomasons. During his campaign, Clinton intervened with Sony (Sony owns Columbia Pictures Television, which owns *Designing Women*) on the Thomasons' behalf against Burke. Clinton convinced Sony executives to cut different deals with Burke and the Thomasons, since what was at stake was revenues for the entire Monday night line-up as well as lucrative syndication rights, prizes worth many millions of dollars to those involved.[24] In all these narratives, Burke was a signifier of feminine excess. But the term means different things to different people, and its very ambiguity became exploited in the press about *Designing Women*. Although Burke remained a kind of "placeholder" for this type, she shifted in different discourses, depending on the values attached to a mutual relationship between femininity and feminism. For Hollywood businessmen, she was portrayed as a wicked woman who had overstepped her place, whereas for audiences of women's magazines, she was either a feminist champion for the rights of fat women or a recovering victim.

The ways that *Designing Women*'s narratives—both inside and outside the episodes—name and organize feminist knowledge has important political implications. It may be possible to recover a pleasurable feminist reading here. But if it is made possible through the effacement of black subjectivity in a white racist culture and of lesbian subjectivity in a heterosexist culture, then we need to attend to how feminist pleasures are contained by the TV discourse that allows for and even encourages such slippages. Such slippages appear to be a structural element in the feminist sitcom. However, while *Designing Women* depends on a relationship between femininity and feminism to establish a definition of cultural and political feminism, *Murphy Brown* stages feminism differently.

From its beginning, *Murphy Brown* was promoted as the "feminist-minded" product of creator-producer Diane English and as a star vehicle for actress Candice Bergen. The advance publicity and critics' descriptions even before the show aired promised a new quality show with high production values, well-developed characters, and quick wit that would rival *The Mary Tyler Moore Show*.[25] It was placed in CBS's evening line-up of other already successful feminist sitcoms (including *Designing Women*) that were key to the network's fiscal health. Several months later, the show won Emmy nominations and three awards. By that time, *Murphy Brown* had achieved all the criteria associated with "quality" and an uncompromised status as a feminist product.

Murphy Brown's contribution to the feminist sitcom is that it demotes the feminine excess and feminist extreme between female characters to a secondary position or, as the show evolves, evacuates it altogether. Although the potential for such a contrast continues so long as the show maintains the characters of Murphy Brown and Corky Sherwood, it is invoked more infrequently as the sitcom achieves increasingly popular status. If, when the series began, the humor depended on making Corky the femininely excessive butt of Murphy's feminist barbs, this aspect of the series becomes softened once the characters achieve greater psychological depth as well as increased familiarity with viewers.

Even when narratives revolve around the relationship between feminine excess and feminist extremes, they tend to become parody. For example, an early episode features Corky and Murphy as investigative journalists going undercover as hookers. They are shown dressed in loud, tightly fitting clothes, four-inch heels, and wigs of very big hairdos—all markers of feminine excess. Former beauty queen Corky repeatedly gives Murphy advice about feminine costuming and behavior—how to walk,

Murphy Brown's *FYI* news team: Candice Bergen as Murphy Brown on the left.

Murphy Brown: Femininely excessive Corky Sherwood (Faith Ford), left, and Murphy Brown (Candice Bergen), right, as undercover "hookers."

how to arrange her clothes, how to carry her purse. Murphy uses the occasion to joke about feminine excess and to put on a parodic performance of the feminine. Throughout those parts of the episode in which they appear in these get-ups, Murphy self-reflexively makes fun of her masquerade while her coworkers watch her and Corky on a hidden camera. The occasion of her transferral to feminine excess as well as the feminized object of a male gaze becomes ironic, since the point is that she *cannot* act the feminine and, unlike the women of *Designing Women*, cannot be transferred from feminist to feminine extreme. In another example, when Murphy's producer encourages her to appear on a *Sesame Street*–like program in order to soften her tough guy public image with a softer, more feminine, even maternal one, she argues heatedly with a "muppet" and spontaneously rips off its head on national TV. The central humor of *Murphy Brown* depends on Murphy's *in*ability to become excessively feminine as it stages the performance of this inability through a voyeuristic frame of the television screen as a mise-en-abyme (we watch *Murphy Brown*, which internally shows Murphy on a TV set that is also watched within the diegesis).

What *Murphy Brown* does depends on, instead, is an oscillation between the political left and right. *Murphy Brown* may not depend on movements between femininity and feminism for its chief humorous trajectory, although it maintains them as structural oppositions. But movements may frequently transfer Murphy from spokeswoman for liberal left political positions to acting in sympathy or agreeing with conservative positions. Her character embodies these tensions in her extreme individualism. For example, when Murphy thinks her cooperative family of coworkers are each negotiating contracts with rival network news shows, she spurs a competition in which they try to outdo each other for more prestigious career options and thus threatens to dissolve their workplace family. Although she is happily part of a cooperative news team, she is fiercely competitive throughout the series and so aggressively individualistic that the character's personal dynamics may be ambiguously representative of both Democratic sensibilities about collective action as well as Republican beliefs in rugged individualism.

Murphy's shifting position in relation to left and right is best represented in the episodes that lead up to her pregnancy in the latter half of the 1991–92 season. The program adds the character of Jerry Gold (Jay Thomas), a right-wing talk-show host who seemingly opposes Murphy's political beliefs and values. Despite their differences, the two become romantically involved. Their affair lasts through several episodes in which the unlikelihood of their mutual attraction is the subject for both plot lines and jokes about left and right positions on political and cultural topics. Although Murphy is never completely transformed into a conservative Republican, she (like Suzanne Sugarbaker's exceptional moments on *Designing Women*) may articulate jokes that are critical of Democratic party politics, since what she and Jerry Gold have in common is sharp-witted humor and the ability to laugh at themselves. Plots allow occasions for each of them to look equally foolish but also to be the first to deflate his or her own self-importance. In these episodes, Jerry and Murphy are only superficially representatives of the right and left, respectively, since they are more deeply cultural critics or satirists who both use humor to unmask the pretensions of the entire political spectrum.

Jerry's and Murphy's commonalities are underscored by the appearance at the end of the 1991–92 season of Murphy's former husband, a radical leftist guerrilla who travels around the world participating in various unnamed military causes. The predictable love triangle that ensues is slanted by the humorlessness of Murphy's "ex," in sharp contrast to Murphy and Jerry, who get all the punch lines. In a sitcom, characters are only as attractive as their capacity for generating humor. In a scene in which Murphy's ex-husband decorates her living room with hundreds of candles, hires a violinist, and proposes marriage to her while he is handsomely attired in a tuxedo, Jerry Gold appears wearing a penguin suit. Both a visual pun and parody of each other, the two flap around the living room.

The scene, in fact, pits extremes of feminine and feminist heterosexual romantic fantasy against each other in unexpected ways. It is the leftist who represents the romantic Tradition—candles, wine, violin music, romance with a dark handsome stranger, assertions of complete devotion, and a marriage proposal—and the rightist who represents a more feminist-styled courtship reminiscent of screwball comedy: independence, humor, the verbal sparring of equals, the unexpected, and commitment only to a monogamous two-career relationship. The most sustained and explicit reference in the series to Murphy's "sleeping around" establishes and confuses paternity, making fatherhood available to Murphy as either feminine or feminist choice. She chooses Eldin, the meta–house husband, as both her Lamaze coach and child-rearing partner. The fact that the former husband, who is revealed to be the biological father, subsequently drops out of the show, whereas Jerry Gold reappears occasionally the following season, allows for no future legal claims or parental struggle over the baby. Thus, Murphy's personal actions are not linked to problems that women face as a social class but are simply the catalysts for a series of lifestyle choices. She can choose either Corky's dream or her own.

Although this individual scene, representative of the show's narrative premises, may rewrite gender roles in important ways for the 1990s, it also unquestioningly defines Murphy as a postfeminist New Woman for whom "choice" and heterosexuality are both assumed. In fact, the real importance of this scenario may be its exposure of the limits of Murphy's feminism. She may be promiscuous and unsure about which man is the father of her unborn child, but she is most assuredly heterosexual. Thus, her assertiveness, independence, brassiness, and "smart mouth," as well as her tailored and even sometimes androgynous wardrobe, may suggest her capacity as a lesbian or figure for lesbian identification while references to her active, ongoing heterosexual life and desire undercut such signifiers.

Murphy Brown, furthermore, covers its simple left-right, feminine and feminist binary oppositions with its humorous wit about topics of political and cultural currency. *Murphy Brown* is not the first feminist sitcom to thread topical relevancy into its narratives and comedy. When Maude had an abortion (*Maude*) in the mid-1970s, it drew an unprecedented avalanche of publicity and viewer mail for featuring a controversial *political* topic on a situation comedy. *Designing Women* featured its women watching Anita Hill's testimony before Congress and then acting out their responses to it while costumed in character as Bette Davis and Joan Crawford in *Whatever Happened to Baby Jane.* This spectacle was excessive even for a show that specializes in feminine excess. But, *Murphy Brown regularly* capitalizes on slippages between the world of the fiction and the world of the show's viewers. It so frequently confuses fact and fiction that it disrupts the boundaries of representation itself.

Murphy Brown refers to her journalistic colleagues by naming real-life women TV journalists. Indeed, several have appeared on the show (e.g., Linda Ellerbee, Connie Chung, Paula Zahn, Kathleen Sullivan), thus conflating their world of journalism with the fictional world of journalism on the show. In an even stranger mise-en-abyme episode, a Hollywood actress (Morgan Fairchild) comes to visit Murphy's *FYI* show, since she is developing a situation comedy based on Murphy's "real life" as a female network news reporter. Later, after Murphy has flown to Hollywood to make a guest cameo appearance on the sitcom, Connie Chung appears at Murphy's newsroom in a staged duplication of Murphy's Hollywood newsroom appearance to tell Murphy that *she* would never compromise her credentials as a serious journalist by appearing on a TV sitcom.

Through this aggressive mix of the real and the fictitious, the program's feminist statements transcend the realm of fiction and thereby achieve a credibility that makes them dangerous. The best demonstration of this occurred, in fact, in *Murphy Brown*'s season premiere, following the summer-long debate about family values in which the character Murphy Brown offers a retort to Vice President Quayle. In a highly publicized and heavily watched episode, the characters and the audience saw actual TV news broadcasts of Dan Quayle discussing Murphy Brown. *FYI* characters mixed both fictional and real newspapers with headlines about Murphy Brown.[26] Indeed, the *New York Daily News* banner headline: "Quayle to Murphy Brown: You Tramp!" is funnier than any of the fictional ones brought in.[27] Even the prestigious *New York Times* ran a front-page photograph of Candice Bergen as Murphy Brown.[28]

But whereas Quayle landed Murphy in the real world, the show acted as if the debate had taken place entirely within the sitcom world. Murphy's response to Quayle occurred within the format of her show within the show. At the end of the episode, Murphy sits on the *FYI* set and does a news report on "the American family and family values" as a direct response to Quayle's attacks on single motherhood.

In a moment that blurs the representational boundaries between fiction and documentary, the television monitor that frames Murphy's response as "on TV" becomes invisible. As the camera tightens to a close-up of what is on the TV screen, Murphy's direct address to the *FYI* viewers fills the entirety of our TV screens as well. Her speech becomes one of direct address to at-home viewers: "In searching for the causes to our social ills, we could blame the media, or the Congress, or an administration that has been in power for twelve years. Or, we could blame me." This *FYI* report is now occluded with *Murphy Brown* itself and ends with Murphy's introduction of several nontraditional families gathered on the set of *FYI*. The screen goes black, and *Murphy Brown*'s closing credits scroll through a list of the families and thank them for appearing on the show. In other words, they are not Hollywood actors playing nontraditional families. The conventions of closing credits signify that they are *real* families joining a fictional show for the purpose of making a *real* statement.

An even more surprising mise-en-abyme follows the broadcast. In cities across the country, the airing of the episode is reported as hard news on late-evening local broadcasts. In Boston, news anchor Liz Walker reported the story as news and then concluded by asking, "Fact or fiction?" to which her coanchor responded, "Hard to tell." If that weren't confounding enough, Liz Walker is a black unwed mother on whom the Murphy Brown story line is said to be based. Walker almost lost her job in 1987 when she became pregnant.[29]

Murphy's pregnancy and the birth of her son is only available as a topic for humor in the wake of several female newscasters like Walker who have had highly publicized pregnancies or reproductive agendas: Connie Chung's publicly discussed attempts to get pregnant appear to have diminished her credibility as a serious journalist among her peers; Meredith Vereira lost her post on *60 Minutes* when she became pregnant. Walker, Chung, and Vereira are real-life women who work in a field where female journalists are still expected to be attractive, young, and svelte, and to conform to conservative values. Walker's experience makes this all too clear. Their bodies are measured in terms of sexual desire, and their trials with their employers, colleagues, and the public were not due to poor job performance but to attempts to transgress the boundaries of acceptable behavior for women marked as public figures. Yet, in the media blitz that followed Quayle's initial sally, this was all but forgotten. No one talked about the actual struggles of working women journalists and the most famous real cases, or about the fact that the most publicized real cases all involved women of color.

The debate also foreclosed the consideration of single parenthood in terms of class, race, or even sexual orientation. There was little discussion about the degree to which popular culture, in fact, has conformed exactly to Dan Quayle's agenda by encouraging and urging all women to want and to bear children—neither to consider abortion when facing an unwanted pregnancy, nor to choose not to reproduce in a culture that apparently meets women's full participation in the public sphere with biological imperatives. An obsession with women reproducing and mothering saturates American ideology, from its heavy inflection in coverage of the Persian Gulf War (the first war in which women participated as soldiers) to the vilification of crack mothers as the ultimate monsters of our society.[30] Succeeding Murphy Brown's pregnancy in the opening weeks of the 1993–94 and 1994–95 fall television seasons, most highly rated network family sitcoms carried story lines about their leading heroines either wanting to get pregnant or cheerfully discovering that they were pregnant (e.g., *Home Improvement, Roseanne, Coach, Evening Shade,*

Hearts Afire, Designing Women, Cheers, Step by Step). As *Newsweek* columnist Eleanor Clift has pointed out, "The irony is that one area where TV espouses unmistakably conservative values is the very one that Quayle chose to focus on: the family. . . . If TV has any prevailing sin, it is sunny romanticizing of that bond: no matter what the conflicts or crises, family love makes everything come out all right. If Dan Quayle were to look at TV a little more closely, he might find in it the stuff of Republican dreams."[31]

What is at stake here is that women continue to be defined in relationship to reproduction. When the *real* consequences are no less than the State's evolving role in all women's lives, it may seem absurd to reduce the battle to one over a fictional prime-time television comedy. But television's representation of feminism is a central, crucial means by which feminism is framed for the public. Although *Murphy Brown* may be flying along the limits of what can be represented about feminism in the mass media of the 1990s, it pushes the envelope of liberal feminism without ever exploding it. Quayle's attack on *Murphy Brown* may have galvanized both those who wish to maintain and control women's dependency on conservative reproductive agendas and those on the left who would mobilize cultural criticism against conservatives like Quayle. But the real lesson of the Quayle-instigated "family values" debate is that television feminism remains undergirded by a discourse of individualism, a strategy that provides the ultimate ideological safety net for the down-to-earth management of social change.[32]

Notes

1 Dan Quayle, quoted in John E. Yang and Ann Devroy, "Quayle: 'Hollywood Doesn't Get It,'" *Washington Post*, 21 May 1992, A17. With this speech, Quayle fired the first round in what became a summer-long crusade for "family values" as a fixture of the Republican Party's presidential campaign in the summer of 1992 before the Republican Party's national convention.

2 Even when sitcoms have occasionally offered unwed pregnancies, as did *The Days and Nights of Molly Dodd*'s (NBC, 1987–88; Lifetime, 1989–91) less well-known pregnancy one year earlier (because it played to a smaller audience on the cable channel Lifetime), Murphy's pregnancy did not veer from comedy into the vagaries of melodrama, as Molly's did. Like Murphy, unwed Molly got pregnant, delivered a child, and did not initially know which of two lovers was the father. However, the implications of being a white, unwed

mother in love with the African American policeman who turned out to be the father and parenting a biracial baby—whether for comedic or melodramatic purposes—never occurred, since one of the last episodes killed off the lover-turned-fiancé, and the show's demise soon after that relegated Molly and her baby to oblivion.

3 Douglas Jehl, "Quayle Deplores Eroding Values; Cites TV Show," *Los Angeles Times*, 20 May 1992, A1.

4 For further discussion of the economic and institutional data, see Julie D'Acci, *Defining Women: Television and the Case of Cagney and Lacey* (Chapel Hill: University of North Carolina Press, 1994), 63–75.

5 See Todd Gitlin, *Inside Prime Time* (New York: Pantheon, 1985), 203–20.

6 "Progress in Prime Time: TV Says Bye-Bye to Bimbos," *Glamour* 84 (July 1986): 40.

7 See Serafina Bathrick, "*The Mary Tyler Moore Show:* Women at Home and at Work," in *MTM: "Quality Television,"* ed. Jane Feuer, Paul Kerr, and Tise Vahimagi (London: British Film Institute, 1984), 99–131.

8 *Phyllis* (CBS, 1975–77), *One Day at a Time* (CBS, 1975–84), *Alice* (CBS, 1976–85), *I'm a Big Girl Now* (ABC, 1980–81), *Love, Sidney* (NBC, 1981–83), *The Two of Us* (CBS, 1981–82), *Gloria* (CBS, 1982–83), *Goodnight, Beantown* (CBS, 1983–84), and *It's Your Move* (NBC, 1984–85).

9 For an extended analysis of this phenomenon, see Lauren Rabinovitz, "Sitcoms and Single Moms: Representations of Feminism on American TV," *Cinema Journal* 29, no. 1 (fall 1989): 3–19.

10 As Judith Mayne has pointed out in her discussion of *L.A. Law,* what is at stake is *not* the *authenticity* of television's representation of feminism but rather the way that television as a mass cultural form appropriates a politically informed practice of cultural critique (Mayne, "*L.A. Law* and Prime-Time Feminism," *Discourse* 10, no. 2 [spring–summer 1988]: 30).

11 Both Robert H. Deming and Lauren Rabinovitz have analyzed this program as a feminist sitcom: Robert H. Deming, "'*Kate & Allie*': 'New' Women and the Audience's Televisual Archives," in *Private Screenings: Television and the Female Consumer,* ed. Lynn Spigel and Denise Mann (Minneapolis: University of Minnesota Press, 1992), 203–16; Rabinovitz, "Sitcoms and Single Moms," 3–19.

12 Elizabeth Sporkin, "Odd Woman Out," *People Weekly* 36, no. 3 (29 July 1991): 47.

13 This practice is more widespread than in feminist sitcoms. Throughout the history of television, other sitcoms have relied on such characters. Particularly interesting examples of earlier stereotypes include Sue Ann Nivens (Betty White) in *The Mary Tyler Moore Show;* Hot Lips Houlihan (Loretta

Swit) in *M.A.S.H.* (CBS, 1972–83), although her character becomes less excessive as the series evolves; and receptionist Jennifer Marlowe (Loni Anderson) in *WKRP in Cincinnati* (CBS, 1978–82). Before sitcoms featured regular characters as excessively feminine, comic sketches on variety shows frequently relied on the timely appearance of such a character for laughs, a comic stereotype that can be traced back to vaudeville.

14 See, especially, Mary Ann Doane, "Film and the Masquerade: Theorising the Female Spectator," *Screen* 23, nos. 3–4 (September–October 1982): 74–87.

15 Identification with Suzanne became even more complicated through the star discourses circulating outside the text and intertwined with it. For example, Delta Burke stated in a women's magazine interview that acting as Suzanne in an episode ("They Shoot Fat Women, Don't They?") that forced Suzanne to confront her weight gain and measure of self-worth helped her, Delta Burke, deal with her own feelings of feminine inadequacy because of her physical appearance and her inability to conform to Hollywood ideals of femininity and glamour. In this instance, Burke articulates the way that "being" Suzanne becomes a feminist therapeutic agent for her own self-recovery, and she implies that identification with both Suzanne's catharsis and her star embodiment of this psychological self-awareness provide feminist models for women (Vernon Scott, "Delta Burke: Learning To Be Happy the Way I Am . . ." *Good Housekeeping* 210 [May 1990]: 165–67). For further discussion of images of fat women on contemporary television, see Jane Feuer's essay in this volume.

16 My interpretation of this scene disagrees with Alexander Doty's critical response to the same episode, which he sees as a positive moment in *Designing Women*'s ongoing lesbian dynamics, a content he attributes to "the chemistry between the women characters/actors [as] ultimately more important to maintaining the lesbian dynamics . . . than is the presence or absence of (straight) men." He credits *Designing Women*'s "indifferent treatment of men and 'compulsory heterosexuality' [for making] it clear that the narrative fact of straight romance and marriage does not necessarily heterosexualize lesbian sitcoms." In this regard, his conclusions depend entirely on a straightforward, albeit politically identified, content analysis of the show's plots without regard to visual semiotics, comic codes and performance, or star discourse (Doty, *Making Things Perfectly Queer: Interpreting Mass Culture* [Minneapolis: University of Minnesota Press, 1993], 41–43, 57–61).

17 Anthony's regular feminization is not a matter of his becoming a drag queen or of posing as an erotic object. He is most often transformed into a grotesque.

18 For example, see Heidi Yorkshire, "Those Remarkable Designing Women," *McCall's* 115, no. 2 (November 1987): 79, 82; Cathleen Schine, "Don't Weep

for Me, CBS," *Vogue* 177, 3 (March 1987): 144; Fred Bernstein, "Pulling Itself Out of the Ratings Waste Heap, *Designing Women* Becomes TV's Trashy New Smash," *People Weekly* 27, 16 (20 April 1987): 63–64. For a discussion of an analogous situation regarding CBS's *Cagney and Lacey* in which a massive campaign to "save" a television show was orchestrated as a feminist activity, see D'Acci, *Defining Women*, 75–104.

19 A small sampling of the wide-ranging coverage of this situation would include Tracy Young, "What Happens When an Actress Outgrows Her Series?" *Vogue* 181 (March 1991): 284–85; Susan Littwin, "Behind *Designing Women*'s Family Feud," *TV Guide* 38, 50 (15 December 1990): 9–10; Elizabeth Sporkin, "Odd Woman Out," *People Weekly* 36 (29 July 1991): 46–50; Vernon Scott, "Life with Delta," *Good Housekeeping* 212 (June 1991): 58–62.

20 After Burke's accusations, Dixie Carter (Julia Sugarbaker) issued a press release backing the producers. But, in a fall 1990 Joan Rivers talk show, she refused to discuss publicly the situation on the set. Then she reversed herself and gave an interview to *TV Guide* (Susan Littwin, "Not Just Whistlin' Dixie," *TV Guide* 38, 50 [15 December 1990]: 4–9).

21 Susan Littwin, "After Two Years of Marriage Delta Reties the Knot with Her Major Dad," *TV Guide* 39 (22 June 1991): 58–61.

22 Mary Murphy and Frank Swertlow, "Delta Redesigned," *TV Guide* 40 (4 July 1992): 10–16.

23 Jeff Rovin, "Dissing with Delta," *Ladies Home Journal* 109 (September 1992): 166–69; Tom Gliatto, "A New Delta Dawns," *People Weekly* 37 (16 March 1992): 34–35.

24 Murphy and Swertlow, "Delta Redesigned," 12.

25 For early reviews of *Murphy Brown*, see Charla Krupp, "*Murphy Brown*," *Glamour* 86 (November 1988): 184; Jeff Jarvis, "*Murphy Brown*," *People Weekly* 30 (14 November 1988): 19; John Leonard, "*Murphy Brown*," *New York* 21 (14 November 1988).

26 This episode of *Murphy Brown* was watched by 44 million viewers, beating out both ABC's *Monday Night Football* game (23 million) and a made-for-television movie on the British royal family on NBC (18 million).

27 The *New York Daily News* headline was cited in "Dan Quayle vs. Murphy Brown," *Time* 139 (1 June 1992): 20.

28 *New York Times* (May 1991), A1.

29 Rebecca L. Walkowitz, "Reproducing Reality: Murphy and Illegitimate Politics," *Media Spectacles*, ed. Marjorie Garber, Jann Matlock, and Rebecca L. Walkowitz (New York: Routledge, 1993), 51.

30 See, for example, the following on the vilification of crack mothers: Jimmie L. Reeves and Richard Campbell, *Cracked Coverage: Television News, the Anti-*

Cocaine Crusade, and the Reagan Legacy (Durham, N.C.: Duke University Press, 1994); Jean Bethke, "Pregnancy Police," *The Progressive* 54 (December 1990): 26–28; Jan Hoffman, "Pregnant, addicted—and guilty?" *New York Times Magazine* (19 August 1990): 32–35 ff. On motherhood and the Persian Gulf War, see Susan Jeffords and Lauren Rabinovitz, eds., *Seeing Through the Media: The Persian Gulf War* (New Brunswick, N.J.: Rutgers University Press, 1994).

31 Eleanor Clift, "The Murphy Brown Policy," *Newsweek* 119 (1 June 1992): 47.

32 I am indebted to Jane Desmond for framing this conclusion in her commentary on an abridged version of this essay ("The Pregnant Pause of 1992: *Murphy Brown* and the Family Values Debate," paper presented at the panel "Ms.-Representations: How U.S. Television Defines Feminism," American Studies Association, Pittsburgh, Pa., 10 November 1995).

The Oprahification of America

Talk Shows and the Public Sphere

Jane M. Shattuc

> Today I am sitting between two people who have never been this close face to face since one very unforgettable night two years ago. Debbie says that the man sitting across from her locked her in a closed room, held a gun to her, and violently raped her. Jawah says Debbie is lying.
>
> Oprah Winfrey, *The Oprah Winfrey Show,* May 3, 1994

Are daytime TV talk shows simply sensational commercialism, or could they be a new form of political debate? Oprah Winfrey's visceral description from her May 3, 1994, show seemingly relegates the social issues involved in rape to the realm of cheap thrills. But on another level, the program's dramatic and individualized account allows ordinary citizens—in the studio and at home—to enter into a debate about sexual power in their everyday lives, a rare moment on network television.

Traditionally, democratic thought assumes that there must be an independent public arena where political opinion can be formed freely. The arena should be entirely free of the taint of government control as well as that of corporate capitalism. For many Americans, the town meeting is the ideal of participatory democracy: the citizen takes part in the politics of the local community by standing up and speaking up. But such direct communication is becoming less tenable in the age of information technology and global communication.

If TV has become the central communicator of information in late capitalist America, no other public forum replicates the town meeting's democratic sensibility better than the first generation of daytime TV talk shows born in the 1970s and 1980s: *The Oprah Winfrey Show, Sally Jesse Raphael, Donahue,* and even *Geraldo.*[1] Here, "average" Americans debate important, albeit sensationalized, issues that are central to their political lives: racism, sexuality, welfare rights, and religious freedom. Would Jürgen Habermas have included the American talk show as part of the public sphere when he defined the latter as "the realm of our social life in which something approaching public opinion can be formed. . . . A portion of the public sphere comes into being in every conversation in which private individuals assemble to form a public body"?[2] The answer depends on whose definition of politics one invokes.

The concept of the public sphere—the place where public opinion can be formed—looms over all analyses of talk shows. From "The Talk Show Report" in *Ladies Home Journal* to think pieces about tabloid culture in the *New York Times* to a Marxist collective analysis of the genre in *Social Text* to an article on talk and female empowerment in *Genders*, our culture is hyperconscious that daytime TV talk shows are involved in the political arena.[3] They are a rare breed: highly popular programs that depend on social topics and participation from average citizens. However, there is a fear that the programs may be trivializing "real" politics by promoting irrational, victimized, and anomalous individuals as representative of the citizenry. The print press often has pejoratively alluded to the "Oprahification" of America. Yet the popularity of the shows continually begs two questions: Can the content of talk shows be defined as "political"? And, more important, can the shows—the children of corporate media interests—be considered public arenas where the "people" form opinion freely?

Even though the women's movement has shown that politics in the late twentieth century includes the personal, American culture still is uncomfortable with describing the content of daytime talk shows as political. The term *political* is derived from the Latin *politicus*, which means relating to a citizen.[4] A citizen is defined by her or his allegiance to a state, which in return offers protection to the citizen. Obviously, the shows, with their dependence on spectacle, individualism, and sensation, deviate radically from the traditional political discussions about social policy that define citizenship—such as Oxford debates, congressional deliberations, union hall meetings, and even network news, which all emphasize established political institutions. Although the practice of debate has shifted from the Aristotelian model of speaker and listener to the coordinated discussion, the shows are more personal and emotional in content and vertiginous in structure, breaking with traditional structures in political discussion.

Here, American politics moves from the "analytical is political" tradition to "the personal as political" in the latter half of the century.[5]

No other TV genre—not news, prime-time drama, or soap opera—generates more ongoing social controversy than daytime talk shows. Beyond the headline-grabbing *Jenny Jones* murder or Winfrey's cocaine confession, the shows provoke endless debates about everyday experience.[6] Not only does viewer give-and-take occur as part of the shows, but discussions continue on the news, in the workplace, and at home: the popularization of current political, social, and theoretical topics. The shows raise questions about fact versus fiction as the audience tests the credibility of the stories presented. (In the common vernacular: "Are those people for real?") They test the demarcation between entertainment and news, as they mix political issues and personal drama. Finally, the programs use ordinary people to stage social issues that are infrequently discussed elsewhere on television: homosexuality, familial conflict, sexual relations, and racial divisions. As the events of the 1990s bring into the political arena an angry African American underclass, gay activists, and working women, might the *Oprah* audience be the newest incarnation of the public sphere?

Even though Habermas concedes that, historically, the public sphere has been more an ideal than a fact, the concept still influences the assumptions of capitalist democracy. Hopes of a public sphere are evoked whenever a writer bemoans the passing of considered discussion of current events where the commercial pressures for "entertainment" have destroyed objectivity and truth. The *New York Times* represents this stance as the principal defender of "real" news when John J. O'Connor, the paper's TV critic, warns against "trash TV" and talk show sensation:

> There's a battle being waged in television these days and broadly speaking, it's taking place along "us versus them" cultural lines. Depending on your vantage point, the results so far could be interpreted as either democracy taking the offensive or the barbarians . . . are in the business of inventing emotional "wallops," and are openly contemptuous of what they like to refer to as "pointy-headed" journalists, meaning for the most part the college-educated kind that works in non-tabloid print.[7]

Here a newspaperman who writes about television for a traditional news medium suppresses questions about the objectivity in news reporting in favor of charges that tabloid or talk shows are manipulative or promote what another *New York Times* reporter calls "the new kind of dumbness."[8] This nostalgia for the loss for the bourgeois public sphere is deeply intertwined with a kind of politics in which clear categories of power are maintained: a class, culture, and gender hierarchy based on the centrality of the educated white bourgeois male.[9] Not surprisingly, Phil Donahue is often nominated by the written press as the most "responsible" or "trusted" of hosts.[10]

The talk show industry self-consciously trades on the concept of "the people speaking." But when cultural studies critics speak of it as "an active audience," other critics have decried the concept as a "naive, unattainable ideal."[11] Within this pessimistic perspective, the problem of active viewers is twofold. Under a veneer of participation the talk show audience is a passive mass led by commercial interests and self-promoting hosts. The active audience of the shows can also be a forum for social control when the audience taunts, shouts down, and demands conformity of the "guest deviants."

Nevertheless, the feminist movement has launched a thoroughgoing critique of the public sphere and the dichotomy of a serious/trivial split that underpins the discussion about daytime talk shows.[12] From a feminist point of view, the problem lies in the fact that the public sphere is contrasted to the private sphere and therefore produces a not-so-subtle division between masculine and feminine realms: men participate in the serious realm of politics and rational debate; women govern the realm of the domestic arena and emotionalism.[13]

As a result, many feminists have come to champion talk shows as a new public sphere or counter–public sphere. Talk shows not only promote conversation and debate, they break down the distance between the audience and the stage. They do not depend on the power of expertise or bourgeois education. They elicit common sense and everyday experience as the mark of truth. They confound the distinction between the public and the private. Talk shows are about average women as citizens talking about and debating issues and experience.

One of the more politically creative discussions about daytime talk shows as this new counter–public sphere is "Chatter in the Age of Electronic Reproduction: Talk, Television, and the 'Public Mind.'" Authors Paolo Carpignano, Robin Andersen, Stanley Aronowitz, and William Difazio champion the shows for breaking down the clear lines between truth and fiction. The shows reveal that public debate is "no longer civilized nor following the dictates of general interest."[14] They are created to produce controversy and are repetitious, inconclusive, and fragmentary. But because they refuse to speak a simple truth, they reveal the subjective nature of politics.

What is important is that programs such as a *Morton Downey* show on the student massacre at Tiananmen Square allow an expert from the conservative Heritage Foundation to be shouted down by an anarchist squatter group. Carpignano et al. argue that *Downey* provides "a forum for the disenfranchised, especially young white men (working and lower middle class) who are not represented in the current knowledge-based commodity culture."[15] Ultimately, even *Downey* is the child of the women's movement, not only because feminism changed the American "political agenda" but because it challenged the relationship between the public and the private. The authors label the change, the "politicization of the private," which allows even lower-class white men the forum of their experience from which to speak.[16]

Gloria-Jean Masciarotte refines Carpignano's argument about the populism of talk shows and calls for division between programs influenced by the public sphere tradition and the feminist movement. She sees *Donahue* as more closely aligned with traditional politics, whereas *Oprah* promotes "the politics of identity and voice."[17] For her, the latter is based in a "citizen strategy" in which the stories of experience resist simple conclusions and answers.[18] *Donahue* depends on a much more classical debate format that works toward an undifferentiated sense of "the social good" and a belief in "answers," a format that effaces the complexity and hierarchical nature of politics in America.

However, Lisa McLaughlin criticizes the idea that daytime talk shows are a "counter–public sphere." Her analysis of a *Donahue* program on safe-sex prostitution reveals the limits of talk's liberal ideology; it rejects radical structural change and desires to work within existing structures."[19] She describes how *Donahue* sets up controversy through guest choice. The program establishes a binary opposition between several seductively clad prostitutes and Helen, a woman who has repeatedly written *Donahue* to complain that talk shows glorify prostitution. With the announced purpose of giving representation to the silent women in the audience who never voice their displeasure with prostitution, the program allows Helen to lash out at the prostitutes. The (not-so-silent) audience joins in on the vituperation, turning the program into a morality play. McLaughlin concludes that the confrontational style of talk shows leads to "resistive binaries such as male/female, madonnas/whores, good/bad—and having limited the terms of the debate to the acceptability of lifestyles and sexual practices."[20]

Of course, the daytime talk shows are not simply progressive or regressive. They do not represent the death of the public sphere. Although they do not discuss specific governmental institutions, they are clear debates about the public sphere's growing intercession into the family, the home, and the regulation of the individual's body. Further, the genre most explicitly enters the public-sphere debate through its gesture toward participatory democracy with its town meeting structure. Finally, the program maintains the structure of the social debate by always placing the private issue within a social matrix. As a result, the talk show participates in a debate arena comparable to Habermas's public sphere. However, the evidence of social injustice has shifted from rational and distant forms to an intersection that collapses personal experience, physical evidence, and emotion.

To begin with, *Oprah* does challenge the supposed objectivity of traditional patriarchal power. The host—a big, black woman—undercuts the authority of the talk show debate format with her self-confessional style; she routinely admits her early sexual and drug abuse and a chronic struggle with weight loss. Her program also represents a potentially radical public sphere that privileges process over a single truth or closure.

Yet the structure of an *Oprah* program is typical of most daytime talk shows: problem/solution. Most often, the problem is introduced as a personal problem (for example, obesity, HIV positive, a bisexual spouse), but then is generalized to a larger social issue. For instance, an April 15, 1994, program on mothers who want to give up their violent children was generalized by Winfrey as "what really makes a child act this way." Either by taking the opposite side or by teasing out the other view, Winfrey questions the guest to flesh out the problem. The ubiquitous guest labels or

"I.D.s" (in production parlance) underline the social representativeness of the guests; for example, one is a "mother who wants to give away a violent child," another is a "convicted woman who plotted her husband's death." The labeling offers a popularized version of the logic of identity politics, which attempts to break down the hegemonic notion of homogeneity or that "we all are one." Yet not all social divisions are represented; talk shows favor gender, sexual preference, familial, and criminal labels. Race and class remain structuring absences. The audience intuits these categories through the guest's appearance, words, and actions.

After establishing the guest's problem and social representativeness, Winfrey directs the debate through her selection of questioners and specifically through the rhetorical use of the pronouns *you, I,* and *we*. She invokes the audience as a larger social collectivity: "I am sure what mothers out there are thinking"; or "When I first heard about this, like everybody, I wondered what the big deal is"; or (my favorite, because it's Winfrey at her most self-aggrandizing) "The question we all have, I am speaking for the audience here and the audience around the world listening to you." As these quotations reveal, Winfrey engages an audience that actively thinks and adjudicates. It is also important that she positions herself with the audience as one of many outside observers/judges who have a social/personal stake in the issue.

Even though the host changes alignment from being sole authority to being a member of the audience, her/his authority is never relinquished. What many observers celebrate as Winfrey's debunking of her authority —she will even sit in the audience—also can be seen as a subtle move that allows her to orchestrate a collective response from the audience. When Wendy Kaminer in *I'm Dysfunctional, You're Dysfunctional* laments about her experience on *Oprah:* "If all issues are personalized, we lose our capacity to entertain ideas, to generalize from our own or someone else's experiences, to think abstractly," she has missed the point.[21] Such shows continually move from personal identification to larger group identification in order to be popular as a broad commercial medium. The host generalizes the particular experience into a larger social frame to capture the interest of a large audience. For all their individualized narratives, the shows speak in social generalities. They just do not speak about or advocate changing specific social and political institutions.

As much as daytime talk show audiences are purveyed as a representative random sample of American women, they are not democratic entities.[22] First, some programs selectively hand out tickets to the show in order to get a particular type of audience. *Donahue*'s NBC pages seek out middle-class well-dressed women tourists on the streets of New York. *Donahue* wants articulate guests. Often the show audience coordinators call and invite people who have a personal stake in the issue. Guests move from being representatives of social organizations or victims of a similar situation to part of the microcosm of the studio audience, which itself is society.

Therefore, the program creates a flow between stage guests, audience guests, and the audience members that empowers the authority of the audience. So, for example, on an *Oprah* program about violence in schools (April 7, 1994), the audience was dominated by angry schoolteachers. On a show about HIV on February 17, 1994, 60 percent of the audience were HIV positive. A debate about the morality of homosexuality or certain sexual practices did not take place on the latter program, because HIV-positive people were normalized as the majority of the microcosm. Hence, the guests and the studio audience were already united in their acceptance of homosexuality.

To a large degree, the construction of the studio audience results from the identity-politics movement. Identity politics has institutionalized around organizations that represent particular political affiliations. Talk show producers book a guest based on the perception that she or he is on a representative "problem." They call on such organizations as ACT-UP, the National Organization of Women, various battered women's shelters, and the National Association for the Advancement of Colored People in order to line up experts, guests, or audience members for the issue at hand. For example, for a program on nonsafe sex, *Geraldo* worked closely with New York gay rights organizations not only to get guests but to produce a program that would not stereotype gays. It is advantageous for these organizations to stack the audience and therefore the debate, allowing the gay or the black male the rare opportunity to have a majority experience. Nevertheless, the program encourages nonmembers or average members to speak if they disagree. Or as one *Donahue* producer suggested to her studio audience: "We like emotion and controversy."

For all its aura of combativeness, *The Oprah Winfrey Show,* like *Donahue,* usually stacks the debate, thus allowing for a subtle form of closure based on a selected majority rule. The monitoring of questions allows the host to serve a clear gatekeeping function. So, on an *Oprah* program on March 8, 1994, on why girls fall behind in high school, audience questioners were overwhelmingly women teachers and female students who had experienced sexism. Only two of twelve speakers registered any resistance to the premise that sexism was a problem for teenage girls.

In fact, most *Oprah* programs end with solutions offered by the experts and underlined by a pithy remark by Winfrey and/or an audience member. Admittedly, some programs, such as the problem-child program on April 15, 1994, do not end in a resolution/solution. The debate continued over the credits. Such inconclusiveness is a rarity instead of the norm. As *Geraldo*'s executive producer, Martin Berman states: "I will never remove the experts. They give perspective to the program."[23]

For all the dominance of traditional authority, the audience of the talk show does form a critique of the traditional methods of arriving at knowledge or truth through their demand for the test of lived experience. Classical notions of evidence would exclude the personal as subjective and not representative. *The Oprah Winfrey Show* turns around the tradition of rational distance by offering spontaneous and raw evidence. A single program on Prozac (April 14, 1994) is representative of the tension between expertise and experience. The program presents numerous Prozac-taking citizens of Wenatchee, Washington, and their psychologist through direct satellite broadcast. Winfrey introduces the psychologist's abundant prescriptions of Prozac and his patients as potentially either representative or anomalous from the start of hour: "You know our society is always looking for the fastest, the easiest, the quickest fix, but is this right?" It is only the slow process of individual members getting up and testifying to their similar experiences that leads to the concept of a larger community—society at large—and evidence of a social problem or issue.

Almost every daytime talk show starts out a bit at risk: Will the guests be seen as anomalous and alone, and therefore, potential freaks in a sideshow? Or will the audience members spontaneously reveal their shared experiences? Lurking below the surface is the supposition that rational people do not expose their private lives on national TV unless they deem doing so socially important. The show depends on this tension for excitement. Even with an audience populated with Prozac takers, the question remains: Will these women overcome their inhibition or societal repression and testify? The spontaneous breakthroughs increase as audience members in Wenatchee and the studio eagerly jump to the mike and emotionally acknowledge their relation to Prozac. As one woman states: "My secret is out." The rising tide of testimony leads not only to a truth based on sheer numbers but also to a truth based on experiences and not on the expert's numbers and sociological language. The camera's zoom serves as a microscope-like tool with which we at home can judge the veracity of the performance.

The topic of Prozac represents an important test of the authenticity of these displays because of the stated question of whether people are "themselves" on Prozac. A principal pleasure afforded by daytime talk shows is assessing to what degree a guest is authentic or "just an act." Winfrey poses the question, "Does a drug like this hide or enhance who we really are?" The program becomes an exercise in discerning whether it is a person or Prozac speaking. The Prozac takers in the audience argue that they are speaking, but are now "enabled" or "chemically balanced." Yet two experts argue against Prozac's use because it is not "natural." It falls to an expert to close the debate. As the credits roll, Peter Kramer (author of *Listening to Prozac*) argues that the success of clinical therapy and medication is "unarguable," but only for serious situations deemed necessary by a qualified physician. Here, bourgeois expertise still dominates. The audience may be posed as judges listening and weighing evidence based on common sense and personal experience, but it is the expert who most often closes or shuts down the debate.

In general, talk shows do not offer traditional political topics. Rather, they translate politics into the everyday experience of the political. So the shows are rarely overtly "political." They are ultimately feminist not because they say they are but because they are populated by women and they discuss domestic and everyday experience as social problems. They do not follow the classical tradition of the bourgeois public sphere, where, J. B. Thompson maintains, "the authority of the state could be criticized by an informed and reasoning public or 'publicness.'"[24] The audience may or may not connect the discussion of abuse, sexual partners, and interracial conflict to legislation, elections, and news stories.

However, talk shows do offer proof that social experience is not a matter of ideology or false consciousness but, rather, has demonstrable consequences that can be proven through the physical and emotional evidence of its victims. Although the program and the experts establish and resolve the debate, the distant evidence of expert knowledge alone is no longer valid. Nor are the synthetic spectacles of commercial television programming acceptable. Rather, the talk show relies on the tangible or physical signs of the society: testimonials, emotions, and the body as well as laughter, facial expression, and tears. These are forms of argument and evidence available to the nonexperts or underclasses. And they are gaining acceptance as talk shows test the centrality of the educated bourgeoisie to define politics and debate.

Oddly enough, in this age of postmodern simulation, talk shows demand a belief in the authenticity of lived experience as a social truth. Perhaps, this belief is what the "Oprahification" of America really is. As one *Oprah* audience member stated on April 14, 1994: "Don't tell me how to feel. I am my experience."

Notes

1 I want to separate this first generation of talk shows of the 1970s and 1980s from the second generation of the 1990s hosted by Ricki Lake, Richard Bev, Gordon Elliot, Jenny Jones, and Jerry Springer. The phenomenal financial success of *The Oprah Winfrey Show* by 1990 spawned numerous new talk shows. Under the competition, the new programs changed the format considerably by removing the expert and social issues, emphasizing the implicit excess and sensation, and adding a campy or more tongue-in-cheek style. For further discussion of this generic shift, see my book, *The Talking Cure: Women and Talk Shows* (New York: Routledge, 1996).

2 "The Public Sphere: An Encyclopedia Article," *New German Critique* (autumn 1984): 49. For a more thorough discussion of the relation of talk shows to Habermas's public sphere, see Sonia Livingston and Peter Lunt, *Talk on Television: Audience Participation and Public Debate* (London: Routledge, 1994).

3 Barbara Lippert, "The Talk Show Report," *Ladies' Home Journal,* April 1994, 154–56, 210; John Corry, "A New Age of Television Tastelessness?" *New York Times,* 29 May 1988, 1; John J. Connor, "Defining What's Civilized and What's Not," *New York Times,* 25 April 1989, C18; Paolo Carpignano, Robin Andersen, Stanley Aronowitz, and William Difazio, "Chatter in the Age of Electronic Reproduction: Talk Television and the 'Public Mind,'" *Sociotext* 25–26 (1990): 33–55; Gloria-Jean Masciarotte, "C'mon Girl: Oprah Winfrey and the Discourse of Feminine Talk," *Genders* 11 (fall 1991): 81–110.

4 *Webster's New World Unabridged Dictionary*, 2d ed. (New York: Simon and Schuster, 1983), 1392.

5 Masciarotte, "C'mon Girl: Oprah and the Discourse of Feminine Talk," 89.

6 On March 6, 1995, during a taping of a Jenny Jones show on secret admirers, a Michigan man Scott Amedure surprised a male friend, Jon Schmitz, by admitting that he had a crush on him. The next day, Schmitz murdered Amedure, alleging that he had been "humiliated" by the exposure on national television. Jenny Jones and talk shows in general were blamed in the press for being irresponsible for misleading guests. See the cover story, Michelle Green, "Fatal Attraction," *People*, 27 March 1995, 40–44.

Oprah Winfrey, host of *The Oprah Winfrey Show*, "confessed" her use of cocaine in front of a live audience during the taping of a program in late January 1995. The statement was reported on the evening news as well as the printed press. For the tabloid coverage, see cover stories, Jim Nelson, "Oprah and Cocaine: The Shocking Story She Didn't Tell You on TV," *National Inquirer*, 31 January 1995, 5; and Ken Harrell, "Oprah: 'How a Man Made Me Slave to Cocaine,'" *Globe*, 31 January 1995, 37.

7 O'Connor, "Defining What's Civilized and What's Not," C18.

8 Corry, "A New Age of Television Tastelessness?" sec. 2, 1.

9 Consider how a series of binary oppositions surface in these discussions of the liberal news tradition and the exploitative talk show genre: democratic versus biased, independent versus profit-oriented, serious versus trivial, educated versus uneducated, and masculine versus feminine.

10 For an example, see Eric Sherman, "Who's the Best? Donahue? Oprah? Someone Else?" *TV Guide*, 26 March 1986, 26. *Newsweek* describes Phil Donahue as "America's most trusted tour guide across today's constantly shifting social and cultural terrain" (*Newsweek*, 29 October 1979, 78).

11 Michael Schudson, "Was There Ever a Public Sphere? If So, When? Reflections on the American Case," in *Habermas and the Public Sphere*, ed. Craig Calhoun (Cambridge, Mass.: MIT Press, 1992), 143–63.

12 See Nancy Fraser, *Unruly Practices: Power, Discourse, and Gender in Contemporary Social Theory* (Minneapolis: University of Minnesota Press, 1989), 113–43; Masciarotte, "C'mon Girl: Oprah and the Discourse of Feminine Talk," 81–110; and Patricia Mellencamp, *High Anxiety: Catastrophe, Scandal, Age, and Comedy* (Bloomington: Indiana University Press, 1990), 194–229.

13 In *Unruly Practices*, Nancy Fraser outlines this debate: "Consider, first, the relations between (official) private economy and private family as mediated by the roles of worker and consumer. These roles, I submit, are gendered roles. And the links they forge between family and (official) economy are effected as much in the medium of gender identity as in the medium of money"

(Fraser, *Unruly Practices*, 124). According to Fraser, one should also consider how the concept of the "citizen" is one associated with men: "As Habermas understands it, the citizen is centrally a participant in political debate and public opinion formation. This means that citizenship, in his view, depends crucially on the capacities for consent and speech, the ability to participate on a par with others in dialogue. But these are capacities connected with masculinity in a male-dominated, classical capitalism; they are in ways denied women and deemed at odds with femininity" (ibid.). As further evidence, Fraser cites studies on the inequalities in male/female dialogues and the lack of respect women have over consent in marital rape. She concludes by quoting Carole Pateman: "If women's words about consent are consistently reinterpreted, how can they participate in the debate among citizens?" (ibid.).

14 Carpignano et al., "Chatter in the Age of Electronic Reproduction," 52.

15 Ibid., 53.

16 Ibid., 51.

17 Masciarotte, "C'mon Girl: Oprah and the Discourse of Feminine Talk," 83.

18 Ibid., 90.

19 Lisa McLaughlin, "Chastity Criminals in the Age of Electronic Reproduction: Reviewing Talk Television and the Public Sphere," *Journal of Communication Inquiry* 17, no. 1 (winter 1993): 51.

20 Ibid., 52.

21 Wendy Kaminer, *I'm Dysfunctional. You're Dysfunctional: The Recovery Movement and Other Self-Help Fashions* (New York: Vintage, 1993), 38.

22 The preselection of questions during segment breaks is quite controversial among regular studio-audience participants and has led to an internal rebellion in which audiences challenge the process during the warm-up. *Donahue* is the only talk show that does not preselect audience questions. *Sally Jesse Raphael* and *Geraldo* producers tend to preselect when the program topic is controversial. *The Oprah Winfrey Show* selects for all programs. These observations are based on my own numerous visits as a participant/observer in these studio audiences in 1994.

23 Martin Berman, interview by the author, New York City, 7 March 1995.

24 J. B. Thompson, *Ideology and Modern Culture: Critical Social Theory* (Cambridge: Polity Press, 1990), 112.

Averting the Male Gaze

Visual Pleasure and Images of Fat Women

Jane Feuer

> It follows from all this, however, that there *is* such a process *as coming out as a fat woman*. Like the other, more materially dangerous kind of coming out, it involves the risk—here, a certainty—of uttering bathetically as a brave declaration that truth which can scarcely in this instance ever have been less than self-evident. Also like the other kind of coming out, however, denomination of oneself as a fat woman is a way in the first place of making clear to the people around one that their cultural meanings will be, and will be heard as, assaultive and diminishing to the degree that they are not fat-affirmative. In the second place and far more importantly, it is a way of staking one's claim to insist on, and participate actively in, a renegotiation of *the representational contract* between one's body and one's world.
>
> Eve Sedgwick, "Divinity," in *Tendencies* (1993)

Two things happened in the 1980s that led to the increasing visibility of fat women in the mass media: the clothing industry discovered fat women as a market; and the size acceptance movement grew to the point where there existed enough fat women with sufficient self-esteem to fill that market. Thus the impetus for the increased media representation of the fat female body in the 1990s came both from mainstream capitalist market-driven needs and from the more organic needs of fat women to achieve self-respect. This essay analyzes the emergence of the fat woman to a position of visibility in contemporary media representations. My approach to this topic attempts to unite two perspectives central to cultural studies today—the idea of a social movement and the idea of the "male gaze." As a social movement—or rather a bundle of social movements ranging from demands for civil rights to a radical rethinking of body politics—fat liberation resembles but is not identical to black, gay, and women's liberation movements. The parallels between fat acceptance/fat liberation and these other social movements are, however, striking. In fact, fat activism sprang from the women's movement as early as the early 1970s; civil rights activism for fat Americans began even earlier.[1] Both, however, thrived in the 1980s, the supposed era of political inactivity (unless you were gay or fat or both). Resembling other social movements, the "fat movement" has always possessed both a "radical" and a "mainstream" branch: the former questioning the fat phobia of even the most radical lesbian feminists; the latter organizing for civil rights and fat acceptance. (NAAFA was originally called "National Association to Aid Fat Americans." It was later changed to "advance fat *acceptance*," a term long associated with quests for equal rights under the law.) Like gay rights and other civil rights battles, fat politics based on an end to discrimination against fat Americans has anchored itself philosophically in recent "scientific" research showing that fat people are born that way and do not eat more than thin people.[2] In other words, like homosexuality as it is now conceptualized on TV talk shows, fat is nature, not nurture; therefore, it is wrong to discriminate against fat people, since they are *not* merely thin people who eat too much.

On the other hand, the seemingly more radical politics of fat liberation stems from lesbian feminist politics and the failure of these women's movements to critique their own fat phobia. According to Vivian F. Mayer, "So far, feminist fat liberation is the only fat voice that offers a cogent and radical analysis of fat oppression, and that suggests ways to end the oppression that are linked with other human liberation struggles."[3] It was a supposedly radical feminist branch of the fat movement that has been most influenced by psychoanalytical interpretations of why women are fat; Susie Orbach's *Fat Is a Feminist Issue* (1978) promised that the resolution of psychic conflicts would lead to the reduction of compulsive eating and hence weight loss.[4] It should be noted that many lesbian feminist fat activists do not subscribe to Orbach's Freudian disease model of fat; in fact, they prefer not to psychoanalyze at all. That's why the brief history I am giving here is already too binary: one could equally argue that the very rejection of psychological models for fat is the most radical position of all. But that is not the subject of this essay.

The antidieting/fat acceptance movement is a grassroots political movement that was rapidly taken up by capitalist industries. It was the commodification/objectification of the fat body made possible by the fashion industry's constructing the fat consumer as a *market* that enabled this movement to achieve media representation. That is to say, in order for fat women to achieve visual representation in the 1980s, we had to enter into beauty culture. This was accomplished by an expansion of beauty culture and fashion to include women who wore sizes 16 to 26. The plus-size clothing industry expanded at all levels: the older lower-priced chains (such as Lane Bryant) became more trendy; upscale boutiques for fat women sprang up in various cities (for example, The Forgotten Woman in New York, Chicago, and other cities); and a more politicized, feminist branch of the clothing industry provided natural fibers for the very fattest women as well (notably, Making it Big in California) while maintaining a cottage-industry relationship to its mail-order public.[5] Thus it's difficult to say whether the growth of the plus-size fashion industry during the eighties was the cause or the effect of fat affirmative politics insofar as these politics enabled media representation. In other words, how can you be on TV with nothing to wear? But how can you create a market for beautiful clothing for fat women to wear without having first imaged them in an affirmative way? Therefore the fat acceptance movement challenges certain Marxist social movement theories that equate commodification with alienation. It also challenges those feminist theories of representation based on the idea that the objectification and commodification of the female body is necessarily the property of a male gaze that is productive of visual pleasure.

The generally acknowledged mother and father of the theory of the male gaze are Laura Mulvey and John Berger.[6] In spite of the fact that she was writing about classical Hollywood film language and he was writing about a much older tradition of European oil painting, the theories are remarkably similar in their emphasis on the fact of the gaze and the fascination posed by its object. For Berger, a male spectator-owner gazes at the woman in the oil painting; she is aware of being seen and responds with calculated charm. For Mulvey, to put it in Berger's terms, men in classical Hollywood cinema act and women appear. Men forward the narrative; women stop it for the gaze. The Hollywood goddess thus objectified in the gaze becomes the object of a presumed male spectator/subject's scopophilia.

Although I do not deny the value of these views from the 1970s or even their explanatory power for many, many images in today's popular culture, I wonder that neither author ever mentioned that the women portrayed in the oil paintings and in the movies (e.g., Jane Russell) are, by today's standards, decidedly fat. Hollywood pinups of the 1940s are at least zaftig by comparison to the early 1990s "waif look" of model Kate Moss; the women in oil paintings are, by any contemporary standard of measurement, obese.

The theory of the male gaze should always be historicized according to the beauty norms of its period. An exemplary text in this regard is Susan Bordo's essay "Reading the Slender Body," in which she "reads" a cultural shift occurring throughout the eighties and early 1990s from a preference for bodies that are merely thin to ones with "firm bodily margins." As Bordo argues, "Until the 1980s, excess weight was the target of most ads for diet products; today, one is much more likely to find the enemy constructed as bulge, fat, or flab."[7] She refers to a *20/20* show in which ten-year-old boys responded to a slight bulge about the hips of emaciated fashion models by calling them fat.

I seriously doubt that the images cited by Berger and Mulvey would evoke a lustful look in my young male students today, and I know for a fact that the women students (whose body-image standards tend to be thinner than the boys') find them repulsive. So where is the much-touted pleasure in looking that is supposed to evoke the male gaze? Does the male gaze of 1994 look away or make little pig noises when it realizes these Renaissance babes are porkers? That is to say, the Berger/Mulvey theory of the male gaze tends to be used in a manner that is both ahistorical and formalist. It analyzes the fact and direction and subjectivity of the gaze without always considering the simple vulgar content of the image.

To refuse the male gaze is not necessarily to refuse the norms of beauty culture. We need to distinguish among issues involving the male gaze, those involving norms of beauty culture at a given time, and those involving body size per se. In fact, I argue that it is only by approximating other norms of beauty culture and thus evoking a male gaze that fat women today can gain access to representation in a form that does not code them as repellent. I do this by looking at a variety of examples of glamour photography involving both thin and fat, straight and lesbian-coded models.

Consider an ad from *Mirabella* featuring the model Paulina.[8] From a

Mirabella magazine advertisement, "Knowing."

purely formal standpoint and in terms of its manifest content, this ad is transgressive. It denies femininity by posing one of the world's most beautiful women in a masculine stance, in men's evening clothing. The look itself is indebted to Lesbian Chic; the model could be coded as lesbian and thus the ad could represent what Danae Clark analyzes under the advertisers' term "gay window dressing." According to Clark, masculine dress and other forms of subtle lesbian coding also represent the avant-garde of heterosexual female fashion and thus always possess a double meaning.[9] Unlike women in the tradition of oil painting represented by Berger, this woman does not seem to be especially aware of "being looked at." In fact, her own gaze might be said to be that of the "male spectator-owner" gazing directly at a woman who returns the gaze with "calculated charm." The label "Knowing" (also of course the name of the Estee Lauder scent being advertised), also lends to the model a greater sense of agency than is customary in the typical "male gaze" advertisement.

And yet—she is a beautiful, thin woman partaking of all the norms of beauty culture. Because Paulina is Estee Lauder's spokesmodel, she has already been associated in more traditionally feminine ways with their products (as in the ultrafeminine wedding gown pose appearing simultaneously in women's magazines with this one). Her diamond ring, earrings, and bracelets lend an aura of femininity to the masculine tuxedo suit. She has big hair and full makeup; her image is one of flawless perfection. It seems to me that an analysis of this ad in terms of "the look" and "cross-dressing" would find it to be far more transgressive than an analysis that focused on body size and adherence to the norms of beauty culture. And yet, the adherence of the ad to these norms negates, I argue, anything that might appear to critique the norms for what constitutes a beautiful woman in Western culture.

Moreover, the body size of the model is in no way transgressive. This correlates with traditional glamour photography as well as with the newer norms of "lesbian chic" beauty culture epitomized by our new cover girls, Sandra Bernhardt and k.d. lang. As it has always been for straight women in our media world of images, only thin lesbians may become chic lesbians.

Now imagine the same ad with a fat woman. Imagine her in the tuxedo and in the same pose. I argue that such a fat image is much more likely to be decoded as butch and as ugly, even if in every other way the model conforms to the norms of beauty culture (i.e., big hair, makeup, alluring pose).

Now picture our fat woman transformed into a slumping posture with no makeup and a crewcut. Even the jewelry changes the coding and no longer represents femininity. What the fat woman "knows" is no longer the true nature of femininity. In fact, she could not know anything in terms of the languages of advertising in the 1990s, because, in fact, her image is impossible. It takes the ad over the edge from radical chic to repulsive. It no longer smells good.

In fact, it's debatable whether the male gaze at the fat female body produces pleasure or revulsion, as the appearance of fat women on talk shows demonstrates. The fat woman is a masquerade of femininity, as the figure of Divine well parodies. Gaylyn Studlar observes, "[The male viewer] can safely enjoy Divine's 'feminine' outrages against social and sexual convention while using the figure of the grotesque wo/man to confirm his own perfection in masculine normality. . . . Divine's exhibition of 'her' excess ugliness also contributes to reinforcing the comic stereotype of the ugly woman who unknowingly elicits ridicule (rather than desire) when she presumes to satisfy the male gaze."[10]

On a 1992 *Maury Povich Show,* a proud, fat Latina appeared on stage with three formerly fat women now dressed up as parodies of seventeen-year-old skinny girls. The fat woman was dressed in a short silk nightie with see-through negligee and dyed-to-match high heels. Her purpose was to proudly display to the world evidence that at 200-plus pounds, a woman could still be sexy. Both the other women on the panel and some men in the audience were not buying it, although the women protested far more vehemently. In fact, a man in the audience wasn't even hostile; he simply could not understand why this woman liked herself. Finally, an aging blonde in a go-go dress summed it up from the podium, "Let's face it. Men do not find fat sexy." Almost any talk show on the subject of fat will arrive at the same contradictions, despite variations (for instance, Oprah tends more toward probing group-therapy discourse and self display).[11] That is to say, women who are not ashamed to be fat will be placed on the hot seat, using other women guests and audience members as custodians of the male gaze. In almost every case, a contradiction arises between the talk show ethos that in America everyone has the *right* to be themselves and the intuitive knowledge of social power relations that tells us heterosexual women had better be thin if they wish to attract the male gaze that will assure their position in the world. It is still difficult to find an example of a self-loving fat woman whose position is not set up as a *debate* with thin or formerly fat women.

As a more extended example, allow me to share with you the March 11, 1994, edition of *Sonja Live* on CNN. Sonja's first guest is Ken Mayer, author of *Real Women Don't Diet! One Man's Praise of Large Women and His Outrage at the Society That Rejects Them.* Ken is presented as a fashion photographer who takes glamour photos of large women. The book is presented as a picture book.[12] Ken is asked by Sonja how he developed his aberrant preference. He replies, "As far as where it came from, it came from my hormones." Was it his mother? No, his mother was thin. Ken equates size with womanliness—the more the better. If a large man is more of a man, a large woman is more of a woman; she's more powerful, stronger.

Next Sonja introduces Carolyn Strauss—"a beauty but large." Most of the hour-long show consists of a "debate" with a thin woman (Michele Herbert), an aging ponytailed blonde Barbie who captured her husband by losing 30 pounds. Later on, she confesses she would never *gain* weight to get a man. Throughout the show, the fat guest—a large-size model—is shown in the same shot as the Barbie woman.

Ken: We need larger women to survive as a species [his evolutionary argument for fat admiration].

Caller: I applaud his tolerance for heavy women.

Sonja: Since Ken prefers a certain body type, why shouldn't other men prefer only thin women?

[Ken agrees with this, not seeming to realize that it contradicts his previous position.]

Sonja to Carolyn: What a face! Why not diet?

Carolyn: I could be thin if I ate nothing but macrobiotics and worked out 3–4 hours a day, but I have better things to do. [She claims to be genetically fat.]

Caller: How do you get started as a big model?

Ken: You need a photographer who knows how to photograph larger women.

Next, a therapist comes on.

Sonja: Which woman has a healthier attitude?

Therapist: Both do [the obsessive dieter and the self-accepting fat woman].

The therapist analyzes Ken. She thinks it has to do with his mom. But Ken protests again—his mom is thin. Well, then, maybe it has to do with rejecting mom. Ken argues for evolutionary over psychoanalytic analysis. Carolyn declares that each individual woman has to say "enough" to society. A male caller informs us that, on talk shows, wives having problems with mates are usually overweight.

Next Sonja brings on a recovered anorexic (thin, gorgeous) to deal further with issues of eating and control.

Ken: We need more role models. We need more cover girls that are big.

Sonja: Why don't we? But the fact is we don't [allow for a democracy of body types].

A female caller criticizes the media because men dump women when they gain weight. A male caller declares that Carolyn is the most attractive of the three women.

Lest it appear that this summary is unusually chaotic and conflicted, I would hasten to assure my readers who are not daytime TV viewers that this example is typical of the chaotic and contradictory nature of talk show discourse in the nineties. No longer based on the old *Donahue* model of the public forum, talk shows today attempt to create a constant flow of contradictory ideological discourses. Thus nobody ever calls Ken on his logic when he equates *large* women with *strong* women. No one ever challenges the use of Darwinian or vulgar Freudian assumptions, or wonders why Ken and the therapist have trouble reconciling these two positions. No one asks Ken the epistemological question of what it means in terms of the theory of the male gaze to "know" how to photograph large women. (Nor was this question answered to my satisfaction in his book.) Although it is perhaps unfair to extract individual statements from this flow, I would like to focus on the last question (what does it mean to know how to photograph large women?) for the obvious reason that I am asking the same question in this essay.

In terms of theories of the male gaze, Ken provides the classic example of the male photographer behind the camera who fetishizes the female object in front of the lens. So, one might ask, is there really any difference between "thin" and "plus-size" fashion photography that cannot be accounted for under the Mulvey/Berger paradigm? Examining the (actually very nice) portraits in Ken's book, I came to one conclusion: none of the photos of fat women attempted to avert the male gaze in the manner of the Paulina ad and other contemporary "transgressive" shots of beautiful, thin women.[13] Indeed an entire section is devoted to fetishizing (fat) body parts in the form of disembodied legs posed in various positions, an iconography common to mainstream ads for women's shoes, pantyhose, and undergarments. In the book, Ken explains further why advertisers use methods of photography to produce images that no real woman can ever hope to duplicate in life:

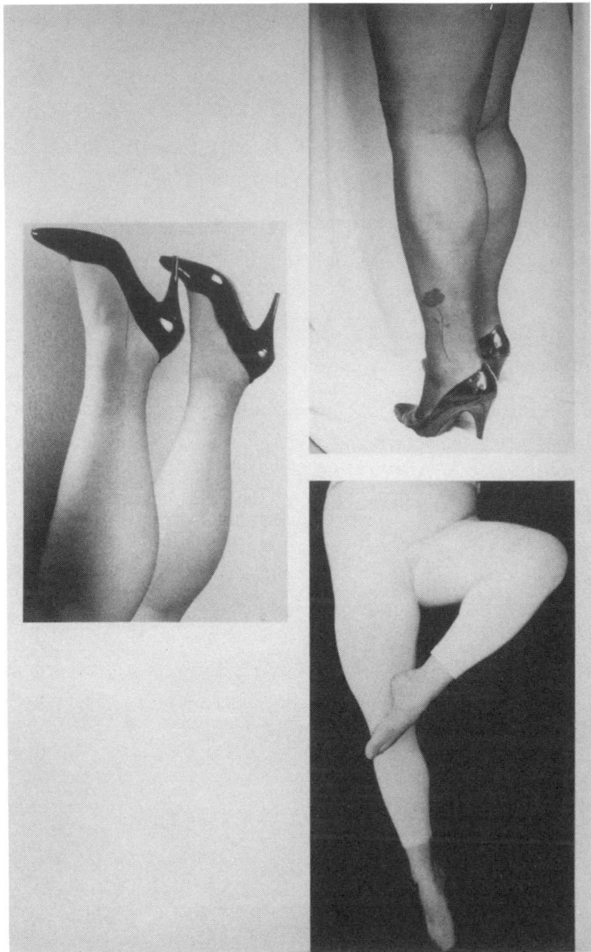

Ken Mayer photos, fetishizing (fat) body parts . . . disembodied legs.

And how are the images actually produced? The photo sessions are arranged by art directors and set designers who create lavish backgrounds and employ elaborate props: brilliantly designed lighting is provided by highly skilled technicians. Talented wardrobe specialists, make-up artists, and hair stylists further cater their services to the models (cover shots can require the model to take up to four hours to prepare). The photographer at the shoot is paid thousands of dollars per day for his skill at using unlimited tricks to perfect the model's look. . . . And the hands, legs, torsos, and heads of the models who specialize in displaying particular body parts are often recombined.[14]

Vanity Fair centerfold of the singing group Wilson Phillips.

Presumably this passage answers the question posed by the caller: to know how to photograph large women is to know how to lavish these same techniques on them. It is to know how to make fat women objects of the traditional male gaze (at a time when the most progressive images of thin women are breaking with these practices).

Several years of random taping (1990–94) have brought me to the following conclusions as to the conditions under which fat women may appear on TV and not be subject to ridicule. Although it has long been acceptable for fat women to serve as objects of pity on TV talk shows (especially when they are holding Richard Simmons's hand), talk show guests may now be fat even if that is not the "issue" discussed on the program, so long as they are coded as "white trash." Oprah Winfrey may be fat, but she cannot at the same time be "svelte" or glamorous or self-fulfilled.[15] Sexy Hispanic fat women may appear in see-through negligees on *Maury Povich*. The faceless heroic rescuers (usually 911 phone operators) of reality TV may be quite fat, as may the mothers of children being rescued (although the actresses playing them in the re-creations are usually thinner). Roseanne, in the role of the blue-collar Roseanne Connor, was welcomed into homes everywhere (*Roseanne,* ABC, 1988–

97). In short, fat women may appear "invisibly" on TV shows when they are also coded as lower class, asexual, and/or nonwhite.[16]

The fat sister in the singing group Wilson Phillips (Carnie Wilson) can appear in the group's music videos but always fully clothed or in a headshot. If the other two appear in bathing suits on the beach, she must appear in a cover-up. When they appear on stage in skimpy dresses, she must be fully jacketed. While the camera eye gazes at the thin singers, it tends to avert its gaze from the fat one. Yet outside MTV, more avant-garde images are possible. There is an interesting centerfold of Wilson Phillips in the June 1992 *Vanity Fair.* The fat sister, Carnie Wilson, occupies the center of the photo and lays claim to not one but two male gazes. She is posed in décolletage, with cleavage, fingers lingering on her own breasts and eyes gazing outward in a sultry glance as two shirtless young men plant kisses on either cheek. To the other side of each man is one of the thinner member of the group, more fully clothed and in the effaced childlike poses of fashion photography. In many respects, however, this photo is a reversal of their more mainstream videos.

Ricki Lake may be fat in the movie *Hairspray* (John Waters, 1988), in *Babycakes* (1989; a made for TV remake of the 1985 German film *Sugarbaby* [Percy Adlon]), and on *China Beach* (for the 1989–90 season), but not as the hostess of her own TV talk show. That is to say, fat women achieve media representation when they are already viewed as nonglamorous on the basis of other exclusions, or when they appear in media already otherwise marginalized. In the case of Ricki Lake, an emergence out of the John Waters/Divine tradition of the grotesque permitted her early screen career. In the case of Jessye Norman, a large woman became a television diva by virtue of her status as an opera singer and the correspondence between her extraordinary body and her extraordinary voice. In her appearances on PBS and even riding in the Macy's Thanksgiving Day Parade, she is thus coded as exotic and "other" for TV viewers.

In the wake of the fat liberation movement, however, a few fat women have attempted to gain entry to mass media representation as an alternative model of beauty. The new Roseanne, still fat by conventional standards, but otherwise substantially altered, occupies an ambiguous position on the cover of the February 1994 *Vanity Fair,* as opposed to the infamous mud-wrestling issue *Vanity Fair* cover of herself and Tom

Annie Leibovitz, *Vanity Fair* covers of Roseanne.

Arnold in December 1990 (both photographed by Annie Leibovitz).[17] In the 1990 incarnation, entitled "Roseanne on Top," Roseanne occupies the grotesque representational space of Divine, a parody of a woman. Her pendulous breasts weigh down on Tom Arnold's chest as she laughs wickedly from under a blonde wig. But the 1994 posttransformation cover is more ambiguous. She poses in a semi-pornographic manner in a black bustier with high heels, stockings, and garter belt. Still a dominatrix, is she still also a parody of a woman? I would argue that the cover photo and the ones inside are readable as "parodies of woman" more in the manner of Madonna than of Divine. That is to say, they are meant to be taken half-seriously as glamour photos. Like Madonna in a similar pose, they may be interpreted as parodic but also erotic. The 1994 cover at least invites a male gaze; the 1990 cover crushes an actual man underneath Roseanne's fat body. Drawing on imagery from fat pornographic videos and magazines for "fat admirers," these eroticized images of fat women have met with mixed reactions from feminists. Yet as Laura Kipnis argues, "pornography's celebration of fat, even its "objectification" of fat women, is in defiance of all societal norms and social controls. . . . Pornography's insistence on visibility for fat forces the spectacle of fat as fat, rather than as an array of connotations. Fat is what our culture, for all of the reasons suggested, doesn't want to look at. Pornography, in response, puts it on view." [18]

I would like to focus some of these issues of the impact of fat liberation on media representations on the TV series *Babes* broadcast on the Fox network from fall 1990 to spring 1991. "Hammocked" between *The Simpsons* and *Beverly Hills 90210,* the show failed in the ratings—although it's hard to imagine that either Bart fans or Dylan fans would be fascinated by a vulgar, physical comedy about three fat sisters named Charlene, Darlene, and Marlene. And yet external evidence reveals that fat women, especially lesbians, managed to take visual pleasure in the program. The program was mentioned favorably in *Radiance* magazine, the mouthpiece of the fat acceptance movement, and the producers solicited feedback from *Radiance* readers.[19] How can this be?

Babes may easily be read as something less than fat-affirmative. This reading is based on the show's numerous sight gags and fat jokes, often overcoded by being done in tandem, a practice that may be verified by citing all the sight gags/fat jokes from the opening segment of the pilot episode. As star Wendy Jo Sperber (Charlene) appears in a gold spandex bustier, her sister Darlene enters saying, "Damn, I forgot my bicycle pants."[20] Darlene physically overpowers her sister Charlene's boyfriend. Darlene explains that she's moving into Charlene's tiny but funky studio apartment in New York City because her husband Wilbur joined fat busters and she found him in bed with his counselor—"116 pounds down from 321." Charlene responds, "How long did it take her?" Next, the third sister, Marlene, arrives after losing her job. "Losing a job isn't easy but you cannot eat yourself to death. I tried sticking my head in the oven but there was a cake in it." The sisters bed down together on Charlene's sofa bed. As they reminisce about "that summer in Hershey, P.A.," the bed collapses, combining the joke with the sight gag. Some fat women found these jokes offensive, but at least they were penned by a female writing-producing team (including Gail Parent,[21] a well-known comedy writer). It may be objected that these are thin women's fat jokes, but they at least take a woman's point of view. In some respects, the fat jokes (which invite identification with compulsive eating behaviors) may be read against the sight gags (in which the fat sisters invoke laughter without identification).

Moreover, visual codes make possible another reading based on an appreciative "male" gaze. If we consider fat women as a subculture, this reading would involve the same kinds of partial decodings practiced by other disenfranchised groups. The three women are represented as beauty objects with their glamorous clothes. The show provides access to visual pleasure based in the adorned fat body, a pleasure that is legible despite the narrative context of a vulgar Fox sitcom or perhaps because of it—one can shut out the crude sitcom framework even if one finds it offensive. In this way, fat women viewers could use *Babes* as a shopping channel. The clothes make the show available for alternate readings, especially from a fat woman's and/or lesbian's subject position.

Babes could also be read as one of many sitcoms about female bonding, a setup always amenable to lesbian decodings as well. For example, the morning after the bed collapses, Darlene says, "I couldn't get comfortable all night," and Charlene replies, "I know. You kept fluffing up my breasts." Although every effort is made to code all three sisters as heterosexual, the fattest sister (Darlene) is constantly outrunning this codification—as in the episode when she must learn to control her use of physical force against her ex-husband. This facilitates a slippage into a lesbian reading. Any Amazon outside the norms of beauty culture may be labeled a lesbian, whether for the positive goal of identification or the negative one of revulsion.

Ironically, Charlene works as a makeup artist, so that when a 200-pound plus-size model, the "Hefty Hose Girl," has liposuction, her beautiful sister Marlene gets the job. "I need a very large, very sexy, beautiful girl," the boss says. Marlene, who in a previous job-hunting scene was referred to as the elephant in *Fantasia,* fits the bill, but not before undergoing a transformation of body-image consciousness completely indebted to the fat acceptance movement. For Marlene, a typical fat girl with "such a pretty face," does not initially possess the self-assurance of Carolyn Strauss, the plus-size model on *Sonja Live.*[22] She tells her sisters, "I wanted to be Susan Dey in the Partridge family. Not some fat girl stuffed into the world's largest pair of pantyhose." But her sisters deliver a fat-affirmative lecture reminiscent of the new fat discourse on TV talk shows: "Don't be ashamed of who you are. Now get your fat ass out there." When the boss says, "Great, I got a porker with zero personality," her sisters are appalled and come to Marlene's defense.

Transformed by their confidence in her, we see Marlene emerge into beauty culture. She becomes a conventionally sexy "voguing" model whose male-gaze image is freeze-framed onto the billboard of a bus passing by the apartment building that the sisters are exiting. This final pose represents perhaps the furthest extent to which the politics of fat liberation has thus far entered into the world of the sitcom. Marlene's accession to billboard status is depicted as a narrative of liberation inspired by fat-positive politics. In fact, we witness the taking of the billboard photo, using exactly the same techniques of enhancement that Ken describes in his book. Indeed, the final product closely resembles the photos in Ken's book; taken from a male-gaze position, it resembles examples of actual plus-size advertising photography.

And yet when she "vogues" in her role as a plus-size model, the fat woman may not bear the same meanings as Cindy Crawford does.

Charlene Gilbert (Wendy Jo Sperber) is the sister who dances in several episodes. In a *Fantasy Island* parody she does classical ballet dancing in a dream sequence with a man. In the narrative, Charlene is considering a fat male suitor as a possible partner. She imagines them dancing a pas de deux right out of *The Sleeping Beauty.* But because he is fat and clumsy, the dance becomes a farce. The boisterous laugh track codes this dream ballet as farce: she is too heavy to lift; ultimately, he drops her, as Charlene returns to reality with a thud. In another episode, Wendy Jo parodies ballet yet winds up triumphing (without self-mockery) as a tap dancer. In the presence of her old dancing teacher, she raises her leg up on the barre and gets stuck—like a fat Lucy. Yet at the end of the show, she appears before a cheering audience as the lead dancer in a tap recital backed up by a chorus of seven year olds. Despite the ridiculousness of the situation, the feeling is like that of the finale of a backstage musical, when we find out that Ruby Keeler really is a trouper. In addition, the narrative codes the tap dance as a moment of self-actualization: Charlene has overcome her childhood demons by tap dancing on stage.

This raises the question: can a fat woman dance? Yes, she can tap dance, because tap is culturally coded as an individualized, male, even phallic dance form. This is why Eleanor Powell could never find an appropriate male partner. Ballet, on the other hand, is about femininity and its display; ballet codes the fat woman as nonfeminine in part because she does not project the illusion of weightlessness when jumping or being lifted. The pas de deux is partner dancing for heterosexual lovers only.

When the original female producers and writers for *Babes* were replaced by men, it was felt that any reference to the women's size would be construed as insulting or "sad." Said the new producer Jeff Stein, "We don't have to do jokes about Mallomars. And at this point, we're not doing fat issues. Why would we make these women look sad? There's nothing sad about them. These are three vivacious girls."[23] Note the equation of fat issues with fat jokes. Yet the fat-positive early episodes already demonstrated that these are not the same. *Babes,* potentially the most radical comedy on television, was transformed into a sitcom about three large sisters whose size was no longer a situation for comedy. The show descended into strident and vulgar affirmations of the women's heterosexuality. Even so, the program was endorsed by leaders of the fat acceptance movement and continued to provide a source of visual pleasure to fat women spectators. In this sense, the humanistic rendering of the fat woman, her mere ascendancy to representation, must be viewed as a necessary first step to more complex representations such as Darlene Cates's performance in *What's Eating Gilbert Grape?* (Lasse Hallstrom, 1993). Cates's reputation from the film as a very fat and very good dramatic actress in turn influenced television, as when she appeared on the short-lived Fox medical series *Medicine Ball* in the spring of 1995. Cast as a patient whose obesity makes her undiagnosable by the thin young doctors in the show's cast, Cates functions as a veritable mouthpiece for fat liberation politics (one senses this in spite of the script). Meanwhile, the book *Women en Large: Images of Fat Nudes* goes a long way toward transforming the tradition of fat pornography into a feminist erotics. Not especially eroticized for a male gaze and definitely not beautified or airbrushed, the fat female images in *Women en Large* are so transgressive the authors had difficulty finding a publisher.[24] And, I suspect, very few women will be prepared to find these images as attractive as they are intended to be for all the reasons this essay has given.

For fat women at this historical conjuncture, representation as objects of visual pleasure is progressive; especially when read by a female/lesbian spectator. Such objectification may well not be progressive for conventionally thin and/or heterosexual women. Thus cinema-based theories of the male gaze need to be adapted to the television medium and to specific struggles such as the fat acceptance movement. At this time, the struggles of thin/fat and lesbian/straight women/feminists may not be equivalent. When straight, thin women are objectified for a male gaze, the problem is not necessarily that of objectification but rather that of the heterosexuality of the gaze. But when the lesbian gaze focuses on Wendy Jo Sperber or Carnie Wilson, identification and objectification may occur simultaneously. At this historical moment (the mid-nineties) beauty culture for fat women must be viewed as progressive, regardless of whether it is recuperable by capitalism, and regardless of whether it occupies the now unfashionable categories of "positive role model" or "humanist subjectivity." Indeed, I argue that fat women must *become* humanistic subjects before they can hope to be represented at all. For those of us subject to what might be called "visual oppression," representation is the necessary first step toward liberation.

Notes

1 See the pioneering collection, Lisa Schoenfielder and Barb Wieser, eds., *Shadow on a Tightrope: Writings by Women on Fat Oppression*, foreword by Vivian Mayer (Boston: Spinsters/aunt lute, 1983).

2 Much of this research has been published in medical journals. It was widely

popularized by William Bennett, M.D., and Joel Gurin in *The Dieter's Dilemma: Eating Less and Weighing More: The Scientific Case against Dieting as a Means of Weight Control* (New York: Basic Books, 1982).

3 Schoenfielder and Wieser, *Shadow on a Tightrope,* x.

4 Susie Orbach, *Fat Is a Feminist Issue: A Self-Help Guide for Compulsive Eaters* (Berkeley: University of California Press, 1978).

5 The upscale boutique branch of the fat clothing industry appears to be contracting in the mid-1990s. Three such shops folded in Pittsburgh recently, including two from the Forgotten Woman and Audrey Jones chains.

6 Laura Mulvey, "Visual Pleasure and Narrative Cinema," *Screen* 16, no. 3 (autumn 1975): 6–18; and John Berger, *Ways of Seeing* (London: BBC and Penguin, 1972).

7 Susan Bordo, "Reading the Slender Body," in *Unbearable Weight: Feminism, Western Culture, and the Body* (Berkeley: University of California Press, 1993), 189.

8 I am indebted to my student, Sherie Olenik, for bringing this ad to my attention insofar as it works against Berger's theory. This ad appeared across a spectrum of glossy though slightly trendy magazines in 1994.

9 Danae Clark, "Commodity Lesbianism," *Camera Obscura* 25–26 (January/May 1991): 183.

10 Gaylyn Studlar, "Midnight S/Excess: Cult Configurations of 'Femininity' and the Perverse," *Journal of Popular Film and Television* 17, no. 1 (spring 1989): 8.

11 See, for example, the essay by Jane Shattuc in this volume.

12 Actually, as I discovered when I raced out to buy it, it's an $18.95 hardback with tiny black-and-white photos and consists primarily of Ken's Ideas about Men and Women. (Ken Mayer, *Real Women Don't Diet! One Man's Praise of Large Women and His Outrage at the Society That Rejects Them* [Silver Spring, Md.: Bartleby Press, 1993]).

13 Well, actually one does: a snapshot of Heidi and her baby daughter. But this photo is not as "flattering" as the others.

14 Mayer, *Real Women Don't Diet!* 52.

15 Ironically, whereas the caucasian Ricki Lake is not permitted to be fat on her TV talk show, Oprah Winfrey appears to be less popular with some audiences when she is thin, as her ratings and several stories in the tabloids seem to indicate.

16 The issue of race, body size, and beauty is very complex and beyond the scope of the present inquiry. See, however, Kim Shayo Buchanan, "Creating Beauty in Blackness," in *Consuming Passions: Feminist Approaches to Weight Preoccupation and Eating Disorders,* ed. Catrina Brown and Karin Jasper (Ontario: Second Story Press, 1993), 36–51.

17 In this case, *Vanity Fair* qualifies as "mass" because the Roseanne covers, like those with Demi Moore, were widely quoted and discussed on tabloid TV and because her new image carries over into her appearance on the sitcom. Of course these images are far more extreme than anything that would be produced for TV.

18 Laura Kipnis, "Life in the Fat Lane," in *Bound and Gagged: Pornography and the Politics of Fantasy in America* (New York: Grove, 1996), 120–21.

19 William J. Fabrey, "'Babes,' Planes, and Automobiles," *Radiance* 8, no. 2 (spring 1991): 25. In his regular column, Fabrey wrote the following: "*Babes* has succeeded in going beyond the stereotypes, and has been very well received according to my many informal interviews. . . . The actresses themselves say that the show is about self-esteem and self-acceptance. . . . Finally, according to NAAFA's Fat Activism Task Force, the show's producer has asked for feedback from those in the size acceptance movement."

20 The actress, Susan Peretz, had previously played a serious role as a fat attorney suing her firm for discrimination in an early episode of *L.A. Law*.

21 A best-selling novelist and Emmy award–winning writer for *The Carol Burnett Show*.

22 Carolyn Strauss had in fact auditioned for the part of Marlene but was told she was not funny enough as a fat woman (Carolyn Strauss, personal communication to author, undated).

23 Monica Collins, "Babes trims the fat jokes," *TV Guide* 38, no. 46 (17 November 1990): 54.

24 Laurie Toby Edison and Debbie Notkin, *Women en Large: Images of Fat Nudes* (San Francisco: Books in Focus, 1994).

Selected Bibliography

Allen, Robert C. *Horrible Prettiness: Burlesque and American Culture*. Chapel Hill: University of North Carolina Press, 1991.

———. *Speaking of Soap Operas*. Chapel Hill: University of North Carolina Press, 1985.

———, ed. *Channels of Discourse, Reassembled: Television and Contemporary Criticism*, 2d ed. Chapel Hill: University of North Carolina Press, 1992.

———, ed. *To be continued : Soap Operas around the World*. New York: Routledge, 1995.

Anderson, Christopher. *Hollywood TV: The Studio System in the Fifties*. Austin: University of Texas Press, 1994.

Anderson, Kathryn, Susan Armitage, Dana Jack, and Judith Wittner. "Beginning Where We Are: Feminist Methodology in Oral History." *Oral History Review* 15 (spring 1987): 103–27.

Ang, Ien. *Watching Dallas: Soap Opera and the Melodramatic Imagination*. Translated by Della Couling. New York: Methuen, 1985.

Armitage, Susan. "The Next Step." *Frontiers* 7 (1983): 3–8.

Baehr, Helen, and Gillian Dyer, eds. *Boxed In: Women and Television*. London: Pandora Press, 1987.

Barnouw, Erik. *History of Broadcasting*. 3 vols. New York: Oxford University Press, 1966, 1968, 1970.

———. *Tube of Plenty: The Evolution of American Television*. 2d rev. ed. New York: Oxford University Press, 1990.

Bathrick, Serafina. "*The Mary Tyler Moore Show:* Women at Home and at Work." In *MTM: "Quality Television,"* edited by Jane Feuer, Paul Kerr, and Tise Vahimagi, 99–131. London: British Film Institute, 1984.

Bennett, Tony. "Texts, Readers, Reading Formations." *Bulletin of the Midwest Modern Language Association* 16 (spring 1983): 3–17.

Bennett, Tony, and Janet Woollacott. *Bond and Beyond: The Political Career of a Popular Hero*. New York: Methuen, 1987.

Berger, John. *Ways of Seeing*. London: BBC and Penguin, 1972.

Bergstrom, Janet, and Mary Ann Doane, eds. *Camera Obscura* 20–21 (1989). Special issue, "The Spectatrix."

Boddy, William. *Fifties Television: The Industry and Its Critics.* Urbana: University of Illinois Press, 1990.

Bordo, Susan. *Unbearable Weight: Feminism, Western Culture, and the Body.* Berkeley: University of California Press, 1993.

Breines, Wini. *Young, White, and Miserable: Growing Up Female in the Fifties.* Boston: Beacon Press, 1992.

Brown, Mary Ellen. *Soap Opera and Women's Talk: The Pleasure of Resistance.* Thousand Oaks, Calif.: Sage, 1994.

———, ed. *Television and Women's Culture: The Politics of the Popular.* London: Sage, 1990.

Brown, Wendy. "Reproductive Freedom and the Right to Privacy: A Paradox for Feminists," in *Families, Politics, and Public Policy,* edited by Irene Diamond, 311–88. New York: Longman, 1983.

Brunsdon, Charlotte. "Crossroads: Notes on Soap Opera." *Screen* 22, no. 4 (1981): 32–37.

———. *Screen Tastes: Soap Opera to Satellite Dishes.* London: Routledge, 1997.

Brunsdon, Charlotte, and David Morley. *Everyday Television: Nationwide.* London: British Film Institute, 1978.

Brunsdon, Charlotte, Julie D'Acci, and Lynn Spigel, eds. *Feminist Television Criticism: A Reader.* London: Oxford University Press, 1997.

Buchanan, Kim Shayo. "Creating Beauty in Blackness." In *Consuming Passions: Feminist Approaches to Weight Preoccupation and Eating Disorders,* edited by Catrina Brown and Karin Jasper, 36–51. Ontario: Second Story Press, 1993.

Caine, Barbara, and Rosemary Pringle, eds. *Transitions: New Australian Feminisms.* New York: St. Martin's Press, 1995.

Carpignano, Paolo, Robin Andersen, Stanley Aronowitz, and William Difazio. "Chatter in the Age of Electronic Reproduction: Talk Television and the 'Public Mind.'" *Sociotext* 25–26 (1990): 33–55.

Cassata, Mary, and Thomas Skill. *Life on Daytime Television: Tuning in American Serial Drama.* Norwood, N.J.: Ablex, 1983.

Chisholm, Brad. "Red, Blue, and Lots of Green: The Impact of Color Television on Feature Film Production." In *Hollywood in the Age of Television,* edited by Tino Balio. Boston: Unwin Hyman, 1990.

Clark, Danae. "Commodity Lesbianism." *Camera Obscura* 25–26 (January/May 1991): 181–201.

Condit, Celeste Michelle. *Decoding Abortion Rhetoric: Communicating Social Change.* Urbana: University of Illinois Press, 1990.

Coontz, Stephanie. *The Way We Never Were: American Families and the Nostalgia Trap.* New York: Basic Books, 1992.

D'Acci, Julie. *Defining Women: Television and the Case of Cagney and Lacey*. Chapel Hill: University of North Carolina Press, 1994.

Doane, Mary Ann. "Film and the Masquerade: Theorising the Female Spectator." *Screen* 23, nos. 3–4 (September–October 1982): 74–87.

Doty, Alexander. "The Cabinet of Lucy Ricardo: Lucille Ball's Star Image," *Cinema Journal* 29, no. 4 (summer 1990): 3–34.

———. *Making Things Perfectly Queer: Interpreting Mass Culture*. Minneapolis: University of Minnesota Press, 1993.

Dudziak, Mary. "Josephine Baker, Racial Protest, and the Cold War." *Journal of American History* 81, no. 2 (September 1994): 543–68.

Dyer, Richard. *White*. New York: Routledge, 1997.

Ehrenreich, Barbara. *For Her Own Good: 150 Years of the Experts' Advice to Women*. Garden City, N.Y.: Anchor Books, 1978.

Enloe, Cynthia. *Bananas, Beaches, and Bases: Making Feminist Sense of International Politics*. Berkeley: University of California Press, 1989.

Feuer, Jane. "Melodrama, Serial Form, and Television Today." *Screen* 25 (1984): 4–16.

———. "Reading *Dynasty:* Television and Reception Theory," *South Atlantic Quarterly* 88, no. 2 (spring 1989): 443–60.

Fiske, John. *Television Culture*. New York: Methuen, 1987.

Fiske, John, and John Hartley. *Reading Television*. London: Methuen, 1978.

Flitterman, Sandy. "Thighs and Whiskers, the Fascination of *Magnum, P.I.*" *Screen* 26, no. 2 (1985): 42–58.

Foucault, Michel. *The Archaeology of Knowledge*. Translated by A. M. Sheridan Smith. New York: Pantheon, 1972.

———. *Power/Knowledge: Selected Interviews and Other Writings, 1972–1977*. Edited and translated by Colin Gordon. New York: Pantheon, 1980.

Franklin, Sarah, Celia Ury, and Jackie Stacey, eds. "Part 3: Science and Technology." In *Off-Centre: Feminism and Cultural Studies*, 129–218. London: Harper Collins Academic, 1991.

Fraser, Nancy. "Rethinking the Public Sphere." In *The Phantom Public Sphere*, edited by Bruce Robbins, 1–32. Minneapolis: University of Minnesota Press, 1991.

———. *Unruly Practices: Power, Discourse, and Gender in Contemporary Social Theory*. Minneapolis: University of Minnesota, 1989.

Fried, Marlene Gerber, ed. *From Abortion to Reproductive Freedom: Transforming a Movement*. Boston: South End Press, 1990.

Frisch, Michael. *A Shared Authority: Essays on the Craft and Meaning of Oral and Public History*. Albany: State University of New York Press, 1990.

Garber, Marjorie. *Vested Interests: Cross Dressing and Cultural Anxiety.* New York: Routledge, 1992.

Garber, Marjorie, Jann Matlock, and Rebecca L. Walkowitz, eds. *Media Spectacles.* New York: Routledge, 1993.

Geraghty, Christine. *Women and Soap Opera.* Cambridge: Polity Press, 1991.

Gitlin, Todd. *Inside Prime Time.* New York: Pantheon Books, 1985.

Glick, Sherna Berger, and Daphne Patai, eds. *Women's Words: The Feminist Practice of Oral History.* New York: Routledge, 1991.

Gordon, Linda. *Woman's Body, Woman's Right: Birth Control in America.* New York: Penguin, 1990.

Gray, Herman. *Watching Race: Television and the Struggle for "Blackness."* Minneapolis: University of Minnesota Press, 1995.

Hall, Stuart. "Encoding/decoding." In *Culture, Media, Language,* edited by Stuart Hall, Dorothy Hobson, Andrew Lowe, and Paul Willis, 126–38. London: Hutchinson/Centre for Contemporary Cultural Studies, 1980.

Hall, Stuart, Ian Connell, and Lidia Curti. "The 'Unity' of Current Affairs Television." In *Cultural Studies 9: Working Papers in Cultural Studies,* 51–93. Birmingham, U.K.: Centre for Contemporary Cultural Studies, 1976.

Hammond, Charles. *The Image Decade: Television Documentary, 1965–1975.* New York: Hastings House, 1981.

Haralovich, Mary Beth. "'Champagne Taste on a Beer Budget': Series Design and Popular Appeal in *Magnum, p.i.*" *Journal of Film and Video* 43, nos. 1–2 (spring–summer 1991): 123–34.

———. "Too Much Guilt Is Never Enough for Working Mothers: Joan Crawford, *Mildred Pierce,* and *Mommie Dearest.*" *Velvet Light Trap,* no. 29 (spring 1992): 43–52.

Hartley, John. *Understanding News.* London: Methuen, 1982.

Harvey, Brett. *The Fifties: A Women's Oral History.* New York: HarperCollins, 1993.

Hilmes, Michele. "Born Yesterday: Television and the Academic Mind." *American Literary History* 6, no. 4 (winter 1994): 791–802.

———. *Radio Voices: American Broadcasting, 1922–1952.* Minneapolis: University of Minnesota Press, 1997.

Hobson, Dorothy. *Crossroads: The Drama of a Soap Opera.* London: Methuen, 1982.

Houston, Beverle. "Viewing Television: The Metapsychology of Endless Consumption." *Quarterly Review of Film Studies* 9, no. 3 (summer 1984): 183–95.

Huyssen, Andreas. *After the Great Divide: Modernism, Mass Culture, Postmodernism.* Bloomington: Indiana University Press, 1986.

Jeffords, Susan, and Lauren Rabinovitz, eds. *Seeing Through the Media: The Persian Gulf War.* New Brunswick, N.J.: Rutgers University Press, 1994.

Jenkins, Henry. *Textual Poachers: Television Fans and Participatory Culture*. New York: Routledge, 1992.

Jensen, Katherine. "Woman as Subject, Oral History as Method." *Frontiers* 7, no. 1 (1983): 84–87.

Jhally, Sut, and Justin Lewis. *Enlightened Racism: The Cosby Show, Audiences, and the Myth of the American Dream*. Boulder, Colo.: Westview Press, 1992.

Joyrich, Lynne. *Re-viewing Reception: Television, Gender, and Postmodern Culture*. Bloomington: Indiana University Press, 1996.

Kaplan, E. Ann, ed. *Regarding Television—Critical Approaches: An Anthology*. Frederick, Md.: University Publications of America, 1983.

———. *Rocking around the Clock: Music Television, Postmodernism, and Consumer Culture*. New York: Methuen, 1987.

Kipnis, Laura. *Bound and Gagged: Pornography and the Politics of Fantasy in America*. New York: Grove, 1996.

Kisseloff, Jeff. *The Box: An Oral History of Television, 1920–1961*. New York: Viking, 1995.

Kuhn, Annette. "Women's Genres." *Screen* 25 (January–February 1984): 18–28.

Lawrence, Amy. *Echo and Narcissus: Women's Voices in Classical Hollywood Cinema*. Berkeley: University of California Press, 1991.

Leibman, Nina C. *Living Room Lectures: The Fifties Family in Film and Television*. Austin: University of Texas Press, 1995.

Lewis, Lisa A. *Gender Politics and MTV: Voicing the Difference*. Philadelphia: Temple University Press, 1990.

———, ed. *The Adoring Audience*. New York: Routledge, 1992.

Liebes, Tamar, and Elihu Katz. *The Export of Meaning: Cross-Cultural Readings of Dallas*. New York: Oxford University Press, 1990.

Livingston, Sonia, and Peter Lunt. *Talk on Television: Audience Participation and Public Debate*. London: Routledge, 1994.

Lopate, Carol. "Daytime Television: You'll Never Want to Leave Home." *Radical America* 11 (January–February 1977): 33–51.

Luker, Kristin. *Abortion and the Politics of Motherhood*. Berkeley: University of California Press, 1984.

Lynd, Staughton. "Oral History from Below." *Oral History Review* 21 (spring 1993): 1–8.

MacCannell, Dean. *Empty Meeting Grounds: The Tourist Papers*. New York: Routledge, 1992.

MacDonald, J. Fred. *Blacks and White TV: Afro-Americans in Television since 1948*. Chicago: Nelson-Hall Publishers, 1983.

Marc, David. *Comic Visions: Television Comedy and American Culture*. Boston: Unwin Hyman, 1989.

———. *Demographic Vistas: Television in American Culture.* Philadelphia: University of Pennsylvania Press, 1984.

Marchand, Roland. *Advertising the American Dream.* Berkeley: University of California Press, 1985.

Margolis, Maxine. *Mothers and Such: Views of American Women and Why They've Changed.* Berkeley: University of California Press, 1984.

Masciarotte, Gloria-Jean. "C'mon Girl: Oprah Winfrey and the Discourse of Feminine Talk." *Genders* 11 (fall 1991): 81–110.

May, Elaine Tyler. *Homeward Bound: American Families in the Cold War Era.* New York: Basic Books, 1988.

Mayne, Judith. "*L.A. Law* and Prime-Time Feminism." *Discourse* 10, no. 2 (spring–summer 1988): 30–48.

McChesney, Robert. *Telecommunications, Mass Media, and Democracy.* New York: Oxford University Press, 1993.

McKay, Anne. "Artificial Voice Amplification and Women's Struggle for a Public Presence." In *Technology and Women's Voices: Keeping in Touch,* edited by Cheris Kramarae. New York: Routledge and Kegan Paul, 1988.

McLaughlin, Lisa. "Chastity Criminals in the Age of Electronic Reproduction: Reviewing Talk Television and the Public Sphere." *Journal of Communication Inquiry* 17 (winter 1993): 41–55.

McRobbie, Angela. "Settling Accounts with Subculture: A Feminist Critique." In *Culture, Ideology, and Social Process: A Reader,* edited by Tony Bennett et al., 113–23. London: Open University Press, 1981.

Mellencamp, Patricia. *High Anxiety: Catastrophe, Scandal, Age, and Comedy.* Bloomington: Indiana University Press, 1990.

———. "Situation and Simulation: An Introduction to *I Love Lucy.*" *Screen* 26, no. 2 (March–April 1985).

———, ed. *Logics of Television: Essays in Cultural Criticism.* Bloomington: Indiana University Press, 1990.

Modleski, Tania. "The Search for Tomorrow in Today's Soap Operas: Notes on Feminine Narrative Form." *Film Quarterly* 33 (fall 1979): 12–21.

———, ed. *Studies in Entertainment: Critical Approaches to Mass Culture.* Bloomington: Indiana University Press, 1986.

Montgomery, Kathryn C. *Target Prime Time: Advocacy Groups and the Struggle over Entertainment Television.* New York: Oxford University Press, 1989.

Morley, David. *Family Television: Cultural Power and Domestic Leisure.* London: Comedia, 1986.

———. *The "Nationwide" Audience: Structure and Decoding.* London: British Film Institute, 1980.

Morrison, Toni, ed. *Race-ing Justice, En-gendering Power: Essays on Anita Hill,*

Clarence Thomas, and the Construction of Social Reality. New York: Pantheon, 1992.

Morse, Margaret. "Talk, Talk, Talk—the Space of Discourse in Television." *Screen* 26, no. 2 (1985): 2–15.

Mulvey, Laura. "Visual Pleasure and Narrative Cinema." *Screen* 16, no. 3 (autumn 1975): 6–18.

Mumford, Laura Stempel. *Love and Ideology in the Afternoon: Soap Opera, Women, and Television Genre.* Bloomington: Indiana University Press, 1995.

Murray, Michael D., and Donald G. Godfrey, eds. *Television in America: Local Station History from across the Nation.* Ames: Iowa State University Press, 1977.

Nightingale, Virginia. *Studying Audiences: The Shock of the Real.* London: Routledge, 1996.

Nochimson, Martha. *No End to Her: Soap Opera and the Female Subject.* Berkeley: University of California Press, 1992.

Perez Firmat, Gustavo. *Life on the Hyphen: The Cuban-American Way.* Austin: University of Texas Press, 1994.

Petchesky, Rosalind. *Abortion and Woman's Choice: The State, Sexuality, and Reproductive Freedom.* Rev. ed. Boston: Northeastern University Press, 1990.

Petro, Patrice. "Mass Culture and the Feminine: The 'Place' of Television in Film Studies." *Cinema Journal* 25, no. 3 (1986): 5–21.

Press, Andrea. *Women Watching Television: Gender, Class, and Generation in the American Television Experience.* Philadelphia: University of Pennsylvania Press, 1991.

Pribram, E. Deidre, ed. *Female Spectators: Looking at Film and Television.* London: Verso, 1988.

Rabinovitz, Lauren. "Sitcoms and Single Moms: Representations of Feminism on American TV." *Cinema Journal* 29 (fall 1989): 3–19.

———. "Soap Opera Bridal Fantasies." *Screen* 33, no. 3 (autumn 1992): 274–83.

Radner, Hilary. *Shopping Around: Feminine Culture and the Pursuit of Pleasure.* New York: Routledge, 1995.

Radway, Janice A. *Reading the Romance: Women, Patriarchy, and Popular Literature.* Chapel Hill: University of North Carolina Press, 1984.

Reeves, Jimmie L., and Richard Campbell. *Cracked Coverage: Television News, the Anti-Cocaine Crusade, and the Reagan Legacy.* Durham, N.C.: Duke University Press, 1994.

Schatz, Thomas. "Desilu, *I Love Lucy,* and the Rise of Network TV." In *Making Television: Authorship and the Production Process,* edited by Robert J. Thompson and Gary Burns. New York: Praeger, 1990.

Schwichtenberg, Cathy. *The Madonna Connection: Representational Politics, Subcultural Identities, and Cultural Theory.* Boulder, Colo.: Westview Press, 1993.

Sedgwick, Eve. *Tendencies.* Durham, N.C.: Duke University Press, 1993.

Seiter, Ellen C. "Promise and Contradiction: The Daytime Television Serials." *Film Reader* 5 (1982): 150–63.

———. "The Role of the Reader: Eco's Narrative Theory and Soap Opera." *Tabloid* 6 (1982): 35–43.

———. "To Teach and To Sell: Irna Phillips and Her Sponsors, 1930–1954." *Journal of Film and Video* 41 (spring 1989): 21–34.

Seiter, Ellen, Hans Borchers, Gabriele Kreutzner, and Eva-Maria Warth, eds. *Remote Control: Television, Audiences, and Cultural Power.* New York: Routledge, 1989.

Shattuc, Jane M. *The Talking Cure: TV Talk Shows and Women.* New York: Routledge, 1997.

Silj, Alessandro. *East of Dallas: The European Challenge to American Television.* London: British Film Institute, 1988.

Sipe, Dan. "The Future of Oral History and Moving Images." *Oral History Review* 19, nos. 1–2 (spring–fall 1991): 75–87.

Skeggs, Beverley, ed. *Feminist Cultural Theory: Process and Production.* Manchester: Manchester University Press, 1995.

Spigel, Lynn. "From Domestic Space to Outer Space: The 1960s Fantastic Family Sitcom." In *Close Encounters: Film, Feminism, and Science Fiction,* edited by Constance Penley, Elisabeth Lyon, Lynn Spigel, and Janet Berstrom, 203–35. Minneapolis: University of Minnesota Press, 1991.

———. "From the Dark Ages to the Golden Age: Women's Memories and Television Reruns." *Screen* 36, no. 1 (spring 1995): 16–33.

———. *Make Room for TV: Television and the Family Ideal in Postwar America.* Chicago: University of Chicago Press, 1992.

Spigel, Lynn, and Denise Mann, eds. *Private Screenings: Television and the Female Consumer.* Minneapolis: University of Minnesota Press, 1992.

Sterling, Christopher H., and John M. Kitross. *Stay Tuned: A Concise History of American Broadcasting.* 2d ed. Belmont, Calif.: Wadsworth, 1990.

Studlar, Gaylyn. "Midnight S/Excess: Cult Configurations of 'Femininity' and the Perverse." *Journal of Popular Film and Television* 17, no. 1 (spring 1989): 2–14.

Thompson, J. B. *Ideology and Modern Culture: Critical Social Theory.* Cambridge: Polity Press, 1990.

Thompson, Paul. *The Voice of the Past: Oral History.* London: Oxford University Press, 1978.

Torres, Sasha, ed. *Living Color: Race and Television in the United States.* Durham, N.C.: Duke University Press, 1998.

Tulloch, John, and Manuel Alvarado. *Doctor Who: The Unfolding Text.* New York: St. Martin's Press, 1983.

Watson, Mary Ann. *The Expanding Vista: American Television in the Kennedy Years.* New York: Oxford University Press, 1990.

Weddington, Sarah. *A Question of Choice.* New York: Penguin, 1993.

West, Cornel. *Keeping Faith: Philosophy and Race in America.* New York: Routledge, 1993.

White, Mimi. *Tele-Advising: Therapeutic Discourse in American Television.* Chapel Hill: University of North Carolina Press, 1992.

Woll, Allen L., and Randall M. Miller. *Ethnic and Racial Images in American Film and Television: Historical Essays and Bibliography.* New York: Garland Publishing, 1987.

Zimmermann, Patricia. "Hollywood, Home Movies, and Common Sense: Amateur Film as Aesthetic Dissemination and Social Control, 1950–1962." *Cinema Journal* 27, no. 4 (summer 1988): 23–44.

Contributors

Julie D'Acci is Associate Professor of Communication Arts and Women's Studies at the University of Wisconsin—Madison and a founder of the Annual Conference on Television, Video, and Feminism: Console-ing Passions. She is the author of *Defining Women: Television and the Case of Cagney and Lacey* and various articles on television, and is a coeditor of *Feminist Television Criticism: A Reader.*

Mary Desjardins is Assistant Professor at Dartmouth College, where she teaches film, television, and women's studies. She is writing a book titled *Recycled Stars: Hollywood Film Stardom in the Age of Television and Video.*

Jane Feuer is Associate Professor of Film Studies in the English Department at the University of Pittsburgh. She is the author of *Seeing through the Eighties: Television and Reaganism* (1995) and *The Hollywood Musical* (1993), and is coeditor of *MTM: "Quality" Television* (1985). She has written numerous essays on film and television and is a member of the advisory board for the Annual Conference on Television, Video, and Feminism: Console-ing Passions.

Mary Beth Haralovich is Associate Professor of Media Arts at the University of Arizona in Tucson and a founder of the Annual Conference on Television, Video, and Feminism: Console-ing Passions. She has published studies of 1950s suburban family comedies and the popular appeal of *Magnum, p.i.*; her studies of film include film advertising, color in 1950s melodrama, and the proletarian women's film of the 1930s.

Michele Hilmes is Associate Professor of Communication Arts at the University of Wisconsin—Madison. She is the author of *Hollywood and Broadcasting: From Radio to Cable* (1990) and *Radio Voices: American Broadcasting, 1922–1952* (1997). She is currently working on a study of American and British cross-influences in broadcasting structures and formations.

Moya Luckett is Assistant Professor of Film Studies in the English Department at the University of Pittsburgh. She is currently finishing a manuscript titled *Cities and Spectators: An Historical Analysis of Movie Going in Chicago, 1907–1917*, working on a book on representations of single femininity in 1960s films and television, and coediting an anthology on gender and sexuality in 1960s popular culture.

Lauren Rabinovitz is Professor of American Studies and Film Studies at the University of Iowa and a founder of the Annual Conference on Television, Video, and Feminism: Console-ing Passions. She is the author of *For the Love of Pleasure: Women, Movies, and Culture in Turn-of-the-Century Chicago* (1998) and *Points of Resistance: Women, Power, and Politics in the New York Avant-Garde Cinema, 1943–1971* (1991). She is coauthor of the award-winning CD-ROM *The Rebecca Project* and coeditor of *Seeing Through the Media: The Persian Gulf War* (1994).

Jane M. Shattuc is Associate Professor at Emerson College. She is the author of *The Talking Cure: TV Talk Shows and Women* (1997) and *Television, Tabloids, and Tears: Fassbinder and Popular Culture* (1994).

Mark Williams is Assistant Professor at Dartmouth College, where he teaches film and television. He has authored several articles on the early history of television.

Index

20/20, 184
227, 148
Abby the Postmistress and Her Black Mountain Boys, 40
ABC: celebration of women's suffrage, 143 n.54; production of *Abortion*, 123, 125, 139 n.16; production of *Peyton Place*, 77, 78; production of *Population and the American Future*, 130, 134, 135, 142 n.48
Abortion, 8; African American feminists and, 120, 128–30; class and, 124, 132; on *Maude*, 160; race and, 121, 132, 133–34; and television documentaries, 121, 123–26, 128. See also *Abortion and the Law; Population and the American Future; Population: Boom or Doom;* Reproductive choice
Abortion and the Law, 123–26
ACT-UP, 175. *See also* Homosexuality
Advertising: female audiences and, 26–29, 145; gender distinctions in, 19–20, 88; sponsors' criticism, 44; television networks and, 31, 41
Agency, 8–10
Allen, Gracie, 4
Allen, Robert, 39
Amos 'n' Andy, 21
Anderson, Christopher, 31
Armitage, Susan, 38, 47
Arnaz Luckenbill, Lucie, 58, 66–68, 73 n.20
Arnaz, Desi, 56–72; press coverage, 72 n.7. *See also* Hispanic ethnicity; Marriage and star couples
Arnaz, Desi, Jr., 58, 69, 72 n.7
Arnold, Tom, 192–94
As the World Turns, 77
Ashe, Arthur, 100, 114 n.6
Audience, 5–7; identity politics and, 174–75; public sphere and, 168–78. *See also* Female audiences
Avengers, The, 100

Babes, 194–97
Babycakes, 192
Baehr, Helen, and Gillian Dyer, 5
Baker, Josephine, 101–2, 117 n.12
Ball, Lucille, 4, 9, 56–72; films with Bob Hope, 73 n.12; press coverage, 72 n.7; television pregnancy, 73 n.8; in relation to Vivian Vance's body, 73 n.15. *See also* Marriage and star couples
Bambara, Toni Cade, 129
Barbara Tate, 40
Barnett, J. M., 23
Barnouw, Eric, 99, 101
Bathrick, Serafina, 4
Before the Laughter, 66–67
Bennett, Tony, 5

Bennett, Tony, and Janet Woollacott, 5, 114 n.5
Berg, Gertrude, 26
Berg, Moe, 100
Bergen, Candice, 144, 156, 161
Berger, John, 183–85, 189
Berman, Martin, 176
Bernhardt, Sandra, 186
Bertha Brainard Broadcasts Broadway, 21
Beverly Hills 90210, 31, 194
Black Women's Liberation Group, 129
Bloodworth Thomason, Linda, 154, 155. See also *Designing Women*
Bob Hope Show, The, 57, 62
Boddy, William, 31
Bond, James, 100, 112, 114 n.5
Bordo, Susan, 184
Brainard, Bertha, 21, 23–24, 27. See also *Bertha Brainard Broadcasts Broadway*
British cultural studies. *See* Cultural studies
Brown, David, 81
Brown, Mary Ellen, 5
Bruce, Lenny, 100
Brunsdon, Charlotte, 6
Burke, Delta: feminine excess and, 149; weight and employment, 148, 154–55, 165 n.15, 166 n.20. *See also* Marriage and star couples; Women's bodies

Cagney and Lacey, 7, 166 n.18
Carpignano, Paolo, Robin Andrews, Stanley Aronowitz, and William Difazio, 172
Carrington, Elaine, 30
Carter, Dixie, 149, 166 n.20
Cates, Darlene, 197–98
Catholic Church: abortion and, 127, 130, 133, 135
Cavalcade, 40
CBS, 30, 56, 66; and abortion documentaries, 130, 135; and celebration of women's suffrage, 143 n.54; feminist sitcoms, 148, 156, 166 n.18; production of *Abortion and the Law,* 123
Central Intelligence Agency (CIA), 101, 116 n.8
Charles in Charge, 147
Cheers, 162
China Beach, 192
Chisholm, Shirley, 129
Chung, Connie, 160, 162
Citizens' Committee on Population and the American Future, 128–30, 134, 140 n.33
Civil rights: television's civil rights activism, 9, 98; U.S. foreign policy and, 101–2, 113. *See also* Race relations
Clara, Lu and Em, 26
Clark, Danae, 185
Clift, Eleanor, 162
Clinton, Bill, 155
CNN, 187
Coach, 162
Codell, Martin, 24
Cold War, 127; *Cold War File,* 100; in television spy fiction, 103–6, 116–17 n.8, 117 n.9
Columbia Pictures Television, 155
Commission on Population Growth and the American Future, 126–35, 141 n.38
Communications Act of 1934, 28

Condit, Celeste, 136
Confidential, 62, 63
Confidential File, 123
Cook's Corner, 41–45. *See also* Monty Margetts
Cooper, Lester, 125
Cornely, Paul, 133–34
Coronation Street, 77, 78
Cosby, Bill: comic wordplay, 118 n.15; television racial integration and, 99–100, 114 n.3, 118 n.16
Cosmo girl, 82
Cosmopolitan: interview with Hugh Hefner, 90–91; liberated female sexuality, 75–76, 80–81; single women in the city, 85–86; single women in the public sphere, 88, 93 n.26. *See also* Helen Gurley Brown
Cronkite, Walter, 123
Crossroads, 6
Crusinberry, Jane, 30
Culp, Robert, 99–100; civil rights activism, 9, 102, 118 n.13; hipster wordplay, 118 n.15
Cultural studies, 5, 53 n.5, 171
Curtin, Jane, 147
Cuthbert, Margaret, 21

D'Acci, Julie, 7, 8, 164 n.4, 166 n.18
Dallas, 6, 31
Days and Nights of Molly Dodd, The, 163 n.2
Days of Our Lives, 77
Democratic Party, 158
Designing Women, 145, 148–58, 162, 165 nn.15, 16, 17
Desilu, 8, 58, 60, 66, 68–69
Desjardins, Mary, 8, 11
Dey, Susan, 196
Dillon, Valerie, 132, 139 n.16
Divine, 186, 192–94
Doane, Mary Ann, 25
Documentary: "balance" in television documentary, 135–37, 138 n.6, 142 n.48. *See also* Abortion documentaries; *Population: Boom or Doom; Population and the American Future*
Donahue, 168, 180 n.22, 189
Donahue, Phil, 171–73, 175
Doty, Alexander, 56–57, 165 n.16
Downs, Hugh, 128, 131
DuBois, W. E. B., 102, 117 n.12
Dudziak, Mary, 101–2, 117 nn.11, 12
Dyer, Richard, 113
Dynasty, 6

Ed Sullivan Show (*Toast of the Town*), 57, 58, 59, 60, 68
Edwards, Ralph, 40
Ellerbee, Linda, 160
English, Diane, 156. See also *Murphy Brown*
Enloe, Cynthia, 98, 108, 111–12
Episodic drama. See *I Spy, Peyton Place*
Equal Rights Amendment, 92 n.1, 127, 132
Evening Shade, 162

Fairchild, Morgan, 160
"Family values," 144–45. *See also* Marriage
Fantasia, 196
Farrow, Mia, 78, 79, 84, 90
Fat Is a Feminist Issue, 182
Federal Communications Commission (FCC), 131, 134, 138 n.6, 142 n.48
Female audiences: radio, 20, 26–30; television, 42, 45, 85, 145–46

Female desire: displacement of race, 153; liberated sexuality, 84–85, 89, 91–92; in sex tourism, 112
Female spectator, 3–7. *See also* Female audiences
Feminine Mystique, 76
Femininity: mass culture and, 20. *See also* Female audiences; Female desire; Marriage; Motherhood; Sexuality; Women's bodies
Feminism: definition, 1; abortion debate and, 120–22; agency and, 8–10; "family values" debate and, 144–45, 147; female spectator-auditor-subject and, 3–7; historical method and, 1–2, 8–9, 11–12; mid-60s popular, 80; in opposition to femininity, 149–51, 156–60; oral history and, 50–52; in television criticism, 2–3, 7–8; television's role in popularizing, 154, 163
Feminist romance, 159–60
Feuer, Jane, 3, 6, 9, 11
Fisher, Craig, 130, 131, 133–34, 135, 141 n.38, 142 n.48. *See also* Abortion documentaries; *Population and the American Future*
Fiske, John, 4
Flitterman, Sandy, 3, 4. *See also* Flitterman-Lewis, Sandy
Flitterman-Lewis, Sandy, 39
Ford, Faith, 148
Foreman, Carol, 134
Forever Darling, 60–62
Foucault, Michel, 8
FOX, 31, 195, 198
Frawley, William, 60, 62–64
Friedan, Betty, 76, 126, 139 n.22

Gay representation: activism, 175; homophobia, 148; homophobia and race, 151, 153
Geraldo, 168, 175–76, 180 n.22
Get Smart, 100
Gitlin, Todd, 164 n.5
Gledhill, Christine, 4
Goldbergs, The, 26
Golden Girls, 145, 148
Gordon, Linda, 121–22, 140 n.24, 141 n.39
Graham, Billy, 79
Gregory, Dick, 100
Group, The, 76
Guiding Light, 30, 77
Gurley Brown, Helen, 75, 80–85, 88–92, 96 n.40. See also *Cosmopolitan*

Habermas, Jürgen, 34 n.28, 169–70, 173, 180 n.13
Hairspray, 192
Hall, Stuart, 5
Hamburger, Philip, 30
Haralovich, Mary Beth, 4, 7, 8, 10, 92 n.4
Harper, Phillip Brian, 99
Harry, Jackee, 148
Hartley, John, 2
Hearts Afire, 162
Hefner, Hugh, 90–91
Heritage Foundation, 172
Heterosexual imperative, 10–11
Higgins, Ken, 41
Hilmes, Michele, 8, 32 n.1, 35 n.32, 54 n.13
Hispanic ethnicity: Desi Arnaz, 8, 57, 63–64, 68–69, 73 n.13; talk show representation of fat Latina, 186–87, 191
Holmes Norton, Eleanor, 128, 129–30
Home Improvement, 162

Homophobia, 148; homophobia and race, 151, 153
Homosexuality. *See* Gay representation; Homophobia; Lesbian representation
Hope, Bob, 62–66, 73 n.12
Hummert, Frank and Anne, 26, 30
Huyssen, Andreas, 20

I Love Lucy, 11, 56–66
I'm Dysfunctional, You're Dysfunctional, 174
I Spy, 8–9, 10, 98–119

Jackson, Jesse, 132
Jenny Jones, 170, 179 n.6
Jensen, Katherine, 37
Johnson, Lyndon, 123, 138 n.12
Jones, V. A. L., 22
Joyrich, Lynne, 4
Just Plain Bill, 26

Kaminer, Wendy, 174
Kaplan, Caren, 57
Kaplan, E. Ann, 2, 4
Kate & Allie, 145, 147, 164 n.11
KDKA (Pittsburgh), 23
Kennedy, John F., 113
KFI (Los Angeles), 41, 46
KHJ (Los Angeles), 81
Kipnis, Laura, 194
Kirbett, Corley W., 23
Knot's Landing, 31
Kramer, Peter, 177
KSD (St. Louis), 22
KTLA (Los Angeles), 36, 54 n.11
KTTV (Los Angeles), 54 n.11
Kuhn, Annette, 6

Lake, Ricki, 192, 199 n.15
lang, k.d., 186
Laverne & Shirley, 145
Lawrence, Amy, 24–25
Leonard, Sheldon, 8, 9, 98, 114 n.2, 115–16 n.7, 118 nn.15, 17. See also *I Spy*
Lesbian representation, 7; chic, 186; feminist politics, 182; homophobia, 151; lovers, 78; spectators, 195, 198; within heterosexual culture, 156, 160, 165 n.16
Lewis, Lisa, 4
Liebes, Tamar, and Elihu Katz, 6
Livingston, Sonia, and Peter Lunt, 178 n.2
Long, Long Trailer, 58
Lowe, David, 123, 135
Lucille Ball–Desi Arnaz Show, 56
Luckett, Moya, 10
Lucy and Desi: A Home Movie, 57–58, 66–70

MacCannell, Dean, 109, 119 n.25
MacDonald, Fred, 99
Madonna, 4, 194
Magnum, p.i., 4
Mailer, Norman, 81
Male gaze, 183–85, 186, 189, 192, 195, 197
Man from U.N.C.L.E., 100
Marchand, Roland, 19–20
Margetts, Monty, 8, 36–52
Marriage: government agent and, 119 n.25; the maternal and, 81–82; sexual desires within, 76; single women and, 95–97 n.40, 144–45, 146; star couples and, 57–58, 60–62, 66–70, 154–55; woman's need for, 88–89. *See also* Reproductive choice; Sexuality

Martin, John, 131
Mary Tyler Moore Show, The, 145–46, 164 n.13
Masciarotte, Gloria-Jean, 7, 172
Maude, 146, 160
Maury Povich Show, The, 186
Mayer, Ken, 187–91
Mayer, Vivian F., 182
McBride, Mary Margaret, 30
McCarthy, Mary, 76
McChesney, Robert, 28–29
McClanahan, Rue, 148
McHugh, James T., 133–34
McLaughlin, Lisa, 172–73
McRaney, Gerald, 154–55
McRobbie, Angela, 5
Mecklenberg, Marjory, 132
Medicine Ball, 198
Mellencamp, Patricia, 4, 56–57, 63
Melrose Place, 31
Metalious, Grace, 75, 76, 79, 93 n.20
Mexico: in spy fiction, 100, 106–12, 119 n.21; subject tourism and travelogue, 106–9
Minnesota Citizens for Life, 132
Mirabella, 184
Mission: Impossible, 100
Mix, Jennie Irene, 22–23
Modleski, Tania, 3–4, 39
Monash, Paul, 75, 77, 83
Moore, Mary Tyler, 4
Morgan, Helen, 40
Morley, David, 5
Morse, Margaret, 7
Morton Downey Show, 172
Moss, Kate, 184
Motherhood: on *I Love Lucy,* 59, 68, 72 n.7; 73 n.8; identity on talk shows, 173, 174; the maternal and, 81–82, 84, 94–95 n.32. *See also* Abortion; Marriage; Reproductive choice; Sexuality
MTV, 192
Mulvey, Laura, 11, 183–84, 189
Murphy Brown, 144–49, 156–63, 166 n.26
Myrt and Marge, 26

National Association for the Advancement of Colored People (NAACP), 175
National Association of Broadcasters (NAB), 30
National Association to Aid Fat Americans (NAAFA), 182, 200 n.19
National Organization for Women (NOW), 126, 139 n.22, 175
NBC, 21, 26, 66; abortion documentaries, 130; Broadcast Standards Department, 94 n.30; celebration of women's suffrage, 143 n.54; color programming, 100, 115–16 n.7; daytime radio, 27, 30; Far Eastern news staff, 117 n.8; Monty Margetts and, 40, 41; racial integration and, 98
Nevins, Allen, 37
Nielsen ratings, 78, 148
Nixon, Richard, 123, 126, 127–29, 134, 140 n.27, 141 n.38
Norman, Jessye, 192

O'Connor, John H., 170
Oprah Winfrey Show, The, 168, 178 n.1; audience as public sphere, 170, 172–78; selection of audience questions, 180 n.22
Oral history: interviews 36–37, 47–49; public/private space and, 47–48; subjectivity and popular memory, 52; women's history and, 37–38,

54–55 n.22. *See also* Feminism and historical method
Orbach, Susie, 182
Outrageous Opinions, 81

Paley, William, 130
Parent, Gail, 195
Parkins, Barbara, 79, 85, 90
Pastorelli, Robert, 146
Paulina, 184–85, 189
PBS: and abortion documentaries, 136, 142 n.48. See also *Population and the American Future*
Pendrell, Ernest, 123, 125–26, 134, 135. *See also* Abortion documentaries; *Abortion and the Law*
Pepper Young's Family, 30
Persian Gulf War, 162
Petchesky, Rosalind, 121–22, 127
Petro, Patrice, 4
Peyton Place, 10, 75–92
Phenom, 147
Phillips, Irna, 30
Pike, Bishop James, 81
Planned Parenthood, 134
Playboy, 88–89
Poltrack, David, 46
Popenoe, John, 23
Population: Boom or Doom, 133–34. *See also* Abortion documentaries
Population and the American Future, 131–33. *See also* Abortion documentaries
Population Education, Inc., 128
Press, Andrea, 5
Pribram, E. Deidre, 5
Prozac, 176–77
Public and private spheres: female journalists and, 162; gender and high/mass culture, 20, 26; gendered fiction and, 39–40; marriage and, 76; in the practice of oral history, 47–48; public sphere definition, 168–69; in talk shows, 171–72; women's seclusion and, 84, 88

Quayle, Dan, 144–45, 161–63, 163 n.1

Rabinovitz, Lauren, 4, 7, 11, 164 n.11, 164 n.9
Race: abortion and, 129, 132, 133–34, 135, 141 n.39; civil rights activism, 113 n.1; Cold War and, 102–6, 113, 117 n.11, 117–18 n.12; discrimination, 101–2; integration on television, 99, 118 n.13, 163–64 n.2; racism on television, 148, 151–53, 156; sex tourism and, 112; structuring absence on television, 174, 175; white consumer demographic and, 10. *See also* Civil rights; Women of color; Women's bodies
Radio: gender, industry structure, and programming, 17–19, 26–31, 39; producers, 18, 22, 30; station managers, 23–24; women announcers, 20–23, 33 n.12, 33–34 n.20, 34 n.22
Radio Act of 1927, 28
Radio Age, 20–21
Radio Broadcast, 22
Radner, Hilary, 80, 81–82
Radway, Janice A., 5
Reproductive choice, 121–22, 144, 162–63; single motherhood, 144, 147, 161. *See also* Abortion; Marriage; Motherhood; Sexuality
Republican Party, 144, 158, 163, 163 n.1
Respect for Life Committee, 132, 139 n.16

Return to Peyton Place, 76
Revell, Nellie, 30
Reynolds, Burt, 83
Rhoda, 145–46
Rider, John F., 34 n.21
Rigg, M.A., 23
Right to Life Committee, 126
Rivers, Joan, 166 n.20
Robeson, Paul, 101–2, 117 n.12
Robson, Mark, 85
Rockefeller Foundation, 127
Rockefeller, John D., III, 126–30, 133–34, 140 n.33, 141 n.38
Roe v. Wade, 120, 121, 133, 134, 136
Rogers, W. W., 23
Roseanne, 191–94, 200 n.17
Roseanne, 145, 162
Rosie the Riveter, 48
Rule, Elton, 125–26, 134
Russell, Jane, 184

Sally Jesse Raphael, 168, 180 n.22
Sanders, Marlene, 8, 130; documentary "balance" and, 142 n.48, 148 n.55. *See also* Abortion documentaries; *Population: Boom or Doom*
Sassone, Robert, 125–26
Scherick, Edgar J., 77
Schlafly, Phyllis, 51
Schwichtenberg, Cathy, 4
SDS (Students for a Democratic Society), 147–48
Sedgwick, Eve, 181
Seiter, Ellen, 3
Serials. *See* Soap operas
Sesame Street, 158
Sex and the New Single Girl, 92
Sex and the Office, 81
Sex and the Single Girl, 75–76, 81, 88–89
Sex tourism, 110–112
Sexuality: "adult" comedy-variety, 57, 62–66; heterosexual imperative, 11; identity and, 83; morality and, 77–78, 79; race and, 153; sexual desire, 64; sexual fiction, 76; sexual revolution, 80. *See also* Female desire; Marriage; Motherhood; *Sex and the Single Girl;* Sex tourism
Shattuc, Jane, 7, 9
Silverman, Kaja, 25
Simmons, Richard, 191
Simpsons, The, 194
Sipe, Dan, 38
Situation comedies: heterosexual imperative in, 11; progressive potential in, 4. See also *Designing Women; I Love Lucy; Kate & Allie; The Mary Tyler Moore Show; Murphy Brown; Rhoda*
Skyler's Square, 40
Soap opera: consumerist address, 7; daytime radio programming, 26–31, 39; diverse audience readings of 3–4, 12–13 n.7; as "quality" prime-time serial, 77. *See also* Audience; Female audience; Female spectators; Radio, gender, industry structure, and programming
Sonja Live, 187–91, 196
Sperber, Wendy Jo, 194, 196, 198
Spigel, Lynn, 7
Stein, Jeff, 197
Steinem, Gloria, 51
Step by Step, 162
St. James, Susan, 147
Story of Mary Marlin, The, 30
Strauss, Carolyn, 187–89, 196, 200 n.22
Studlar, Gaylyn, 186

Sugarbaby, 192
Sullivan, Ed, 59–60
Sullivan, Kathleen, 160
Susann, Jacqueline, 76

Talk shows: as public forum, 7, 9, 168–79. See also *Donahue; Jenny Jones; The Oprah Winfrey Show; Sonja Live*
Taylor, Meshach, 151
Television criticism, 2–6, 11–12; cultural studies and, 5, 53 n.5, 171; ethnography and, 5–6; female spectators and, 3–7; 9–10. *See also* Feminism; Oral history
Television industry: women's employment in, 5, 9–10. *See also* Radio announcers; Radio station managers; Lucille Ball; Delta Burke; Monty Margetts; Television producers; Television stars; Vivian Vance; Women's bodies
Television producers: as cultural and creative influences, 7, 8–10; replacement of women producers, 197; as subject of television histories 39; 197. *See also* Desi Arnaz; Lucie Luckenbill Arnaz; Diane English; Craig Fisher; Sheldon Leonard; Paul Monash; Ernest Pendrell; Linda Bloodworth Thomason; Radio producers; Radio station managers
Television stars. *See* Desi Arnaz; Lucille Ball; Candice Bergen; Delta Burke; Bill Cosby; Robert Culp; Phil Donahue; Monty Margetts; Wendy Jo Sperber; Oprah Winfrey
This Woman's Secret, 40
Thomas, Jay, 158
Thomas, Marlo, 85
Tiananmen Square, 172
Toast of the Town. See *The Ed Sullivan Show*
Today's Children, 30
Tourism: color television and, 115–16 n.7; television travelogues, 98, 100, 106–12
Truth or Consequences, 40
Tucker, Madge, 21
Twentieth Century–Fox, 77–78
Two of Us, 147

U.S. Catholic Conference, 133
U.S. Coalition for Life, 131
U.S. Office of Education, 133
U.S. State Department, 101–2, 104, 107

Valley of the Dolls, 76, 85
Vance, Vivian, 60, 62–64, 73 n.15
Vanity Fair, 192–94, 200 n.17
Vereira, Meredith, 162
Vietnam, 104, 107
Viewers for Quality Television, 154

Wade, Margaret, 39
Wagner, Gwen, 21
Walker, Liz, 161–62
Wallace, John, 23
Waller, Judith, 21
Warner Bros. Presents, 31
Waters, John, 192
Wattenberg, Ben, 132
WEAF (New York), 21
Weaver, Pat, 30
Weddington, Sarah, 135
Westinghouse, 23
WGBH (Boston), 131
WGN (Chicago), 21
WGR (Buffalo), 23

Whistler, The, 40
White, Helen M., 23
Who's the Boss, 147
Williams, Mark, 8
Wilson, Carnie, 192, 198
Wilson Phillips, 192
Winfrey, Oprah: audience as public sphere, 170, 173–77; drug use confession, 179 n.6; "Oprahification," 168; stardom as creative influence, 9; on subject of fat women, 187; weight and glamour, 191; weight and popularity, 173, 199 n.15. *See also* Public and private spheres; Talk shows; Women's bodies
Witmer, Roy C., 27
WJZ (New York), 21, 23–24
WMAQ (Chicago), 21
Wolf, Thomas, 125–26, 135, 139 n.19, 142 n.48
Woll, Allen, and Randall Miller, 99, 113 n.1
Women en Large: Images of Fat Nudes, 198
Women of color: feminist activism, 121, 128, 129–30; women journalists, 162. *See also* Women's bodies
Women's bodies: fat, 9, 73 n.15, 154–55, 165 n.15, 173, 181–200; feminine excess, 148–51, 156–57; feminine look at, 85–87, 90–91; femininity, 184–186; Latina, 186–87, 191; lesbian chic, 186; race and, 173, 187, 191, 199 n.15; in radio, 25; and sexual desire, 162. *See also* Delta Burke; Male gaze; Oprah Winfrey
Women's movement. *See* Feminism
WOR (New York), 23, 30
WPO (Memphis, Tennessee), 21
WRC (Washington, D.C.), 21–22
WWJ (Detroit), 23

Zahn, Paula, 160
Zimmermann, Patricia, 68

Library of Congress Cataloging-in-Publication Data

Television, history, and American culture : feminist critical essays / edited by Mary Beth Haralovich and Lauren Rabinowitz

p. cm. — (Console-ing passions)

Includes bibliographical references and index.

ISBN 0-8223-2361-3 (cloth : alk. paper).

ISBN 0-8223-2394-X (paper : alk. paper)

1. Television broadcasting—Social aspects—United States.

2. Television and women. I. Havalovich, Mary Beth.

II. Rabinovitz, Lauren. III. Series.

PN1992.6.T414 1999 302.23′45′0973—dc21 99-22693 CIP